Travelling Goods, Travelling Moods

Christian Huck is Professor for English and American Cultural and Media Studies at the University of Kiel, Germany. *Stefan Bauernschmidt* is an associated member at the University of Bayreuth, Germany (Chair of Sociology of Culture and Religion).

Christian Huck, Stefan Bauernschmidt (eds.)

Travelling Goods, Travelling Moods

Varieties of Cultural Appropriation (1850–1950)

Campus Verlag
Frankfurt/New York

Bibliographic Information published by the Deutsche Nationalbibliothek.
The Deutsche Nationalbibliothek lists this publication in the Deutsche Nationalbibliografie; detailed bibliographic data are available in the Internet at http://dnb.d-nb.de.
ISBN 978-3-593-39762-7

Printing office and bookbinder: CPI buchbücher.de, Birkach
Printed on acid free paper.
Printed in Germany

This book is also available as an E-Book.

www.campus.de
www.press.uchicago.edu

Contents

Appropriating Books

Appropriating Machines

Theory Revisited

Preface

We wake up in Swedish beds and Bangladeshi pajamas, shave using American razors and put on French perfume; we eat Danish pastry for breakfast, drink coffee from Ethiopia or sip tee from India; we put on Italian clothes and drive to work in Japanese cars; we communicate using Finnish cell phones, work on American computers and eat lunch at a Mexican restaurant; when we come home we have Thai take-away and an Australian Chardonnay for dinner before we read a Norwegian crime novel, listen to British pop music and return to our Swedish beds. *Does this sound familiar to you?* One of the most immediate and directly felt effects of globalization—at least in the West—can be experienced in our daily encounters with consumer goods. Supermarkets, warehouses and online shops offer consumer goods from all over the globe: one click, and products once thought of as foreign, exotic and almost impossible to obtain are now delivered straight to our doorstep. Today, goods seem to travel light, and it appears to be easy to make the foreign our own.

However, not all of these 'travelling goods' travel the same way, and not all are foreign in the same way. Ikea's Swedish designed beds are mostly produced in China; Honda's Japanese cars are manufactured in plants all around the world, and some ingredients of French Chanel No. 5 are fabricated in Bitterfeld, once the capital of the chemical industry in East Germany. Whereas tee and coffee are indeed grown in their respective countries of origin, our Danish pastry has been made at our local bakery, though according to a recipe created in Vienna, Austria. While the Italian origin of our suit and the Britishness of our music might be of specific importance to our personal identity, the fact that our smart phone is a Finnish product seems less relevant. At the same time, while we all know that our computers and shelves most likely have been produced in China, their American or Swedish provenance matters to us nonetheless.

Why does it matter where things come from—even when they do not *actually* come from there? Goods partake in specific networks: they are conceived by certain people in certain places, they are produced from specific materials using specific techniques and machineries, they are used by certain people in certain ways and they are named and described in relation to similar, familiar things. In short, they are embedded within a specific culture, part of a specific, albeit contingent, fabric of meaning, practice and materiality. Apparently, things are nothing without a context, and by their association with context they are attuned to a certain mood, a certain disposition. When we encounter goods we cannot but react to these moods.

The questions that this volume asks seem simple: what happens to the mood of a good once it travels from one culture to another? What happens to the original mood of a good within a new culture? Is it maintained, dismissed or transformed? Does this process change the good? Does it affect the cultures involved? The process that decides what place a thing shall have within a culture, and at the same time decides on the mood of a good, is what we term *(trans-)cultural appropriation*. What happens when a culture makes an alien good its own?

To answer these questions we examine an historical period (1850–1950) when processes of globalization and the consequent presence of foreign goods on local markets were not as widespread as today, but when this presence was all the more heavily and controversially discussed. The goods we concentrate on in this edited volume fall into three categories: food, books and machines. These represent anthropological necessities (*food*), key cultural products (*books*) and technologies central to modern civilizations (*machines*). Each section comprises three essays preceded by a short introduction outlining the general characteristics of the good in question and the particular perspective of each individual contribution. The volume opens with an introduction to the concept of cultural appropriation by one of its foremost theorists, the ethnologist Hans Peter Hahn. The closing text, by the editors of this volume, revisits the theory of cultural appropriation, taking into consideration what the case studies assembled here can contribute to the understanding of the concept.

In order to comprehend assorted processes of cultural appropriation, research into it must not only be transcultural, but also transdisciplinary. We therefore bring together researchers from anthropology, ethnology, history, media studies, sociology, and from American, Asian, English, German and Scandinavian studies. Accordingly, the different contributions display a wide assortment of approaches to the phenomena in question. We hope this melee of cultures, disciplines and approaches does not confuse readers but inspires them to scrutinize processes of cultural appropriation from a multiplicity of angles. We hope the varieties of cultural appropriation we present here open new perspectives on such travelling goods and travelling moods as readers may encounter them in their research and everyday life.

The editors would like to thank Meltem Gökdemir and Alexander Joachimsmeier for their meticulous work in copy editing the manuscript, as well as John Foulks for his thorough proofreading and his willingness to engage with the manifold arguments presented in each individual article; any remaining errors are the responsibility of the editors. Also, we would like to thank Andreas Walter, Benjamin Frahm and Beke Hansen for their help in setting up the conference that laid the foundations for this book. Furthermore, we would like to thank all participants in the conference for their interesting and most valuable contributions. Most importantly, we would like to thank Nicola Dropmann and Sonja Weishaupt, our fellow members of the Emmy Noether-research group "Travelling Goods // Travelling Moods: A Transcultural Study of the Acculturation of Consumer Goods, 1918–1933," as well as Susanne Scholz, Ulfried Reichardt, Doris Feldmann, Michael Lackner, Anja Schwanhäußer, Angelika C. Messner, Jutta Zimmermann and Felix Konrad for discussing various aspects of cultural appropriation with us. Finally, we would like to thank the *Deutsche Forschungsgemeinschaft* (DFG), without whose generous financial support the production of this edited volume and the research its findings are based on would not have been possible.

Stefan Bauernschmidt and Christian Huck, Erlangen and Kiel, May 2012

Theory

Cultural Appropriation: Power, Transformation, and Tradition

Hans Peter Hahn

Like a parable, the scene of the tea ceremony among the Tuareg reveals several key features of the concept of cultural appropriation. The precious moment, when tea is poured into small glass cups and people start sipping the sweet hot drink, is never missing from any travel report about the Western Sahara. Tea, here, is simultaneously an archetypical 'global good' and a cornerstone of local traditions. The preparation of tea among the Tuareg and the principles of sharing and drinking it while engaging in conversation are among the activities most typically associated with this desert people's traditions. The ceremony has become more than just a tradition; it has gained the status of an image attracting people from elsewhere, that is: tourists. Guided tours in Northern Niger, for example, almost always include such a tea ceremony. The Tuareg tea ceremony conveys an idealized image of African traditions and values. In short, it has achieved the status of an emblematic cultural feature; as such its perception extends far beyond the Western Sahara. The tea ceremony of the Tuareg—like many other cultural traditions—reveals how cultural appropriation deals with the impact of globalization; it shows how a 'global good' can be used to articulate local culture and redefine traditions. The concept of cultural appropriation provides arguments that explain why researchers in history, culture and literature do not believe in cultural homogenization as a necessary consequence of the forceful promotion of uniform cultures worldwide.

This article not only discusses phenomena of cultural appropriation, but also deals with the origins of the concept and some relevant perspectives in current debates about it. Sources from several disciplines will be consulted in order to properly describe the roots of the concept. They all provide case studies of cultural appropriation, sometimes without labeling it explicitly as such. The sweep of different approaches is astonishingly wide. It includes art history and media studies, law and—last but not least—cultural anthropology.

This article also presents some fields of empirical research. Although media studies have contributed substantially to the definition of cultural appropriation, the majority of examples are based in ethnography.[1] More so than other research fields, ethnography highlights the transformation and redefinition of local cultural phenomena through cultural appropriation. Possible approaches to researching cultural appropriation will be explained in more detail.

The final section of this article deals with the legitimacy of cultural appropriation and with unequal power relations. The question of power is crucial to any understanding of the current interest in the concept of cultural appropriation; more than other approaches to cultural transformation, cultural appropriation highlights unequal power relations and the actions of the 'weak.' In general, the appropriation by some powerful actors of (some aspect of) another people's culture has been widely criticized as illegitimate. The extended meaning of appropriation, which can have connotations of theft, has recently gained currency in a heated debate about commodities and cultural objects from American Indian and Aboriginal Arts, among others.[2] Appropriation is shown to be a multidirectional process. For example, European societies throughout history have been appropriating Japanese culture as much as the Japanese were appropriating Western culture.

Transdisciplinary Perspectives

Cultural appropriation is a notion shared among several disciplines. The clearest and most intensely considered use of the term is to be found in art history. Robert Nelson points to the Quadriga of Venice to reveal the importance of actors in the process of cultural appropriation (2003). The bronze monument on a facade of the Basilica of San Marco in Venice depicts a four-horsed chariot; it is the only surviving antique quadriga and had been displayed in Venice since the thirteenth century. In 1797, at a particular historical moment, this famous object was physically appropriated by the French military, i.e. Napoleon's troops carried it off to Paris. (It was returned about fifteen years later.) This forcible act of appropriation shows the usurping and violent dimension of this phenomenon. However, in many places around the world (Berlin, Paris, London), the monument has been appropriated in that it has been copied and adapted to a new setting. In the terminology of art history, this could be labeled a process of 'borrowing' or 'influencing.' However, neither of these terms reflects the relevance of the actor in such processes (Nelson 2003, 172). Actors in processes of appropriation are both those who, for example, physically take the Venetian Quadriga with them and those who reproduce it. It is fair to say that much of art production, worldwide and throughout history, is intentional appropriation of preexisting models (Schneider 2003; Schneider 2006).

Following Nelson (2003, 163), the act of appropriation can be related to Roland Barthes' *Mythologies* (1957). In Nelson's reading, Barthes' 'myths of everyday life' describe precisely these processes of appropriation. In Barthes' theory, the idea of a particular model, concept or technique appears attractive or convincing to such a degree that someone other than the idea's originator is motivated to engage in particular activities that result from accepting the idea. For example, accepting the idea that a good is particularly advanced technologically might lead to the acquisition of a specific product. This process can be interpreted as one of Barthes' everyday myths—a convincing story—or a moment of appropriation. Something to be appropriated is not simply a thing, but a thing desirable and associated with superior value that motivates the act of appropriation. None of the more recent quadrigas is identical to the Venetian original; the eighteenth or nineteenth century artists would insist that their reconfigured quadrigas were even more powerful and impressive than the original. Therefore a myth—an object or a story carrying strong connotative meaning—can be said to lie at the beginning of the appropriation process. However, instances of appropriation are not just symbolic achievements or cognitive activities; they are concrete actions. Typically, such actions take time, they can be partial (fragmented), and they can fail. Consequently, one might compare appropriation to distortion, but one should not equate it with influencing or borrowing. The moment a cultural trait is appropriated, it may become fragmented; subsequently, it can be reestablished in a different form and in a different context.

Currently, the debate about the role of appropriation in the world of art continues. Crucial, but unresolved, questions address the relationship between authenticity and cultural appropriation (Young 2008). Can an object of art be authentic if it is based on models originating elsewhere? Further unanswered questions concern the relationship between the 'original author' and the appropriators. Is appropriation an offensive act (Young 2005)? Do artists need particular strategies to legitimize their practices of appropriating (Schneider 2006)? Recently, the concept of 'Appropriation Art' has been acknowledged as an important trend. 'Appropriation Art' refers to artworks that *explicitly* use or exploit other artists' work (Blume Huttenlauch 2010).

For many art historians, cultural appropriation as a concept is still provocative because it dismisses the idea that an object autonomously moves from one place to another or from one cultural context to another. It is never just an object or a motive or a technology that 'diffuses' among cultures and epochs, but always human agents who act in favor of such changes and actively promote a specific contextualization. Who appropriates something? And what are the motives for such an action?

However, a transdisciplinary approach should abandon the concerns of art historians concerning authorship and legitimacy of shifting objects and ideas. Of a more general interest are the cultural transformations leading to new understandings and contextualizations of particular objects or ideas. 'Cultural appropriation' deals with how new social, shared meanings emerge and how 'newness' is perceived and evaluated.

The most convincing concept of cultural appropriation, when seen as innovation, comes from the French historian Michel de Certeau. In his seminal book *The Practice of Everyday Life* (1984), he describes how ordinary people appropriate things (and ideas or institutions) even without knowing much about them. De Certeau's argument is based on a distinction he draws between *strategies* and *tactics*. Whereas 'strategy' applies, for example, to armies in war, the notion of 'tactics' designates a way of acting when there is no clearly defined goal and no precise knowledge about the matter concerned. Tactics would appear to be the resort of the weak, but since they require very little structure, they may be more powerful in the long run.

When introducing a new product, institution or regulation, a company or governmental organization usually follows a 'strategy.' This means a particular product, institution or idea has to perform predefined tasks; such things result from a powerful structure promoting their future place in society. But—and this is the central tenet of de Certeau's approach—things are very often not adopted as intended, or they attain a meaning in everyday life quite different than intended.[3] These modifications or transformations are 'tactics of everyday acting.' Through their actions, people redefine the product, institution or idea and counter hegemonic structures with everyday routines and—sometimes—by intentionally neglecting rules. Ben Highmore calls the basis of such 'tactics of everyday acting' "situated knowledge" (2007, 16). The unplanned, pragmatic and often spontaneous transformations of products, institutions or ideas are the core of cultural appropriation. The historian

Marian Füssel has put this elegantly with his description of the "art of the weak." (2006, 7)[4]

De Certeau's approach has, of course, been criticized. It has been argued that he takes an anti-essentialist position, neglecting the real power of the powerful, i.e. of the state, corporations, institutions, etc. (Bogue 1986). For many, de Certeau's celebration of the agency of everyday activities seems limited. In this context, Rebekka Mallinckrodt (2004) points out that de Certeau has resonated much more in the US than in Britain or France. In the latter countries, his concept has been criticized much more directly, for not sufficiently addressing questions of power and justice.

In the development of the concept of 'cultural appropriation,' art history and social history are complemented by medieval history, which has provided some of the most provocative arguments. Following Denise Cuthbert (1998), appropriation can be everything between borrowing and stealing.[5] Ashley and Plesch (2002, 7) insist that appropriation is always about cultural relations in the context of an unequal distribution of power. In such a context, appropriation can be a form of 'cannibalizing' culture and may even lead to the vanishing of a culture.

Within cultural anthropology, the notion of cultural appropriation has gained particular relevance in debates about globalization. Anthropology has dealt with the notion of 'vanishing cultures' since its foundation as a discipline. In the nineteenth century, colonialism and modernity were blamed for the destruction of local cultures. Cultures were taken as isolated and autonomous units existing under homeostatic conditions; every influence from outside seemed to have devastating effects. A good example of this idea of homeostasis is Richard Salisbury's book *From Stone to Steel* (1962). Salisbury claims that the introduction of metal tools in New Guinea led to the dissolution of traditional knowledge and social structures. New consumer goods create new and threatening dependencies, forcing the members of the local culture to abandon inherited values. The advent of global goods was equated with the end of 'traditional cultures.' However, history teaches something different; today Salisbury's ideas have been found to be mistaken. Local cultures—including those of Papua New Guinea—have survived, and anthropology has had to learn that the idea of 'vanishing cultures' was an early stereotype within the discipline.

With the advent of globalization, the prophets of doom gained momentum, and many believed that, due to the worldwide impact of globally homogenous cultural traits, anthropology as the study of cultural diversity must come to an end. Faced with globalization, anthropology had to take the task of explaining cultural differences seriously. Anthropological research no longer limited itself to descriptions of different cultures, but began asking why cultures did not vanish and why cultural diversity did not decrease. In the wake of such reasoning anthropology reinvented itself as a discipline and focused on how societies maintain a distinctive identity and simultaneously transform their culture. One important way to do so was by appropriating global consumer goods. The anthropologists' key to highlighting these processes was to investigate forms of transformation and the assignment of distinctive meanings to otherwise globally uniform things (Appadurai 1986a, 1986b; Ferguson 1988). Today, authors with a background in anthropology like Arjun Appadurai, Homi Bhabha, Jonathan Friedman and others are among the leading figures in globalization theory. They explain how globalization transforms local cultures. Resistance is replaced by appropriation, which allows members of a culture to articulate a distinctive identity self-consciously. Anthropology has adopted several terms suited to the task of explaining transformations. 'Cultural appropriation' is one of them. Other terms with a similar meaning are 'domestication,' 'creolization,' 'nostrification' and 'hybridization.' The differences in meaning among them will not be discussed here in detail. For the moment, suffice it to underscore that they all contribute to explaining cultural differences in the context of globally uniform cultural trends.

To clarify the usefulness of these terms for explaining cultural diversity, it may be worthwhile to point out some concepts that assume a totally different understanding of cultural change. A prominent example is *McDonaldization* (Ritzer 1993). This concept suggests that the rationality of modern organizational principles bears substantially on all processes of producing and handling things, on the ways services are executed, and also on politics. Rationality is seen here as a powerful driving force which will erase cultural diversity in the long run. Another example comes from the history of consumption; here, a 'civilizing mission of consumption' is proclaimed, and consumer goods are presumed to have a political impact—that they inevitably influence societies toward higher cultural uniformity (Trentmann 2007). Thus, awareness has grown of cultural appropriation within the ongoing debate about globalization and its apparent homogenizing consequences, as has awareness of domestication, creolization, nostrification and hybridization. Of these concepts 'cultural appropriation' has the particular capacity to reveal something about individual actors and the agency of those who redesign contexts and re-establish meanings of specific things. Furthermore, in contrast to the other terms, appropriation focuses additionally on the transformation of cultures. Cultural appropriation can be a spontaneous process, or it can remain ephemeral, or it can fail. As many historical examples reveal, this process takes time and requires someone's particular effort. It is appropriate, therefore, to speak of the "work of appropriation," as James Carrier (1996, 128) has done in his studies of consumption.

These preliminaries should suffice to give a first impression of the origins of 'cultural appropriation' as a concept. It is time now to turn to more practical aspects of how to design research using the concept of cultural appropriation.

Fields of Research

Beyond its background in the disciplines of history and art history, the concept of cultural appropriation has achieved its widest recognition as a working tool in the field of cultural studies. This can be explained by the particular influence of de Certeau in this field of research. As cultural studies looks for culture in the transient and volatile aspects of a society (and not in its canonical and normative articulations), the notion of cultural appropriation as a 'tactic' of everyday life seems a good fit (Hall 1992). More recently, in light of globalization, appropriation has been widely accepted in media studies as well. Media studies comprise both the study of the reception of media and the analysis of the active use of media in order to give voice to local cultural articulations. Media studies from a more specifically anthropological perspective deal with such different contexts as the consumption of American soap operas in Upper Egypt, Brazilian telenovelas in Trinidad or the production of videos in West Africa (Abu-Lughod 1995; Miller 1992b; Larkin 2008). The list could easily be extended. In all cases, media are not simply 'consumed'; rather, they are thoroughly transformed.

Roger Silverstone has provided a model for how media studies can make particular use of the concept of cultural appropriation. In his seminal book *Consuming Technologies* (1992), he elucidates the concept of appropriation in the way people acquire and subsequently use new technologies on an everyday basis. His approach not only addresses media consumption, but also asks how media are transformed in usage and how societies are transformed by them. In doing so, Silverstone integrates the content side of media with its material aspects. Radios, TV-sets and mobile phones are objects appearing in specific contexts in households and requiring resources in terms of time and awareness. The material side of such objects is closely associated with their transformation. Thus, cultural appropriation describes the transformation of a publicly available commodity into a specifiable object that is part of someone's personal belongings.

Silverstone identifies four empirical fields as possible venues for studying cultural appropriation, not only for media, but for any object perceived at first as strange, foreign or simply innovative, but which then gradually becomes more familiar. These four fields are not successive phases or stages, but possible points of entry for studying cultural appropriation. They can guide a more differentiated research design. These fields describe the mutual changes that the objects and the people dealing with them undergo. The four aspects are 1) material appropriation, 2) objectification, 3) incorporation, and, last 4) transformation. Each aspect is explained in more detail in the following.

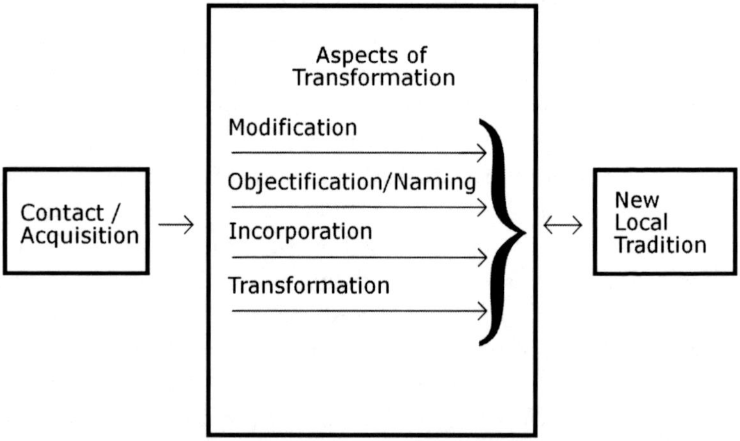

Fig. 1: Aspects of Cultural Appropriation (source: Hahn 2005a, 99)

1. *Material Appropriation and Modification.* Appropriation at the material level is the transition from formal economy (= a commodity has a certain price) to moral economy (= an object has a 'personal' value). Thus, an anonymous commodity becomes the personal possession of individuals and part of the material inventory of a society. This process may also include changes in the (material) form of an item. Examples of modification would be changing the decoration of a bicycle, an alteration of the screen of a mobile phone or

the reverse engineering of a simlock (Hahn and Kibora 2008). In many cases, however, the material appropriation consists solely of some form of internalization, of producing 'familiarity' with something that was previously an external, unknown entity. Material modifications are of particular relevance when it comes to such 'familiarization.' The idea of intentional enhancement is not limited to the "do-it-yourself-practitioners" producing "moded computers" or individually designed bicycles (Knorr 2009). A closer look at everyday routines reveals that the perceived value of many things is not highest when these are acquired, but only after they are used for some time. When someone's laptop is scratched or when the owner knows the idiosyncrasies of its software, the perceived value of this object is even higher. Thus, material appropriation is furthered by material modification.

2. *Objectification and Naming.* All items of material culture are submitted to classification, and only thereby do they come to belong to a cultural category of objects. New things acquire a particular place in the local 'universe of things.' Only then do they enter into contexts that define a culturally specific set of properties and purposes. Contexts, in this case, are fields of meaning that define proximity to or distance from other items. Who is allowed to use the object? Is the object seen as an individual possession or as something shared by several people? What is its role in everyday life? In short, novel objects are categorized and classified according to the same or similar categories as those applied to known objects. The outcome of this process is a reliable and permanent relationship between the object of appropriation and other things. Through this process, for example, an item may become a gendered object, suitable only for men, only for women, or for both sexes (Kirkham 1996).

Evidently, global goods have to be objectified in a culture-specific way. When for example young people acquire new, previously unknown things they consider fashionable, they are seeking to articulate distinction. In Arnould and Wilk's (1984) study, it is only for young people that jeans and tennis shoes are prestigious objects forming a distinctive style and expressing autonomy. For others, these things are not necessarily alluring. Still others ignore the objects completely or reject them because they are unwieldy to use (Hahn 2005b). Such differing or even conflicting evaluations express social differentiation; any objectification of a particular good is the outcome of negotiations.

Objectification also takes into account the naming of things and the ways people talk about them. In some regions of West Africa, for example, bicycles are called 'iron horses.' The naming reveals the way the respective society evaluates the object in question: the bicycle's association in name with horses indicates its high value, something beyond the economic means of most households in rural West Africa (Hahn 2004b). This differs profoundly from the bicycle's German nickname *Drahtesel*, which literally means 'wire donkey.' Another example of locally specific objectification is the German term for a mobile phone, *Handy*. The term *Handy* is an entirely local creation, but it thrives on its linguistic affinity to the Anglophone world. It associates the mobile phone with the ideology of globalism, because English is equated with the globalized world. At the same time *Handy* alludes to something practical, smart, readily at hand; this is apparently what makes the term a good fit for German-speaking mobile phone users (Burkart 2007).

As the examples suggest, material appropriation and objectification are important aspects of cultural appropriation. Becoming familiar with an object and naming it are core elements of appropriation. But they do not suffice to make something a part of one's identity. The following two aspects are of equal importance:

3. *Incorporation.* This term refers to the development of practical routines of use. Often, everyday modes of dealing with things are of habitual character. There is a 'correct way' of holding a pen with the fingers and a proper way of sitting on a bicycle in order to ride safely. Along with objectification, specific modes of habitual usage and corporeal interaction between user and object emerge. The intuitive ways of touching and handling an object establish norms of interacting with these things. The item itself, its operation, impacts people's bodies and thereby the time people spend with it in their immediate physical vicinity. Simultaneously, using the item changes the way people perceive their own bodies.

Again, the bicycle in Africa is a good example. Incorporation includes the physical fitness required to ride a bicycle. Furthermore, as a result of the physical disassembling of bicycles—nearly all removable parts quickly disappear—and of the particulars of their use there, a rider's ability to stop without brakes or balance heavy loads also comes into play. Because brakes often have been removed, the ability to stop a moving bicycle in Africa is quite special, even while it is fairly common for their riders to be carrying loads of up to 100 kilograms.

More directly than the other aspects of cultural appropriation, incorporation refers to processes of appropriation that are by no means strictly or intentionally controlled. The appropriator's body is a partner in a 'dialogue without words' aimed at finding routines to deal with a new object.[6] This is particularly evident in the case of complex technological objects like the bicycle and the mobile phone. For example, the harmfulness of electromagnetic radiation from mobile phones was debated extensively at a particular moment after the introduction of this new device. The result was the widely accepted advice that one should not sleep with one's mobile beside the bed or carry it too close to one's body.

Other pertinent examples refer to the history of certain beverages. In Europe, coffee had been appropriated with a mode of drinking it in cups, preferably of porcelain. The advent of Italian coffee specialties was marked by the distinction of drinking coffee from glasses. The day people are no longer familiar with drinking coffee from a porcelain cup will be the day the incorporation of 'coffee Italian style' is completed. Thus cultural appropriation also explains why innovations do not lead so much to substitution as to an expansion of another way of doing something.

Whereas objectification is primarily relevant with regard to meaning, naming and categorization, incorporation describes more direct forms of interaction with things as well as people, and the corresponding consequences for actors' perceptions. But it should be emphasized that both objectification and incorporation are important at either level, the individual and the social: both focus on human agency, and on social expectations.

4. *Transformation.* Appropriation is a process that leads in some cases—but not in all cases—to irreversible transformations. What initially is an imported commodity gradually becomes part of the local life-world and comes into individual or collective possession. The appropriated object acquires local meanings; it is no longer considered 'foreign.' Appropriation does not, however, always result in the obfuscation of provenance. In some cases, people accept the paradox of knowing about a good's global provenance, yet simultaneously considering it their own.

A closer examination of regional differences between distinct pathways of appropriation can help one understand how spaces of meaning become available, and what motivates the appropriation of new things into particular contexts. A case in point, again with reference to the bicycle, is classification according to gender. In some areas, bicycles would be considered exclusively male objects, whereas elsewhere both men and women ride them. The history of the introduction of bicycles in Germany exemplifies both. Bicycles were initially part of the male domain, and later became an object common to both sexes. In Germany around 1900, the sporting, masculine dimension boosted the vehicle's adoption; its transport and mobility dimension were not yet as relevant as they would become later on (Ebert 2010).

The term 'transformation' underscores that classifications of this kind represent definite processes which are difficult to reverse. 'Transformation' emphasizes the accomplishment of making a thing into something different, new and locally defined, regardless whether or not its (material) form has changed. Transformation also assigns particular relevance to the creation of new traditions. The Tuareg example of drinking tea shows perfectly how appropriation and tradition mutually legitimize each other. Daniel Miller puts this more polemically when he speaks of the 'authenticity' of imported goods (1992a). The establishment of a local tradition combining the appropriated object with a specific story or myth is an integral part of transformation. This is what Robert Nelson refers to in his reading of Roland Barthes' *Mythologies*.

All four aspects explained here—(1) material acquisition and modification, (2) objectification, (3) incorporation and (4) transformation—can be considered as partial processes of cultural appropriation. It is, however, difficult to speak of a 'complete' or definitive appropriation, because the status of an object, institution or idea in any culture remains negotiable. Nothing is immune to redefinition and re-contextualization. Cultural appropriation is therefore related in particular to the status of being in-between, of negotiating specific local meanings for a global good, sometimes for a limited period only. Simultaneously, every appropriated object also constitutes a link to another world, and this link explains the object's particular relevance in a culture's specific and distinctive identity.

Similarity and Diversity

It might be useful to explain why cultural appropriation has only recently been acknowledged as a relevant concept of cultural change. In the history of European thought, the first modern usage of the term 'culture' by Samuel von Pufendorff (Pagden 1995; Stagl 1981, 55), and subsequently by Gottfried Herder (Böhme, Matussek and Müller 2000, 38), designates something uniform and shared by all members of a society. This then dominant concept of culture refers to those phenomena recognized by all members of a society as carriers of this culture. In short, this dominant line of thought is based on similarity, on homogeneity: men and women who have had similar experiences embody similar identities and therefore cohere more than others.

There is, however, another way of reasoning about culture which has its roots in Enlightenment thinking, and which later on becomes a foundational concept in anthropology (Hahn 2000). It takes a different perspective: societies exist *in spite of* an inherent *heterogeneity*. If all men and women were similar, there would be no such thing as 'culture.' One could even say that anthropology, throughout its history as a discipline, has been obsessed with difference. Anthropological investigations started with differences between cultures and differences within societies. From the very beginning of their discipline, anthropologists eschewed conceptual frameworks that integrated these differences into coherent global systems. One such framework, from the nineteenth century, is evolution. Another, more recent and widely acknowledged one is ecology, which explains how peoples and their economies differ due to different environmental factors.

Whereas the similarity paradigm assumes coherence and homogeneity within cultures, and takes culture to be a primordial entity, the diversity paradigm leaves more room for the complexity of processes of cultural change and for intercultural relations. It may not be surprising that anthropology always had a special interest in such complexities. As a consequence, it was more sensitive to the influence of globalization on local cultures. Probably the most important outcome of this anthropological understanding of culture is that now anthropologists assume that homogeneity may never be taken for granted within a given culture. Instead, they take diversity and heterogeneity to be the 'normal condition' of societies. Cultural appropriation is one of the concepts that bring forth how diversity is managed within societies.

Among the more recent approaches dealing with diversity, the work of Michael Taussig in *Mimesis and Alterity* (1993) stands out for its relevance to appropriation. His seminal study of similarity and difference explores how people intentionally make the best use of minimal differences. As he demonstrates, it is in particular those cultural phenomena that seem to be the result of a perfect adoption or assimilation in which the smallest differences can constitute the basis for a distinctive social and political sense of belonging. Coca-Cola provides good examples of this kind of instrumentalization. Anthropologists have produced a number of studies on how Coca-Cola has been appropriated in local cultures. In some of these cases, it has gained a considerable relevance in articulating distinctive local, regional or national identities.[7]

Taussig does not only discuss creative redefinition and the relevance of minor differences. He argues that the tactical, i.e. locally improvised, use of global brands and commodities represents a kind of subversion. People seem to adapt to global patterns but, in doing so, they reject the rationale behind these phenomena; they reject the inherent global character of these items. Coke as a leading brand is well aware of this; it consequently reacted to its customers' desire to consume Coca-Cola as a local product and created regionally specific publicity campaigns for its products. According to Taussig, the so-called global players may perceive the local transformation of their products and brands as a threat to their corporate identity. But in many cases global producers gradually recognize that they must accept such appropriations as a way to create new traditions and, consequently, to expand their markets.

There is more to say about similarity and diversity. Even if specific local cultural forms are created, appropriated objects may be subject to a kind of 'double association.' That is, for those societies that consider themselves marginalized or disadvantaged within the global context, the consumption and appropriation of global goods might be quite desirable. Knowing about innovations from abroad and wanting to acquire foreign goods can be a form of expressing discontent with one's own society. Appropriation, representing the "allure of the foreign" (Orlove 1997), is a tactic for overcoming one's current status and the dominant patterns in one's own society. In these particular contexts, appropriation is a statement about the superiority of the imported. Thus the acquisition of American films and other media can be an expression of local identity (through translation, localizing of places, etc.), but it can also be a manifestation of a particular esteem of the 'American way of life.'

The examples underscore the importance of distinction and difference in cultural appropriation. On the one hand, even the smallest differences are observed and valuated. On the other hand, appropriation is a tactic by which actors may regulate and negotiate difference. One option is to explicitly highlight difference by especially emphasizing the creative side of the process. But another option is to foreground the transcultural connection created through the appropriated object. Difference is important, but similarity comes in when one considers the double association of the appropriated object.

Conclusion: *Regards Croisées* and Unequal Power Relations

Because the last two centuries (and probably even longer) have been dominated by imperialism and colonialism, relations between societies and cultures have often been characterized by uneven power relations. As a rule, exchanges between cultures and societies have been asymmetric and often marked by arbitrary limitations and violence. These aspects are typical of colonialism, in which a powerful colonizer frequently imposes severe restrictions on the colonized in their access to the colonizer's culture. It is not a coincidence that many prominent studies of cultural appropriation are based on case studies from (post-)colonial contexts. These studies show how the powerless use cultural appropriation as a tactic to engage in decision making processes from which they would otherwise be excluded. Appropriation turns out to be a conceptual tool for anthropologists and historians focused on the contradictions of colonial processes and the often overlooked agency of the colonized.[8]

But appropriation is not only a subversive tactic of the powerless. It can also be a self-conscious expression of power exercised by globally dominant groups. Thus, the collection of objects from Africa, South America and elsewhere in ethnographic museums, from the so called 'world fairs' in the nineteenth century (Bayerdörfer and Hellmuth 2003) to the exhibition of 'native art' in Western galleries in the twenty-first century (Myers 2002), are examples of cultural appropriation, too. A current debate in this context centers on the legitimacy of commercializing paintings by non-Western artists. Another example of contested appropriation is the success of 'plastic shamanism,' which comprises traditional shamanistic rituals with neurobiological knowledge, and is used for new (and sometimes fashionable) forms of therapy (Wallis 2003). Vehement critics of such practices are asking for more responsible eclecticism and for mechanisms to make sure that the rights of the true 'authors' are respected.

In their book *Borrowed Power*, Bruce Ziff and Pratima V. Rao (1997) give examples of such questionable appropriations and the corresponding legal issues. They highlight the insatiable thirst of the Western art market for the material and ideational appropriation of non-Western art and call for a more thorough dealing with the legal questions. Much as in the example of the Venetian quadriga mentioned above, it seems that the valuation of these artworks increases with their potential for appropriation. The important difference is, however, that all participating actors know that this practice of appropriating non-Western art can exist only because of unequal power relations on the global level.

It is difficult to organize or to control appropriation. Appropriation is always possible as long as an object or an idea is available to someone who intends to appropriate it. Walter Moser (1996) explains cultural appropriation as a form of cultural recycling: things which have become common property, which are no longer strictly controlled in a particular culture, are adopted by others and gain new and specific meanings (and power) in their hands. The course of an object's value in its journey from one place and culture to the other is bifurcated: the value of the appropriated object decreases in one culture while it rises in another.[9] Once again the actor-centered perspective is worth noting: these shifts only take place through the efforts of actual people. Only through the work of appropriation, in all its facets described here, are new meanings, practices and traditions created.

Of even greater relevance is the bi-directionality underlying appropriation as a concept. As much as indigenous cultures appropriate Western technologies, goods and institutions, the West appropriates things from elsewhere. China and Chinoiseries have been in fashion in Europe for centuries; "Occidentalism" (Carrier 1995) has been the ideology of appreciating European goods and technologies in China and Japan—but it is an ideology that never produces a discontinuity in the transformative processes that contribute to a distinctive Chinese or Japanese identity. The new identity that stands at the end of this particular appropriation process is 'Chinese without rejecting European goods.' Perhaps this example indicates best how much appropriation has to do with power: on a global scale, Japan and China are countries that have been systematically appropriating Western technology. This particular "Occidentalism" contributed substantially not only to their economic success but also to their capacity to express a distinctive, non-Western identity.

Cultural appropriation is a tool to describe both how societies transform objects and ideas and how societies as such are transformed as they integrate new things, and as new local traditions arise. Today, with globalization, no society can escape such transformations, and thus appropriation has become an indispensable tool for understanding the benefits and perils of global cultural relations. The appropriated things, ideas and institutions are no more, and no less, than indicators of change in the society itself.

Notes

1 Previous research and subsequent publications were carried out by the author in the framework of the collaborative research program "Local Action and Global Influences in Africa" (SFB 560) at Bayreuth University. Among the publications related to this research are articles on appropriation (Hahn 2004a, 2008b, 2009, 2012) and alienation (Hahn 2008a).

2 The recent version of the Wikipedia entry is much biased in its focus on legal issues concerning appropriation. http://en.wikipedia.org/wiki/Cultural_appropriation (accessed September 28, 2011).

3 For cultural appropriation in this sense, everyday life, and therefore the understanding of culture as something that happens 'on the street,' is quite relevant. Numerous examples from the history of the quotidian (*Alltagsgeschichte*) and cultural studies bear witness to the need to integrate studies of everyday life with studies of cultural appropriation (Dinges 1987; Highmore 2002; Mackay 1997; Lüdtke 1989; Teuteberg and Wischermann 1985).

4 Füssel (2006, 16) suggests a comparison between de Certeau's notion of appropriation and Bourdieu's concept of *habitus*. De Certeau, however, was highly skeptical of the idea of a habitus defining the valuation of things or the ways people deal with things or institutions. While recognizing an implicit acceptance of powerful structures hidden in the idea of habitus, de Certeau insists that the tactics of cultural appropriation work perfectly without such structuring principles. Cultural appropriation may even undermine and subsequently destroy established lifestyles. One might say that the concept of appropriation does not align with the idea of an existing habitus; but it is a valuable tool for explaining how new forms of habitus come into being and change the social recognition of those creating the new habitus. Bourdieu's approach has a strong bias toward structures; it implicitly presents a static image of societies. By contrast, de Certeau is more interested in the emergence of new cultural phenomena and the fading away of old, established ones (Costey 2004, 12–4).

5 Anthropologists, however, would insist that it can be both at the same time (Strathern 2011).

6 The role of the body in contextualizing things is often underestimated. The interaction between the object and the body is crucial to familiarity with any object (Gatewood 1985).

7 Whereas in Europe Coca-Cola is considered a 'not so healthy' drink for younger people, Robert Foster collected advertisements from Papua New Guinea that illustrate how Coca-Cola has achieved the status of a conveyor of modernity (Foster 2002, 2008). Daniel Miller (1998) presents evidence from Trinidad that Coca-Cola has achieved a status as an appropriate drink for the black (African-American) population; meanwhile yellow or colourless soft drinks are associated with white people. See Alcalde (2009) for Coca-Cola in Peru, Özkan and Foster (2005) for Turkey and Hollensen (2007, 637) for Coca-Cola in Arab countries.

8 Powerless people use appropriation to counter hegemonic power and, simultaneously, to create platforms of self-assertion and resistance. Jean and John Comaroff (1991) have revealed this in documents of missionary communities in South Africa. They find that proselytes undermined the dress code by minute changes: going to church, people would wear the prescribed shirt and trousers, but arrange these in particular ways so that everyone could recognize the difference between the missionaries and the parishioners. These forms of resistance led to other, more efficient forms of resistance and eventually inspired independent African churches.

9 David Napier (1997) is even more explicit in describing the shifting value of things at the moment of their appropriation. He argues that donor cultures of objects appropriated by others are already weakened and fragmented. Only through loss of control does the process of appropriation become possible.

References

Abu-Lughod, Janet L. (1995). The Objects of Soap Opera: Egyptian Television and the Cultural Politics of Modernity. In Daniel Miller (ed.). *Worlds Apart: Modernity through the Prism of the Local*, 190–210. London: Routledge.

Alcalde, Cristina (2009). Between Incas and Indians. Inca Kola and the Construction of a Peruvian-global Modernity. *Journal of Consumer Culture*, 9, 1, 31–54.

Appadurai, Arjun (ed.). (1986a). *The Social Life of Things. Commodities in Cultural Perspective.* Cambridge: Cambridge University Press.

Appadurai, Arjun (1986b). Theory in Anthropology. Center and Periphery. *Comparative Studies in Society and History*, 28, 356–61.

Arnould, Eric J., and Richard R. Wilk (1984). Why do the Natives Wear Adidas? *Advances in Consumer Research*, 11, 748–52.

Ashley, Kathleen, and Veronique Plesch (2002). The Cultural Processes of "Appropriation." *Journal of Medieval and Early Modern Studies*, 32, 1, 1–15.

Barthes, Roland (1957). *Mythologies.* Paris: Édition du Seuil.

Bayerdörfer, Hans-Peter, and Eckhart Hellmuth (eds.). (2003). *Exotica. Konsum und Inszenierung des Fremden im 19. Jahrhundert.* Münster: Lit.

Blume Huttenlauch, Anna (2010). *Appropriation Art—Kunst an der Grenze des Urheberrechts.* Baden Baden: Nomos.

Böhme, Hartmut, Peter Matussek, and Lothar Müller (eds.). (2000). *Orientierung Kulturwissenschaft. Was sie kann, was sie will.* Reinbek: Rowohlt.

Burkart, Günter (2007). *Handymania. Wie das Mobiltelefon unser Leben verändert hat.* Frankfurt/Main: Campus.

Campbell, Colin (1992). The Desire for the New. Its Nature and Social Location as Presented in Theories of Fashion and Modern Consumerism. In Roger Silverstone (ed.). *Consuming Technologies: Media and Information in Domestic Spaces*, 48–64. London: Routledge.

Carrier, James G. (ed.). (1995). *Occidentalism. Images of the West.* Oxford: Clarendon.

Carrier, James G. (1996). Consumption. In Alan Barnard and Jonathan Spencer (eds.). *Encyclopedia of Social and Cultural Anthropology*, 128–9. London: Routledge.

Certeau, Michel de (1984). *The Practice of Everyday Life.* Berkeley: University of California.

Comaroff, Jean, and John L. Comaroff (1991). *Of Revelation and Revolution: Christianity, Colonialism, and Consciousness in South Africa.* Chicago: University of Chicago Press.

Costey, Paul (2004). Pierre Bourdieu, penseur de la pratique. *Tracés. Revue de Sciences humaines*, 7, 11–25.

Cuthbert, Denise (1998). Beg, Borrow or Steal: the Politics of Cultural Appropriation. *Postcolonial Studies*, 1, 2, 257–62.

Dinges, Martin (1987). Materielle Kultur und Alltag—die Unterschichten in Bordeaux im 16./17. Jahrhundert. *Francia*, 15, 257–79.

Ebert, Anne-Katrin (2010). *Radelnde Nationen. Die Geschichte des Fahrrads in Deutschland und den Niederlanden bis 1940.* Frankfurt/Main: Campus.

Ferguson, James (1988). Review Essay: Cultural Exchange. New Developments in the Anthropology of Commodities. *Cultural Anthropology*, 3, 488–519.

Foster, Robert J. (2002). Globalization. A Soft Drink Perspective. In Robert J. Foster (ed.). *Materializing the Nation: Commodities, Consumption, and Media in Papua New Guinea*, 151–74. Bloomington: Indiana University Press.

Foster, Robert J. (2008). *Coca-Globalization. Following Soft Drinks from New York to New Guinea.* New York: Palgrave Macmillan.

Füssel, Marian (2006). Die Kunst der Schwachen. Zum Begriff der 'Aneignung' in der Geschichtswissenschaft. *Sozial.Geschichte. Zeitschrift für historische Analyse des 20. und 21. Jahrhunderts*, 21, 3, 7–28.

Gatewood, John B. (1985). Actions Speak Louder than Words. In Janet Dougherty (ed.). *Directions in Cognitive Anthropology*, 199–219. Urbana: University of Illinois Press.

Hahn, Hans P. (2000). Zum Begriff der Kultur in der Ethnologie. In Siegfried Fröhlich (ed.). *Kultur: ein Interdisziplinäres Kolloquium zur Begrifflichkeit*, 149–64. Halle: Landesamt für Archäologie.

Hahn, Hans P. (2004a). Global Goods and the Process of Appropriation. In Peter Probst and Gerd Spittler (eds.). *Between Resistance and Expansion. Explorations of Local Vitality in Africa*, 211–30. Münster: Lit.

Hahn, Hans P. (2004b). Die Aneignung des Fahrrads. In Kurt Beck et al. (eds.). *Blick nach vorn. Festgabe für Gerd Spittler zum 65. Geburtstag*, 264–80. Cologne: Köppe.

Hahn, Hans P. (2005a). *Materielle Kultur. Eine Einführung.* Berlin: Reimer.

Hahn, Hans P. (2005b). Stil und Lebensstil als Konzeptualisierungen der Bedeutungen materieller Kultur. In Tobias L. Kienlin (ed.). *Die Dinge als Zeichen: Kulturelles Wissen und materielle Kultur*, 41–52. Bonn: Habelt.

Hahn, Hans P. (2008a). Appropriation, Alienation and Syncretization: Lessons from the Field. In Afeosemime Unuose Adogame et al. (eds.). *Unpacking the New: Critical Perspectives on Cultural Syncretization in African and Beyond*, 71–92. Münster: Lit.

Hahn, Hans P. (2008b). Diffusionism, Appropriation, and Globalization. Some Remarks on Current Debates in Anthropology. *Anthropos*, 103, 191–202.

Hahn, Hans P. (2009). Consommation, modèles et appropriation en Afrique. In Dominique Darbon (ed.). *La politique des modèles en Afrique—Simulation, dépolitisation et appropriation*, 75–88. Paris: Karthala.

Hahn, Hans P. (2012). Circulating Objects and the Power of Localizing Strategies: Appropriation and Hybridization. In Philipp W. Stockhammer (ed.). *Conceptualizing Cultural Hybridization. A Transdisciplinary Approach*, 27–42. Berlin: Springer.

Hahn, Hans P., and Ludovic O. Kibora (2008). The Domestication of the Mobile Phone. Oral Society and New ICT in Burkina Faso. *Journal of Modern African Studies*, 46, 1, 87–109.

Hancock, James F. (1992). *Plant Evolution and the Origin of Crop Species*. Englewood Cliffs, NJ: Prentice Hall.

Highmore, Ben (2002). *Everyday Life and Cultural Theory*. London: Routledge.

Highmore, Ben (2007). An Epistemological Awakening: Michel de Certeau and the Writing of Culture. *Social Anthropology*, 15, 1, 13–26.

Hollensen, Svend (2007). *Global Marketing. A Decision-Oriented Approach*. Englewood Cliffs, NJ: Prentice Hall.

Kirkham, Pat (1996). *The Gendered Object*. Manchester: Manchester University Press.

Knorr, Alexander (2009). Die kulturelle Aneignung des Spielraums: Vom virtuosen Spielen zum Modifizieren und zurück. In Matthias Bopp (ed.). *Shooter. Eine multidisziplinäre Einführung*, 217–46. Münster: LIT.

Larkin, Brian (2008). *Signal and Noise: Media, Infrastructure, and Urban Culture in Nigeria*. Durham: Duke University Press.

Mackay, Hugh (ed.). (1997). *Consumption and Everyday Life*. London: Sage.

Mallinckrodt, Rebekka von (2004). 'Discontenting, surely, even for those versed in French Intellectual Pyrotechnics.' Michel de Certeau in Frankreich, Deutschland und den USA. In Rebekka Habermas and Rebekka von Mallinckrodt (eds.). *Interkultureller Transfer und nationaler Eigensinn*, 221–41. Göttingen: Wallstein.

Miller, Daniel (1992a). Imported Goods as Authentic Culture. In Reinhard Eisendle (ed.). *Produktkulturen: Dynamik und Bedeutungswandel des Konsums*, 271–88. Frankfurt/Main: Campus.

Miller, Daniel (1992b). The Young and the Restless in Trinidad. A Case of the Local and the Global in Mass Consumption. In Roger Silverstone (ed.). *Consuming Technologies: Media and Information in Domestic Spaces*, 163–82. London: Routledge.

Miller, Daniel (1998). Coca-Cola: A Black Sweet Drink from Trinidad. In Daniel Miller (ed.). *Material Cultures. Why some Things Matter*, 169–87. Chicago: University of Chicago Press.

Moser, Walter (1996). Le recyclage culturel. In Claude Dionne, Silvestra Mariniello and Walter Moser (eds.). *Recyclages. Économies de l'appropriation culturelle*, 23–53. Montréal: Balzac.

Muensterberger, Werner (1995). *Sammeln, eine unbändige Leidenschaft. Psychologische Perspektiven*. Berlin: Berlin-Verlag.

Myers, Fred R. (2002). *Painting Culture. The Making of an Aboriginal High Art*. Durham: Duke University.

Napier, A. David (1997). Losing One's Marbles: Cultural Property and Indigenous Thought. In Jeremy MacClancy (ed.). *Contesting Art—Art, Politics and Identity in the Modern World*, 165–83. Oxford: Berg.

Nelson, Robert S. (2003). Appropriation. In Robert S. Nelson and Richard Shiff (eds.). *Critical Terms for Art History*, 160–73. Chicago: University of Chicago Press.
Orlove, Benjamin S. (ed.). (1997). *The Allure of the Foreign. Imported Goods in Postcolonial Latin America.* Ann Arbor: University of Michigan.
Özkan, Derya, and Robert J. Foster (2005). Consumer Citizenship, Nationalism, and Neoliberal Globalization in Turkey: The Advertising Launch of Cola Turka. *Advertising & Society Review*, 6, 3, n. pag.
Pagden, Anthony (1995). The Effacement of Difference: Colonialism and the Origins of Nationalism in Diderot and Herder. In Gyan Prakash (ed.). *After Colonialism: Imperial Histories and Postcolonial Displacements*, 129–52. New Jersey: Princeton University Press.
Ritzer, George (1993). *The McDonaldization of Society: an Investigation into the Changing Character of Contemporary Social Life.* Thousand Oaks: Pine Forge.
Salisbury, Richard F. (1962). *From Stone to Steel. Economic Consequences of a Technological Change in New Guinea.* Melbourne: Melbourne University Press.
Schneider, Arnd (2003). On 'Appropriation': A Critical Reappraisal of the Concept and its Application in Global Art Practices. *Social Anthropology*, 11, 2, 215–29.
Schneider, Arnd (2006). *Appropriation as Practice. Art and Identity in Argentina.* New York: Palgrave.
Silverstone, Roger, Eric Hirsch, and David Morley (1992). Information and Communication Technologies and the Moral Economy of the Household. In Roger Silverstone (ed.). *Consuming Technologies: Media and Information in Domestic Spaces*, 15–31. London: Routledge.
Stagl, Justin (1981). *Kulturanthropologie und Gesellschaft. Eine wissenschaftssoziologische Darstellung der Kulturanthropologie und Ethnologie.* Berlin: Reimer.
Strathern, Marilyn (2011). Sharing, Stealing and Borrowing Simultaneously. In Veronica Strang and Mark Busse (eds.). *Ownership and Appropriation* (= Association of Social Anthropologists Monographs, 47), 23–41. Oxford: Berg.
Taussig, Michael T. (1993). *Mimesis and Alterity. A Particular History of the Senses.* London: Routledge.
Teuteberg, Hans J., and Clemens Wischermann (1985). *Wohnalltag in Deutschland, 1850–1914. Bilder, Daten, Dokumente.* Münster: Coppenrath.
Trentmann, Frank (2007). Citizenship and Consumption. *Journal of Consumer Culture*, 7, 2, 147–58.
Wallis, Robert J. (2003). *Shamans/Neo-Shamans. Ecstasy, Alternative Archaeologies, and Contemporary Pagans.* London: Routledge.
Young, James O. (2005). Profound Offense and Cultural Appropriation. *Journal of Aesthetics and Art Criticism*, 63, 2, 135–46.
Young, James O. (2008). *Cultural Appropriation and the Arts.* London: Blackwell.
Ziff, Bruce, and Pratima V. Rao (eds.). (1997). *Borrowed Power. Essays on Cultural Appropriation.* New Brunswick, NJ: Rutgers University Press.

Appropriating Food

Introduction

Doris Feldmann

It has become commonplace to say that "we are what we eat" (Long 2009, 3). In the context of contemporary cultural studies, this old adage takes on a new significance. In that it defines individual and group identities (Camp 1980, 141), the consumption of food is part and parcel of identity politics. Because they offer people ways to create and communicate cultural meanings, including distinctions on an intra- and intercultural level, the choices a person makes in their food consumption can signify a host of identity positions, including national, ethnic, gendered, and religious ones. If culture is a signifying practice, then food and eating are basic semiotic strategies, basic acts of representation (Döring et al. 2003, 2–3). Hence, food functions (almost) like a language—it conveys meaning via (structural) difference. It is therefore appropriate that food has been analyzed both as a system of communication and a semantic field. More specifically, we might consider how food functions as a 'myth of everyday life' in Roland Barthes' sense. 'National cuisines' are prime examples of the operation of such myths. They are produced discursively and have political effects in that they help people define their national identities and stereotype perceived outsiders (Mintz 2003, 32) (as, for instance, when foreigners are called 'krauts,' 'frogs' or 'limeys'). Even if so-called national cuisines may be described as "for the most part merely the artificial sticking together of regional dishes" (ibid., 25), they nevertheless help construct an imagined food community.

Once we start considering the appropriation of foreign food, as the three papers assembled here do, the conceptual and methodological complexities multiply. The consumption of foreign food may be experienced as a performative act of identification, as a pleasurable form of affirming an identity or as "the commodification of 'Otherness'" (hooks 1998, 181)—often all at the same time. It may even be an empowering act of nostrification: the ingestion—and, perhaps, the incorporation—of cultural difference. In the end, what exactly the difference is "between cultural appreciation and cultural appropriation" (ibid., 200) remains an open question.

This question already indicates how complex 'taking food' is, whether as bodily ingestion or as an object of cultural analysis. One reason for this has to do with methodology. As an emergent interdisciplinary field, the study of food is very much governed by competing theories and approaches. After all, the very word 'food' refers both to "the raw materials" used to prepare meals and to "the meals themselves" (Camp 1980, 142), so that "the study of food [...] is both object- and behaviour-oriented" (ibid., 151). As a cultural practice, 'food' includes tastes, habits, and patterns of production and consumption—all of which have been conceptualized within different disciplinary frameworks. From a sociological perspective, food and eating can serve as social markers, as a means of 'distinction.' We also have to consider issues of food production and distribution—what Appadurai calls 'gastro-politics' (1981). Socio-economically, food is a commodity, albeit one that has been claimed to play a unique role in everyday life "in contradistinction to all other commodities" (Mintz 2002, 24). Both politically and economically, it is part of a consumer culture; it has developed into a massive economic undertaking and has become one of the biggest industries among Western national economies. Historical analysis may seek to trace this development to the emergence of a distinct consumer culture beginning in the eighteenth century; but when it comes to food, historical approaches are fraught with difficulties, and any historical analysis must be conducted in a very careful manner (Versteegen 2009, 227). For example, the claim that foreign influences on 'national cuisines' were strong even in the nineteenth and early twentieth centuries is in itself convincing—but was food really perceived as having a nationality at that time, or is this an anachronistic projection? In historical analyses, food mostly tends to be a symptom: it is 'milked' for its significance as a key to larger social and economic trends, while the dominant line of cultural studies analyzes or 'reads' food symbolically, as a representation of complex negotiations of self-definition.

To continue the brief overview of the different theoretical frameworks, one might also claim from a psychological perspective that food is a site of desire, that eating is "our most frequently indulged pleasure" (Belasco 2002, 2). Food then also appears as a site of anxiety and may provoke rejection or even disgust. In this context, the consumption of food challenges the binary opposition between inside and outside, between subject and object. With all the critical attention being paid to the cultural characteristics of food, we might still miss another crucial point, one easily forgotten in light of the commodification of food as a 'good.' Food must not only be taken both figuratively and literally, as both a trope and a material object; it has not only a sensual oral aspect but is also an important anthropological and biological factor. Eating is a fundamental act, and as "the first of the essentials of life" (ibid.), food blurs the distinctions between nature and culture. In fact, food and eating may be "prone to symbolic investiture" precisely because they are so fundamental (Mintz 2003, 32). If cultural contact, migration and cultural hybridity are old phenomena, and if food has always been involved in the daily practice of cultural translation, then, surely, the appropriation of 'foreign food' has a (pre)history longer than that of appropriation of foreign books, cars or other 'modern objects.'

Each of the three essays in this section examines a different cultural transmission of food, and they all do so from an historical perspective: they focus on the migration of German food to Britain, on the marketing of British food in Germany, and on the appropriation of Chinese food by New Yorkers. None of these forms of cultural contact is quite the same as the other, and each comes with a healthy amount of theoretical and methodological baggage.

In the first essay, *Margit Schulte Beerbühl* argues that the appropriation of foreign food in Britain should not be regarded as a new phenomenon. The foreign influence she studies is that of German butchers moving to Britain in the nineteenth century. In tying the migration of food to the immigration of people, her analysis of cultural appropriation of foreign food immediately faces a challenging set of questions about the exchange between 'Self' and 'Other.' A first question concerns the British 'Self': when German sausage moved to Britain, what did it find there? Was there a distinctive 'national British cuisine'? Victorian society was characterized by distinctions of class, and the consumption of pork or sausage was part of the Victorians' identity politics, marking and constructing their economic and social status. Schulte Beerbühl also discusses family patterns, transnational networks, transport systems, agency systems and new production methods in order to reveal the complexity of the appropriation processes.

The second paper focuses on an example of the limits of cultural translatability. *Ole Sparenberg* charts failed attempts to market British fried fish at shops in Germany in the 1920s and explores reasons for that society's resistance to foreign food and eating habits. Again, the protagonists in the exchange programs between 'Self' and 'Other' turn out to be less clearly delimited or stable than perhaps initially expected. In the early twentieth century, 'fish and chips' had not yet come to be associated with British national identity[1] (Panayi 2008, 18) and lacked the 'exotic aspects' of an 'ethnic' food like Chinese. Resistance to cultural translation and foreign eating habits also indicates food as a marker of social difference, as shown by the case of fish and chips, a dish rooted in British working-class culture. According to Sparenberg, class differences include different ideas about family meals, and thus about domesticity and gender. Those who tried to transfer the concept of the fish-and-chips shop to Germany, however, faced multilayered problems. Sparenberg sheds light on these through an examination of the language-specific problems of translating the term into German, the lack of capital backing for the industry, and the training and marketing practices employed.

In the third paper, *Sonja Weishaupt* shows how ethnicity in the form of Chinese immigrant food has influenced American eating habits and thus the practices of everyday life. The appropriation of Chinese food by New Yorkers into their own kitchens was a highly gendered activity involving ideologies of health and household management as well as entertainment rituals. The essay explores the 'exotic' aspect of 'ethnic food'[2] and the Orientalist strategies which might have been at work here.[3] Weishaupt also tackles the difficult question of appropriation or 'Americanization': how authentic can Chinese cuisine in America be, when "[s]ome dishes have been adapted beyond recognition" (Pang 2003, 55)? The larger methodological question here is whether it is important to know something about 'authentic' origins or 'roots' of food or dishes at all, since a national (or ethnic) cuisine is arguably just another dynamic construct "in constant flux." (ibid., 67)

Here is much food for thought. This has been only an appetizer: onwards to our first course.

Notes

1 Fish and chips allegedly has French-Jewish origins (Panayi 2008, 17).

2 Provocatively called 'food pornography' by Frank Chin (qtd. in Pang 2003, 55).

3 'Orientalist style' is a reference to, and a manipulation of, enduring and essentialist stereotypes of the 'Orient.' (Pang 2003, 60)

References

Appadurai, Arjun (1981). Gastro-Politics in South India. *American Ethnologist*, 5, 3, 494–511.

Belasco, Warren (2002). Food Matters: Perspectives on an Emerging Field. In Warren Belasco and Philip Scranton (eds.). *Food Nations: Selling Taste in Consumer Societies*, 2–23. London: Routledge.

Camp, Charles (1980). Foodways. In Milton Thomas Inge (ed.). *Handbook of American Popular Culture*, vol. 2, 141–59. Westport: Greenwood Press.

Döring, Tobias, Markus Heide, and Susanne Mühleisen (2003). Introduction: Writing/Eating Culture. In Tobias Döring, Markus Heide and Susanne Mühleisen (eds.). *Eating Culture: The Poetics and Politics of Food*, 1–16. Heidelberg: Universitätsverlag Winter.

hooks, bell (1998). Eating the Other: Desire and Resistance. In Ron Scapp and Brian Seitz (eds.). *Eating Culture*, 181–200. Albany: State University of New York Press.

Long, Lucy M. (2009). Introduction: Food and Identity in the Americas. *Journal of American Folklore*, 122, 483, 3–10.

Mintz, Sidney W. (2002). Food and Eating: Some Persisting Questions. In Warren Belasco and Philip Scranton (eds.). *Food Nations: Selling Taste in Consumer Societies*, 24–32. London: Routledge.

Mintz, Sidney W. (2003). Eating Communities: The Mixed Appeals of Sodality. In Tobias Döring, Markus Heide and Susanne Mühleisen (eds.). *Eating Culture: The Poetics and Politics of Food*, 19–34. Heidelberg: Universitätsverlag Winter.

Panayi, Panikos (2008). *Spicing Up Britain: The Multicultural History of British Food.* London: Reaktion Books.

Pang, Ching Lin (2003). Beyond 'Authenticity': Reinterpreting Chinese Immigrant Food in Belgium. In Tobias Döring, Markus Heide and Susanne Mühleisen (eds.). *Eating Culture: The Poetics and Politics of Food*, 53–70. Heidelberg: Universitätsverlag Winter.

Versteegen, Heinrich (2009). Spicing up Britain: the Multicultural History of British Food—By Panikos Panayi. *Economic History Review*, 62, 1, 226–8.

Cook at Home in Chinese: Mediating Chinese Food for American Kitchens

Sonja Weishaupt

Chinese restaurants had already been popular in the United States for several decades when English-language Chinese cookbooks were first published. The cookbooks were an avenue of entry for Chinese products and recipes into households, a development that marks the last of various stages in the process of appropriation of Chinese food from a cuisine originally produced and consumed by Chinese immigrants into a popular addition to the American dinner repertoire.

But the integration of foreign cuisines is not an automatic process, nor does their entry go uncontested. That one enjoyed eating Chinese at a restaurant did not mean one was willing or able to reproduce the dishes in one's own household. First of all, cooking Chinese at home required knowledge of cooking techniques and access to ingredients. Second, the food needed to be materially and symbolically transformed in order to fit the culinary desires and needs of American consumers.[1]

Part of the methodological challenges of working with historical sources is that they do not always answer the questions that appear most relevant to the researcher. From an ethnological point of view, for example, the individual appropriation of Chinese food by the consumer ought to be the focus. This study, however, relies principally on food articles published in newspapers and magazines, and on Chinese cookbooks published for an English speaking market; but except for the evidence provided by an occasional second-hand account of consumers' attitudes and a handful of letters-to-the-editor, these sources do not reveal why women wanted to obtain Chinese recipes or buy Chinese cookbooks, nor whether they really cooked the dishes according to the instructions given in an article or cookbook recipe.

Instead, the sources point to another, more collective form of appropriation performed by the authors of the cooking articles and books in their function as mediating agents of appropriation. The sources reveal steps of appropriation in that their Chinese and American authors tried to adapt

Chinese cuisine according to what they believed to be the consumer's needs and knowledge. In doing so they had to take into account both the financial situation of their target audience as well as contemporary culinary and cultural discourses.

Early Forms of Eating Chinese at Home

Chinese food first came to the United States with the arrival of Chinese immigrants around the mid-nineteenth century. For decades it remained a cuisine of immigrants who, by means of their culinary knowledge and a promptly established food distribution network, were able to maintain their traditional diet remarkably unaltered. Chinese entrepreneurs rented farms outside big cities. Here they grew a vast number of Chinese vegetables, and import firms supplied shops in Chinatowns with canned vegetables, dried seafood, sauces and spices. A number of firms manufactured noodles and tofu, and butchers specialized in roast meats (Hsu 2006; Chin 1939, 54). Chinese restaurants quickly arose in all of the Chinatowns in the USA. But for a long time, they catered almost exclusively to a Chinese clientele. It was not until the 1880s that urban Americans began to sample Chinese food. With the popularity of slumming—excursions of well-to-do Americans into the ghettos of immigrant neighborhoods—and with the sudden fame of certain Chinese dishes, especially Chop Suey and Chow Mein, Chinese restaurants around the turn of the century boomed. The popularity of Chinese food grew continuously over the following decades. After WWI there were hundreds of Chinese restaurants spread all over New York.[2] It was not long before the editors of housekeeping pages began receiving letters requesting recipes for the most prominent Chinese dishes (Norton 1916). And yet the integration of Chinese food in the home was not a linear, automatic process. It came about in a number of different ways.

First, cooking was not the only form of eating Chinese at home, nor was it the beginning. That distinction falls to Chinese take-out, probably the first way Chinese food entered the homes of New Yorkers.[3] Restaurants also occasionally provided catering service for private dinner or luncheon parties. Chinese theme parties were a variation on the costume balls that came into vogue at the beginning of the twentieth century (Levenstein 1988, 61–2; Durante 1931, 189–90). These costume balls were held at hotels, restaurants or at the homes of wealthy New Yorkers. The special appeal of such a party was its exotic theme. Rooms were decorated thematically with Chinese or Japanese elements, and hosts and guests dressed up in Chinese costumes and often acted accordingly. The food—just one, albeit crucial element of such parties—was chosen to match the party's theme, but the hostess typically did not cook it herself, preferring to have it delivered from a restaurant or cooked by Chinese chefs on site and, if possible, served by Chinese waiters. This would add some Oriental color.

Chinese luncheons or tea parties remained popular throughout the 1920s and 30s, though their grand and expensive scale diminished. The fashion of the mid-twenties was the Mah-Jong party. Women would convene at home to play the game, very much as with Bridge, also popular then. These parties resembled the earlier costume balls: Mah-Jong, "being an Oriental game" (Wills 1923, 10), called for decorations of Chinese or Japanese character, as an article from a 1923 issue of the magazine *The Hostess* suggested, and could be turned into a Chinese or Japanese costume affair as well. The Oriental theme was carried through to the refreshments served before or after the game. In the article, *The Hostess* suggested procuring "a host of appetizing and appropriate dishes" (ibid., 11) such as Chop Suey or Chow Mein from a nearby restaurant. But this time a suggestion was offered for the lunch menu in case a hostess wanted to cook herself (ibid., 11):

Fruit Cocktail
Cream of Celery soup
Rice Moulds filled with Chopped Chicken and
Halved Small Button Mushrooms
Covered with Cream Sauce
Crisp Rolls
Pistachio Ice Cream
Rice Wafers / Almond Cakes
Crystallized Fruits / Crystallized Ginger
Lichee Nuts
Tea

For this menu the hostess clearly need not have possessed any knowledge of the Chinese cuisine—as a matter of fact she probably did not have any if she served it. Some of the dishes suggest exoticness (the fruit cocktail, the pistachio ice cream); others use common ingredients of Chop Suey or Chow Mein such as mushrooms, celery, chicken and rice. The only truly Chinese items on the menu are the desserts: crystallized fruits, crystallized ginger, lichee nuts and almond cakes, all of which were easily purchased in New York.

Cooking

Even though having Chinese catering at a party still seemed preferable to cooking Chinese oneself, by the twentieth century Chinese recipes had found their way onto domestic meal plans. The reasons people cooked Chinese at home are at first glance identical to those that drew Americans to eat at Chinese restaurants: it had exotic appeal, prices were low, the food wholesome and tasty. But the two activities are not the same, first and foremost because cooking was a highly gendered matter. Before the turn of the century, eating at Chinese restaurants was a men's activity. Chop Suey restaurants were linked to vice and deemed inappropriate for 'ladies.' But by the 1920s, they were being frequented by both sexes. Entertaining guests at home, on the other hand, was leisure activity mainly for females. The planning and—unless there was domestic help—preparation of the family meal in general was also considered to be the duty of the housewife. Seeing to healthy and nutritional food was part of the female domain, for women were not only supposed to control their own weight but also ensure the physical well-being of their loved ones by providing appropriately for their nutrition. More attention was therefore paid by women to the nutritional benefits of Chinese foods. Women, the managers of household affairs, also placed greater emphasis on the cost of ingredients and the practicality of recipes.

In a broad sense, developments in science and industry, political and economic circumstances all influenced how Americans and New Yorkers cooked and ate. In the aftermath of the Great Depression, for example, cooking—as opposed to eating out—had again become an economic necessity. Housewives had to learn how to cook and save on food (anon. 1933). New developments in food processing led to the creation of canned products that were heavily marketed to consumers.

In the wake of these developments, Chinese food gained the attention of food writers and housewives as a source for new and innovative practices that would fulfil the requirements of modern cooking. Recipes for Chinese dishes were tested out, and Chinese ingredients and to a lesser extent even cooking techniques were experimented with. Three aspects of modern cooking were linked to Chinese food and made it attractive: it was exotic, inexpensive and nutritious.

Qualities of Chinese Food

Chinese food was attractive in part because it had an exotic allure. It provided a theme for parties, teas and luncheons, which could then be 'different.' And even if it was not lending its character to an expensive party or fancy invitation, Chinese food was still perceived as something out of the ordinary, an exotic deviation from the daily fare at home.

It was not just any kind of cooking that became fashionable during the 1930s; the rage was international cooking. 'Eating around the world' became a hobby of New Yorkers, and it did not just mean going to international restaurants. The cuisines of immigrants were also explored at home, for inspiration and to break up the dullness of "endless rounds of lamb chops and potatoes and green vegetables." (anon. 1939a)

As with the Chinese theme parties that had gone before, it was not necessary to serve an authentic Chinese menu or even one genuine Chinese dish in order to give an Oriental touch to an invitation or family meal. As one cookbook from 1936 suggests, even a salad *à la Chinese*—that is, one with a spiced-up dressing, perhaps of mayonnaise with soy sauce—would do the trick:

"Salad à la Chinese may be the answer to your oriental party that requires something different and good without calling for too great a lengthening of the purse string. In these days you need not give a nine-course dinner or even a chop suey or chicken noodle supper to give your 'social' the oriental touch. Just as you may give your hall the oriental motif by the use of lanterns over your lights, so may you depend on a good salad served the Chinese way to give the sense of taste the enchanting atmosphere of the Orient." (Au 1936, 41)

Chinese cooking was not desired only for its exotic appeal but also for its nutritional qualities, which fulfilled contemporary tastes and perceived nutritional needs. As mentioned above, apart from its exotic allure, two qualities were frequently mentioned in conjunction with Chinese food: price and nutritional value.

Price, as the above quotation demonstrates, was an important factor in the appeal of Chinese cooking. Chinese food had been known and valued for its cheapness from its earliest days as a restaurant food. This quality of Chinese food made it especially attractive during the tough economic times of the Great Depression. It was an important presence in the cookbooks and articles addressed to female readers, because women were the ones who had to economize household expenses.

In search of inspiration for novel and cheap dishes, journalists and state authorities such as the Department of Public Markets, Weights and Measures examined the immigrants' cuisines. Chinese food or, more specifically, the popular Chinese dishes, were particularly attractive. Because they contained little meat and lots of vegetables, they were comparatively inexpensive, and the Chinese cooking method of stir-frying saved both time and fuel. Chop Suey, whose recipe was much in demand among American housewives, gained currency as a smart way to use up leftovers (anon. 1937). Chop Suey by then was not so much a distinct dish as a loose concept, according to which all kinds of diced ingredients could be thrown together—a reputation that was not always to the advantage of the Chinese restaurant business, whose restaurateurs were rumored to incorporate old kitchen scraps into their dishes (Johnson 1924). But for the household it was precisely this quality that recommended the dish to the thrifty housewife.

Healthy eating was another important concern when it came to Chinese food. Nutritional science had begun transforming American eating around the turn of the century. New developments in the production and distribution of food made food products easily storable and readily available. The rise of big food companies such as Heinz and Campbell's contributed to the spread of processed, canned and ready-made food. The government passed laws to ensure that standards of food hygiene and purity would be maintained, and it funded research on what a nutritionally balanced diet might be and what new food sources might combat malnutrition. This trend continued well into the 1920s and 1930s, and gained in importance as various vitamins were newly discovered. The results of the research did not stay within academia but became common knowledge. Middle-class housewives in particular had been trained in the new science, and during the 1920s such education had begun to bear fruit (Levenstein 1988, 30–43).

Hardly a cookbook or article on cooking could be found that did not mention calories or vitamins. Commercial food producers used the topic extensively in their advertising. Gone were the days of indulging in rich and heavy foods; the momentary food fads demanded less meat, and lighter, nutritionally valuable and easily digestible foods.

In this context not only the Chinese diet but also Chinese food products came to be scrutinized by food researchers and writers. Chinese cooking was praised for its balanced combination of different foods, its low meat content and its sparing use of oils and fats. The method of stir-frying vegetables received some attention not only for gustatory reasons, but also because researchers attested that this method of cooking preserved the vitamins. (Traditional ways of cooking vegetable sides, still very common in that day, used to denature any vitamins by boiling the vegetables into a mushy mess.) Besides, the sheer quantity of novel food products, vegetables and fruits that the Chinese had imported into and cultivated in the USA seemed intriguing. Scientists explored the different botanical varieties of vegetables and were especially enthusiastic about soy products like soy sauce, soy flour, soy milk and even tofu, which they found to be high in protein, low in calories and fats, and cheap to produce, and thus an excellent substitute for animal protein (Kaempffert 1937; anon. 1924). These attestations to the healthfulness of Chinese food helped gain consumer trust and made it easy to justify cooking with Chinese ingredients or using Chinese techniques.

Obtaining Information and Ingredients

Chinese food, even at the beginning of the 1920s, had been shrouded in a strange and mysterious aura. The secrets of Chinese cookery, it was believed, were only known to Chinese chefs. But not only did non-Chinese cooks and food companies very soon attempt to unveil these secrets in order to profit from the popularity of Chinese dishes, but consumers, too, started to flood the editorial desks of cooking and housekeeping columns and magazines with requests for recipes for their favorite Chinese dishes (Wilson 1921). The magazines responded with some of the earliest obtainable recipes in the English language. Cookbooks were soon to follow. An English-language Chinese cookbook written in 1911 was probably the first, and by 1939 it had been followed by about two dozen cookbooks and booklets that featured Chinese cuisine (Newman 1987).

Their authors, intentions and scopes were remarkably varied. They were both Chinese and Western women living in China, chefs of Chinese birth living in the United States, or food companies instructing on how to use their products. The scope of the recipes varied as well: a couple of cookbooks, and all of the booklets edited by food companies, concentrated purely on the popular Chinese restaurant dishes, but many others did not shy away from more authentic recipes such as dried oysters with tofu (Au c.1936, 40) or Chinese liver sausage with bok choy (Low 1938, 186).[4]

Besides providing recipes, most cookbooks and articles gave their readers basic instructions and information about Chinese cuisine and cooking. They pointed out differences between Chinese and American eating habits, fundamentals such as the absence of dairy from Chinese cooking, the non-sweetening of tea and the staple status of rice instead of bread. Some books also tried to entertain audiences with stories from China or Chinatown, or attempted to educate them about Chinese table manners, seating order and the correct use of chop sticks. Information and pictures on how to decorate tables and serve and eat the food were not only educationally valuable, but could also be used as a guide to creating an authentic Chinese atmosphere in a dinner invitation. Many books also included drawings or photographs of ingredients, cooking utensils and preparation methods. They gave advice on how and where to buy the ingredients, ignorance of which was the second major hindrance on the way to cooking Chinese.

The Chinese had, since the beginning of their immigration to America, established an elaborate food distribution network selling the combination of imported goods—sauces, spices, dried sea food, canned or bottled preserves and vegetables—and a variety of Chinese vegetables grown on farms they had leased near the big cities. These products allowed for a remarkably authentic cuisine, and in New York they could be purchased by everyone in the stores of Chinatown. Most New York-based authors suggested buying the ingredients there; some described shopping excursions to Chinatown and advised readers on where to buy what kind of vegetable or spice (Wells 1922; S. H. 1935, 64). Cookbooks often included the addresses of Chinese stores in bigger cities; some even included a glossary in which the names of Chinese products were written in Chinese characters so they could be copied for ordering Chinese products by mail or in person. Such lists, the authors held, were necessary because of the language barrier that posed such a problem for American shoppers (Low 1938, 6). Not all Chinese shop keepers were fluent in English, and even if they were, most ingredients did not have a standardized English name, and not even a Latin transcription of the Cantonese word would help, because it could not convey the fundamental tonal aspect of Chinese phonology.

Most consumers, even New Yorkers, it seems, shunned all this trouble that getting the right ingredients would incur. And ultimately, they would be spared the effort. As the letters to the editors of cooking columns of various newspapers and magazines prove, readers usually demanded the recipes of just the most popular dishes. These did not call for many ingredients, most of which would soon be easily obtainable as processed food.

Shrewd entrepreneurs—Chinese or no—had quickly realized the potential of marketing basic Chinese ingredients to the American consumers and had, as early as the 1910s, started companies that imported and produced specifically for a non-Chinese clientele.[5] The biggest of these was LaChoy, founded by two Americans, one Korean-born, in 1920. They sold everything necessary to cook popular Chinese food, from soy sauce to mixed Chop Suey-vegetables, and offered cooked rice and crisp Chow Mein noodles in cans. They published recipe booklets in which they gave suggestions on how to use their products—and not only for Chinese dishes (fig. 1).

Fig. 1: LaChoy: The Art and Secrets of Chinese Cookery (1937)

Adaptations

Most authors on cooking apparently surmised that, for an American housewife trying out Chinese dishes, obtaining the right ingredients and recipes would not be enough. Almost every author of a cookbook or cooking article, Chinese or no, found it necessary to modify the dishes or at least give alternative methods of preparation or hints on how to substitute ingredients. Most stated that without these alterations, Chinese dishes would be too strange or complicated, the ingredients too costly or too difficult to obtain. Instead of obscuring these alterations, authors presented modifications not only as necessary, but also as being in the consumer's interest. Adaptations had previously been applied in the restaurant business, and with success. Dishes such as Chop Suey or Chow Mein evolved out of simple Chinese dishes; Americanized Chinese dishes, for instance, often used more sugar and gravy, and restaurants gradually modified the order of items on their menus according to American tastes. But modifications in cookbooks and articles were even more pronounced. In the following some forms of adaptation will be pointed out that are typically found in cookbooks.

One type of modification came in the structure and content of cookbooks themselves. First, only those recipes were printed which authors thought suitable for American cooks. As the author of one cookbook states, "even the inexperienced housewife can prepare Chinese dishes of great flavor and delicacy" (Chan 1917, 4). Articles and cookbooks made ample use of words and descriptions like "simplicity" (Lu 1939, introduction), "facility of preparation" (Lamb 1936, blurb) or "strictly practical" (Low 1938, foreword) to coax timid cooks. Recipes that required days of preparation or that would make use of too unfamiliar or seemingly disgusting ingredients were explicitly omitted.

Many cookbooks also included traditional American recipes to be cooked with Chinese ingredients. Recipes for the previously mentioned Oriental-style salads were given by some books because the authors thought salads—which are not a staple of Chinese cooking—were too important to be excluded from any cookbook. Authors of articles in particular felt free to include other dishes like creamed bean sprouts or rice au gratin in which Chinese ingredients were cooked American-style.[6]

Modified or, as it was more popularly called, 'Americanized' Chinese dishes are more difficult to pinpoint, because there are few established 'authentic' Chinese dishes one could compare 'Americanized' ones with; also, alterations are seldom mentioned by the authors themselves. So-called 'Chinese brown gravy,' which appears in quite a few cookbooks, is one case in point. It is a simple sauce, usually made of stock, soy sauce and starch. Rather than being cooked along with the ingredients, which would be the Chinese method, it was served, like American gravy, on the side, for example with the popular Foo Young Dan, an egg omelet which, ironically, the Cantonese preferred to eat 'dry.' (Low 1938, 193)[7]

The most common form of modification was to leave out certain Chinese ingredients or to substitute them with more familiar or readily available ones. In some of the recipes, for example, olive oils or butter are used, both of which are unknown to traditional Chinese cooking. The reasons for doing so were often of a practical nature. Some authors stated that it was fear of buying too many costly foreign products that kept American housewives from trying out Chinese recipes:

> "Frequently, budget-wise meal planners hesitate to undertake the making of chop suey, popular as it is in their households, for fear the preparation will involve the purchase of too many exotic ingredients not regularly stocked in the pantry. If a simplified recipe is used, the difficulty is obviated very easily." (anon. 1939b)

Others left out certain products that seemed too strange or hard to procure. This was not only the case with more exotic products like oyster sauce, dried abalone or shark fins, which cookbooks rarely included, but also with the most familiar and commonly used Chinese products: water chestnuts, bean and bamboo sprouts. The substituting ingredient was most commonly chosen because of its purported resemblance in texture, taste or appearance to the one it replaced. Water chestnuts for example, according to one author, resembled apples in taste, and thus could be substituted by them (Wong 1930). Often the only ingredient left to identify a dish as Chinese was soy sauce, and even that, as it turned out, could be substituted by Worcestershire sauce, to which soy sauce had been compared from the start.[8]

Authenticity

The subject of adaptation, of course, raises the question of whether authenticity as a concept was part of the 'ethnic food' equation in the 1920s and 1930s. This is difficult to assess, especially since no coherent idea prevailed about what defined authentic Chinese cooking, nor had the value of authenticity been fully determined.[9] A discourse on the subject, begun in the 1920s, was continued through and culminated at the end of the 1930s. To a certain extent it was set off by the 'discovery' that Chop Suey was not a truly Chinese dish.[10] The move towards authentic Cantonese cooking was also the result of economic and political events that influenced the restaurant business and forced Chinese restaurants to reconceptualize. One new concept was to offer 'genuine Chinese cooking' in marked distinction to the familiar Chop Suey Palaces. Whatever the reasons for the turn to authenticity, value lay in selling the 'real deal.' Most authors tried to capitalize on the subject in one way or another. Non-Chinese authors had to establish that they had obtained their recipes from authentic sources. Fredric Girnau, an American who claimed fourteen years' experience as a Chinese chef in the best American clubs, pointed out in the introduction to his cookbook that his recipes were "authentic translations of the recipes for leading Chinese dishes, obtained from the leading Chinese chefs of the Orient and translated from the original Chinese into the American language" (Girnau 1931, introduction). Even food producers like LaChoy, who were by far the most liberal interpreters of Chinese cuisine, promised that with the help of their products it would be "possible for you to prepare authentic Chinese recipes in ten minutes that will rival the magic creations of those practiced in the art of the Chinese cuisine." (LaChoy 1937)

Chinese authors as 'born experts' did not need to prove their knowledge of authentic Chinese cuisine, but occasionally their working experience as Chinese chefs was also highlighted (Low 1938, preface). But this did not necessarily correspond with the contents of their books. Even Chinese authors adapted their dishes, at least to a certain extent, and virtually all of the cookbooks still gave recipes for Chop Suey and Chow Mein, even though both dishes had by then come to be ridiculed as a culinary joke. And although Americanized dishes were frowned upon, these modified dishes would be the favorite ones to eat and cook for decades to come. Practicality and taste preferences, it seems, ultimately reigned over authenticity.

Conclusion

Appropriating Chinese food into daily life in form of self-cooked meals required more than just familiarity with and a liking for Chinese food, something the habit of eating out at Chinese restaurants had already established. The American housewife had to obtain information about the ingredients, on where to get and how to cook them. This is where newspapers, magazines and newly appearing Chinese cookbooks stepped in. They did not simply offer, in one-to-one transfer, recipes of the dishes cooked in China or at Chinese restaurants in the United States. Their authors, as mediating agents of appropriation, selected, adapted and culturally translated the dishes to suit them to their readers' needs and desires, real or imagined. In doing so, they linked Chinese food to the nutritional, economical and aesthetical culinary concerns of their time. Their strategies reflected the integration of Chinese food on a more collective level that had to take into account the current gendered discourses surrounding eating and cooking.

In linking Chinese food to nutritional quality, low cost and exotic distinctiveness, these authors not only made cooking Chinese attractive, but also made it seem reasonable. The information provided by the authors about how to cook and how to obtain ingredients made home-cooked Chinese food possible. Adaptations made cooking Chinese less intimidating, less complicated, and more practical. These factors, combined, allowed for the transformation of a once-foreign food into a still-exotic yet familiar part of the everyday diet of New Yorkers and Americans alike.

Notes

1 This is not to negate the innovative and transformative potential that Chinese food had. Its impact on American eating habits has been substantial both at home and in restaurants, though its form has been a hybrid.

2 There are no official or otherwise reliable numbers; the given number is an estimate based on my own research.

3 Some accounts mention New Yorkers taking food home from restaurants in pails as early as 1901. But it was not until the 1930s that take-out and later home delivery of Chinese food became a highly-advertised service of New York's Chinese restaurants. This may have been due to a need to economize during the Great Depression.

4 There is no recognizable development from popular to more authentic cookbooks or vice versa.

5 The New York based Chinese-American Food Company, Chinese-founded and run, already existed in 1914 (anon. 1914).
6 This was not only done to Orientalize American dishes, as in the case of the salads, but also to make Chinese ingredients easy to use even in non-Chinese dishes.
7 Low gives a Cantonese version of the dish, which he terms "Omelet Cantonese" and which "is never served with gravy" (Low 1938, 194). The pancake shape of the omelet in most recipes and restaurants is another modification from the original scrambled version.
8 Worcestershire sauce, a British invention, contains soy sauce, but also spices and vinegar that blend the soy taste. In the mainly Anglo-American cuisine of the United States, it was widely known and popular long before soy sauce was introduced.
9 Authenticity was often used incoherently and sometimes even in contradictory ways by restaurateurs, food producers and consumers alike. This can be attributed to the lack of sophistication on the part of consumers, who were receptive to this new trend but still clung to dishes like Chop Suey. Chinese producers and restaurateurs faced a dilemma, as they marketed 'authentic cuisine' but had to rely on popular and modified Chinese dishes for commercial reasons.
10 There is an ongoing controversy, even among scholars, about the origin of the dish, whether it was a Sino-American invention or evolved from an authentic Cantonese dish (Höllman 2010, 235; Yu 1987).

References

Anderson, Eugene (1988). *The Food of China*. New Haven et. al.: Yale University Press.

anon. (1914). Celestial Canned Goods. *The Edison Monthly*, 6, 11, 441–3.

anon. (1924). Soy. *The Scientific Monthly*, 18, 1, 109–11.

anon. (1933). Mrs. America Back in the Kitchen, *The Villager*, May 18, 6.

anon. (1937). Fish Now Abound in the New York Market. *The New York Times*, January 3, D9.

anon. (1939a). For Gourmets and Others: Dining Abroad in the City. *The New York Times*, January 22, 45.

anon. (1939b). Yankee Chop Suey. *Brooklyn Daily Eagle,* May 2, 6.

Au, Man Sing (c.1936). *The Chinese Cook Book*. Reading: Culinary Arts Press.

Chan, Shiu Wong (1917). *The Chinese Cook Book*. New York: Frederick A. Stokes Company.

Chin, Henin, and James Boyle (eds.). (1939). *Official Chinatown Guide Book*. New York: Publication Division of Henin & Company.

Cummings, Richard Osborn (1941). *The American and his Food. A History of Food Habits in the United States.* Chicago: University of Chicago Press.

Durante, Jimmy and Jack Kofoed (1931). *Night Clubs*. New York: Alfred A. Knopf Inc.

Girnau, Fredric H. (1931). *Girnau's Chinese Chop Suey*. Los Angeles: Fredric H. Girnau Publishing Company.

Höllmann, Thomas O. (2010). *Schlafender Lotos, trunkenes Huhn. Kulturgeschichte der chinesischen Küche*. Munich: Beck.

Hsu, Madeline (2006). Trading with Gold Mountain. *Jinshanzhuang* and Networks of Kinship and Native Place. In Sucheng Chan (ed.). *Chinese American Transnationalism. The Flow of People, Resources, and Ideas between China and America during the Exclusion Era*, 22–33. Philadelphia: Temple University Press.

Johnson, Nunnally (1924). One Word After Another. *Brooklyn Daily Eagle*, March 6, 24.

Kaempffert, Waldemar (1936). The Week in Science. Chemistry's Expanding Field. *New York Times*, April 19, XX4.

LaChoy (1937). *The Art and Secrets of Chinese Cookery.* Detroit: La Choy Food Products, Inc.

Lamb, Corrinne (1936). *The Chinese Festive Board.* New York: Frederick A. Stokes Company.

Levenstein, Harvey A. (1988). *Revolution at the Table. The Transformation of the American Diet.* New York, Oxford: Oxford University Press.

Low, Henry (1938). *Cook At Home in Chinese*. New York: The Macmillan Company.

Lu, Gwei-djen (1939). *The Epicure in China*. San Francisco: Colt Press.

Newman, Jacqueline M. (1987). *Chinese Cookbooks. An Annotated English Language Compendium.* New York et. al.: Garland Publishing.

Norton, Jeanette Young (1916). Chinese Delicacies and How to Prepare Them. *The New York Tribune Sunday*, December 31, IV.

S. H. (1935). Markets and Menus. Mixed Greens. *The New Yorker*, June 1, 62–4.

Wells, Mildred (1922). A Real Chinese Dinner May Be Served in Any Home, But it Requires Special Marketing, *New York Tribune*, March 26, 10.

Wills, Mary Adelaide (1923). A Ma-Jong Party and How to Give It. *The Hostess*, Thanksgiving Number, 10–1.

Wilson, M. A. (1921). Want to Try Out Some Chinese Dishes? Mrs. Wilson Gives Mandarin Recipes. *Brooklyn Daily Eagle*, August 18, 5.

Wong, Nellie Choy (1930). Chinese Recipes Suitable for American Cooks. *The Christian Science Monitor*, August 8, 6.

Yu, Renqiu (1987). Chop Suey: From Chinese Food to Chinese American Food. In Chinese Historical Society of America (ed.). *Chinese America: History and Perspectives*, 87–99. San Francisco: Chinese Historical Society.

How the Germans did not Appropriate Fish and Chips: the Case of the *Fischbratküche* in the 1920s and 1930s

Ole Sparenberg

The nineteenth and in particular the twentieth centuries saw an increased transfer of consumer goods and styles of consumption, but because different cultures appropriate things differently, this did not (always) lead to a homogenization of cultures. Furthermore, the history of 'travelling goods' and 'travelling foods' does not solely comprise success stories, as not all of these transfers proved successful in the long run. Rather, goods or styles of consumption sometimes fail to gain acceptance in a new cultural environment despite their popularity in their country of origin. This is actually not such a rare occurrence, and even today, multinational corporations with huge marketing budgets frequently do not succeed in establishing their products in new markets (Hellmann 2003, 152–6). Hartmut Kaelble rightly identified the analysis of 'failure' as an important challenge for the historiography of cultural transfers (2006, 10). Although often overlooked, failure constitutes an integral part of the history of 'travelling goods,' and the transfer of fish and chip shops from Great Britain to Germany in the 1920s is a case in point.

Fish and chips, or the fried fish trade, has long been regarded as something typically British (Panayi 2008, 16–8; Walton 1992, 1–3). Following the British model, a considerable number of fried fish shops, so-called *Fischbratküchen*, opened in Germany in the mid to late 1920s. The German fishing industry had high hopes for these fried fish shops as a new marketing channel, but only a few years later the initial enthusiasm turned to disillusionment, as German customers had not appropriated this 'travelling food.'

This article will outline the background of the German fried fish trade and examine what made this form of catering appear attractive to its German advocates in the fishing industry and beyond. It will then describe the spread of the *Fischbratküchen* in Germany, how the British model was modified and adapted in this process and how the trade nevertheless proved a severe disappointment that did not live up to the expectations placed on fried fish.

Finally, the article will discuss possible reasons why, in this case and as compared to other foreign foods, cultural appropriation did not take place.

Finding a name is an essential part of any cultural appropriation. In the case of fish and chip shops in Germany, the designation *Fischbratküche* (literally 'fish-frying kitchen') became the most widespread. Less common names were *Fischbraterei*, *Fischbackstube*, *Fischbäckereien* or *Bratfischladen*.[1] Initially, but without lasting success, the industry proposed the term *Friedfisch* for the meal itself and *Friedfischlokal* or *Friedfischladen* for the shop (Sterner 1924, 3; Stahmer 1925, 160; Huth 1926). This was a simple adoption of the English term 'fried fish,' and this slightly awkward German neologism was meant to be pronounced the English way (Huth 1926, 6). Otherwise, if one pronounces the first syllable the German way, the term *Friedfisch* might be completely misunderstood as 'peace fish' or 'non-predatory fish.'

Background

Probably unlike most 'travelling food,' in the case of the fish and chip shops the introduction to Germany can be traced back to an idea of one man: Hans Lübbert (1870–1951), the head of the Hamburg state fishing authority (Watermann 1992, 126–9). Lübbert first proposed adopting the British concept in 1910, but his suggestion met with little enthusiasm. He continued to pursue the idea after WWI, and based on his proposal the first German fried fish shop opened in Hamburg in 1924 (Lübbert 1924; Sterner 1924, 6; Fischmarkt Cuxhaven GmbH 1926, 8; Stahmer 1943, 277).

A long lasting sales problem (or overcapacity problem) of the German fishing industry formed the background for Lübbert's idea. To a certain degree fish caught at sea were generally a 'travelling' or newly introduced food in Germany. Only since the mid-1880s had the combination of steam trawlers, ice to preserve the fish and railway transport begun to make fish caught at sea available all over Germany, or at least in all major towns. In the following decades, the German deep-sea fishery underwent rapid development, and the number of trawlers as well as the total catch grew fast (Sarrazin 2002, 137–42; Heidbrink 2004, 31–43; Teuteberg 2008). After the first German steam trawler, launched in 1885, the fleet grew to 123 trawlers in the year 1900 and finally 263 at the outbreak of WWI in 1914 (Walter 1999, 64). The total catch of the German fisheries in the North Sea and North Atlantic rose from 64,452 tons in 1905 to 166,161 tons in 1910 and further to 221,217 tons in 1924, in which year Germany's catch ranked fourth after Norway, England and Scotland among the nations of north-west Europe. The catch figures of these countries had been growing only slowly or even decreasing, while Germany's fisheries had been expanding rapidly since the late nineteenth century (Schnakenbeck 1928, 214).

The demand for fish, however, did not always keep pace with the rising production despite various marketing efforts (Sarrazin 2002, 140; Heidbrink 2006, 137). In coastal areas, people traditionally consumed fish caught at sea, but consumers in the interior of Germany were mostly unfamiliar with it (other than salted herring) or disliked it. In 1896, a dedicated fish cookbook lamented, "[m]any households do not know how to make use of the valuable fish and in particular the saltwater fish. The fish appears in the marketplace almost like an alien good in which one has no trust." (Westdeutscher Fischerei-Verband 1896, 3)[2] Forty years later, a similar publication directed at canteens still came to the same conclusion (Keune and Ziegelmayer 1939, 8).

After WWI, the situation deteriorated for the German fishing industry. Demand for fish, which had been high during and immediately after the war due to the scarcity of meat, collapsed when meat—cheap imports of frozen meat in particular—became readily available again, while the trawler fleet had quickly more than compensated for the loss of ships during the war with the help of state subsidies. The result was a severe sales problem, and the ship owners had to decommission trawlers temporarily and try to sell the fish in foreign ports or process it to fishmeal. The fishing industry urgently needed to find a way to make Germans eat more fish (Sarrazin 2002, 152–3; Heidbrink 2006, 138–40).

Hans Lübbert, head of the Hamburg fishing authority, and others thought that adopting the British fried fish shops might be the way to increase fish consumption in Germany. The fish and chip trade formed a huge business in Great Britain, and it was of fundamental importance both in the diet of the working class and for the fishing industry. Its origins are obscure, but the trade evolved sometime in the early nineteenth century. Hardly any history of fish and chips fails to refer to its first mention in Charles Dickens' *Oliver Twist* (first published 1837–1839) (Lübbert 1924; Loftas 1931, 1; Priestland 1972, 61; Walton 1992, 23). Even though the British fried fish trade is older, its breakthrough came only with the introduction of steam trawlers towards the end of the nineteenth century. Since then, the British trawler fleet and the fried fish trade grew in tandem and depended on each other. The trawlers provided a large and steady supply of fish, while the fried fish shops guaranteed a high and stable demand. Roughly 35,000 fish and chip shops existed in Britain around 1927 and were claimed to consume more than half of the British catch of whitefish[3] (Walton 1992, 5–7).

High Hopes

Because the fried fish trade created a broad and reliable foundation for the marketing of fish in Great Britain, Lübbert and others in the German fishing administration and industry thought it could work the same way in Germany, too. Conditions seemed to be even more favorable, because in Germany, the population and thus the potential market were larger, but the trawler fleet smaller than in Britain. A contemporary German publication assumed that a modest number of 800 *Fischbratküchen* would be sufficient to have the German trawler fleet working at full capacity (Schmidt 1925/26, 341).

The British fried fish trade consumed large quantities of fish, especially pollock and smaller sizes of cod, haddock and ling. These fish made up a high percentage of the British and German trawlers' catches but were unpopular with consumers. In Britain, however, the fish and chip shops had created a demand for those sizes and species, because they were very suitable for frying (Lübbert 1924; Schmidt 1925/26, 341; Loftas 1931, 8). Before this fish found a market in the fried fish trade, fishermen on German trawlers often would throw pollock back (Ehrenbaum 1936, 110). When a new *Fischbratküche* opened in Hamburg in 1926, invited guests were served fried fish made from various species and, according to a newspaper article reporting on the event, the fried pollock tasted just as good as fried turbot, which was in general a highly priced delicacy (h. 1926).

Of course, as its advocates pointed out, the *Fischbratküche* had something to offer the consumer as well, as a serving of fish, batter and potatoes represented a combination of protein, carbohydrates and fat, considered ideal at the time (Lübbert 1924). Furthermore, some authors ascribed the disappearance of rickets in Great Britain to the widespread consumption of vitamin-rich fried fish (Schmidt 1925/26, 342; Fischmarkt Cuxhaven GmbH 1926, 28). German articles on fried fish emphasized as a more tangible benefit how filling it was in combination with potatoes, because this was what many consumers had been missing when eating fish (Schmidt 1925/26, 342; Biegler 1932, 67).

Another major selling point of fried fish was its character as a convenience food. In the past consumers often had eschewed fish because they were unfamiliar with its preparation or disliked the smell.[4] Fish served in the *Fischbratküche*, which could be consumed on the premises or at home, was by contrast a convenient and ready-to-eat meal (Sterner 1924, 4; Huth 1926, 6). Women and in particular working mothers were a group of customers the advocates of *Fischbratküche* especially had in mind. In Britain, fish and chip shops eased the workload of many working-class women, because they could get a cheap take-away meal from these shops once or twice a week instead of cooking themselves (anon. 1926b; Loftas 1926, 253; Loftas 1931, 10; st. 1926; Stahmer 1943, 278).

Furthermore, it was argued that the German economy as a whole would benefit from *Fischbratküchen*, which allegedly would create many new jobs (Fischmarkt Cuxhaven GmbH 1926, 30; Schmidt 1926). At least this was the hope, since the British fried fish shops employed at least 90,000 people in the 1920s (Loftas 1931, 7). Some authors even expected a wider benefit to the national economy. If fish consumption could be raised, Germany would be able to curtail meat imports and thereby improve an unfavorable balance of trade in addition to creating jobs in the fishing industry (Schmidt 1925/26 341; h. 1926; Fischmarkt Cuxhaven GmbH 1926, 29). In short, from 1924 onwards a number of articles in trade journals and newspapers portrayed fried fish shops as a cure-all for the grievances of the fishing industry and beyond.

Diffusion and Appropriation of Fried Fish in Germany

Based on Lübberts initiative, a ship owner and two fishmongers set up the first German *Fischbratküche* in Hamburg in March 1924. The results were disappointing from the start, and this first shop soon had to close again; but others, also in Hamburg, followed quickly. The idea finally gathered momentum after a model shop, established in Cuxhaven in 1925 by the local fish-market administration, had proven the concept (Fischmarkt Cuxhaven GmbH 1926, 8–9; Schmidt 1926). Fried fish was displayed at several trade fairs during 1923 and 1924 (Lübbert 1924; Sterner 1924, 6), and in 1924 the German government granted 75,000 marks to promote this new form of catering

(Sarrazin 2002, 153). According to British sources, there may have been a second point of origin apart from Hamburg, namely in the Rhineland under the British occupation after WWI (Walton 1992, 39). The Rhineland later became one of the centers of the German fried fish trade; however, German sources—whether deliberately or not—did not mention any connection to the occupation.

Over the following years, Lübbert and the Hamburg Fishing authority remained active in this field. The authority sponsored the founding of a new company in 1926, and Lübbert gave a lecture at the opening of a new large *Fischbratküche* in 1932 (h. 1926; Biegler 1932, 67). Furthermore, the Hamburg fishing authority invited a British expert, William Loftas, to Germany in 1926 and 1928. Loftas, a leading figure in the National Federation of Fish Fryers (NFFF) in Great Britain, was a trade journalist and himself owned a fish and chip shop in Manchester (Walton 1992; Loftas 1926, 245). In 1926, he gave at least two public lectures, one in Hamburg and one in Bremerhaven, which Lübbert translated sentence by sentence to the audience (anon. 1926a; anon. 1926b; 1926c; st. 1926; Struve 1926, 84–8). Loftas returned to Germany two years later, in 1928, to inspect the progress made in the trade since his last visit. After visiting more than twenty *Fischbratküchen* on a tour through the Rhineland and Westphalia, he reported his findings in another public lecture in Hamburg, again translated by Lübbert (anon. 1928a; anon. 1928b; bg. 1928; st. 1928).

By 1926, the *Fischbratküche* had already spread across the country, and an article from 1926 mentioned more than 33 German towns where fried fish shops had been established (Schmidt 1926). Most of them were located in north and north-west Germany, including at the seaports, but a considerable number of places in the heart of Germany were on the list, too. Frankfurt, with 15 or 16 *Fischbratküchen* in 1926, actually emerged as a center of the fried fish trade, surpassing even Hamburg (Loftas 1926, 245; H. 1926, 8). An article from 1932 mentioned Hamburg, Frankfurt, the Rhineland and the Lausitz (Lusatia) as the places where fried fish shops were most common (Biegler 1932, 67). Information on the total number of *Fischbratküchen* in Germany, and on when their number was highest, is contradictory and only sketchy. However, numbers apparently climaxed at around 300, and the consensus seems to be that the trade grew fastest around 1926 (Fischmarkt Cuxhaven GmbH 1926, 9; Biegler 1932, 67; Stahmer 1943, 227).[5]

As *Fischbratküchen* spread across Germany, the fried fish trade soon began to organize itself. By 1927, shop owners had already joined forces and had founded the *Verband deutscher Fischbratrestaurateure* ('Association of German Fish Fryers'). It was certainly not a large organization, as only around thirty members—including Hans Lübbert—were present at its meeting in January 1927 (Siebs 1927). The chairman of the association, Daniel Wischer, also participated, together with Lübbert and others, as a lecturer in the training program for prospective fish fryers, which was held at the research institute of the fishing industry in Altona starting in 1927 (Siebs 1927; F. 1927, 21).

While fish was obviously available in Germany, given the fishing industry's overcapacity problem, transferring the British concept of fried fish shops also necessarily involved other elements. One was the oil for frying; by 1926, the German company Brinckmann & Mergell was already offering a variety of oil specifically aimed at *Fischbratküchen* (Fischmarkt Cuxhaven GmbH 1926, 19). Gas-fired frying ranges or ovens were another key element. German industry again reacted quickly to this new, promising market, and several producers offered ovens built to purpose (Fischmarkt Cuxhaven GmbH 1926, 8, 16; Siebs 1927; Biegler 1932, 67). However, Loftas, the British expert, advised German fryers to use well-proven British frying ranges instead of domestic products (Loftas 1926, 251).

Just as in those days in Britain, the price of fried fish was relatively low in the *Fischbratküchen*, with a complete meal costing around fifty to sixty *pfennig* (Schmidt 1926). In both Germany and Great Britain, fried fish shops served meals for take-away and for consumption on the premises. White-collar workers and civil servants of both sexes frequented the *Fischbratküchen*-type restaurants during their lunch breaks if they did not have an opportunity to return home for lunch (Stahmer 1943, 278; anon. 1926d). In Northern Germany restaurants dominated, while in Frankfurt and in the Rhineland, the shops mostly focused on take-away meals (Stahmer 1943, 278; Fischmarkt Cuxhaven GmbH 1926, 11), which demonstrates that German *Fischbratküchen* already had begun a regional diversification.

German fried fish shops were not slavish imitations of the British model, but over the course of their cultural appropriation changed and adapted to their cultural environment and local tastes. Fried potatoes (or chips), the typical side dish in British fried fish shops, were being offered in Germany too, under designations like *gebackene Kartoffelschnitzel.* However, potato salad soon became the prevailing side dish in German *Fischbratküchen* (Stahmer 1943, 278; Fischmarkt Cuxhaven GmbH 1926, 22). Around 1926 or 1927, this new form of catering and promising marketing channel for the fishing industry was surrounded by optimism. As a newspaper proudly reported, even a British trade journal predicted a bright future for the German fried fish trade and advised young fish fryers to go to Germany and open a shop there (Schmidt 1926).

Disillusionment

Only a few years later, the optimistic mood had evaporated, only to be replaced with profound disillusionment, as many of the fried fish shops had had to close down again soon. Reportedly, only 150 of the nearly 300 *Fischbratküchen* in existence after 1926 remained so in 1930 (Stahmer 1943, 277). In 1933, a trade journal recalled the "flooding of Germany with *Fischbratküchen*" and wondered how much public and private money had been frittered away for this purpose (anon. 1933, 152). In the 1930s, newspapers and trade journals were no longer publishing enthusiastic reports. Instead, the introduction of fried fish shops in Germany was considered an impracticable, expensive and ill-fated idea unlikely to solve the enduring sales problem of the German deep-sea fishery (Valten 1933, 200; anon. 1933, 152).

Some of those shops did survive, though, and especially in Hamburg and Bremerhaven *Fischbratküchen* still exist today that trace their origins to the mid-1920s (Brockmann 2009). Furthermore, Germany's largest fish retailer, *Nordsee*, operates restaurants for casual dining and fast food in many towns today. In terms of the concept and the food offered these resemble the *Fischbratküchen* (Brandes 1998, 12–3). Booths selling fried fish are also still a common sight at markets and fairs, at least in Northern Germany. Nevertheless, fried fish shops never became an important branch of the German catering trade, and they achieved very little toward raising demand for fish.

What went wrong with fried fish in Germany? Why did German customers hardly appropriate this 'travelling food'? The unfavorable economic environment comes to mind first in thinking about the late 1920s. Most *Fischbratküchen* were launched around 1926 in the short phase of stabilization and relative prosperity, only to be hit by the world economic crisis shortly afterwards. The history of the German fried fish trade might have taken a different course if it had taken place in a more stable economic environment and had thereby had more time to iron out any teething problems. However, it is noteworthy that none of the contemporary observers blamed the failure of the fried fish trade on the general condition of the national economy.

Despite widespread optimism, some voices pointed out early on that a number of fried fish shops had quickly run into trouble. One author, Max Stahmer, was very quick to dismiss the whole idea. According to Stahmer's publication from 1925, *Fischbratküchen* had not lived up to even the modest expectations, and he blamed this on the difficulties of transferring specific forms of catering from one country to another (Stahmer 1925, 160). In 1927, a trade journal ran that a number of *Fischbratküchen* had become insolvent, and it expressed concern that the whole of the new and promising trade might be discredited by these insolvencies. The journal, however, still considered the concept viable if shops were established by qualified personnel in suitable locations (anon. 1927a, 28). Later the same year, the trade journal repeated this point and stressed the difficulties of changing habits and customs in the field of food (anon. 1927b, 61).

After visiting more than twenty *Fischbratküchen* in the Rhineland and Westphalia during his second journey to Germany in 1928, William Loftas, the British expert on fried fish, also came to a critical assessment. Loftas pointed out that German fish fryers did not know how to treat fish properly, prepare batter or save costs operating the gas-fired ovens. He also advised them to mind hygiene and fatty odors. In short, he criticized their lack of qualification. Nevertheless, he did notice improvements compared to his first visit and considered the industry's prospects to be generally good (anon. 1928a; anon. 1928b; bg. 1928; st. 1928).

According to an article from 1933, most *Fischbratküchen*, "which had mushroomed here in Germany roughly eight years ago," disappeared again quickly (Valten 1933, 200). The article blamed the German fish fryers for simply copying the British model without considering that German customers were used to higher levels of hygiene than were average Englishmen. Furthermore, the article claimed many people had opened up a *Fischbratküche* without sufficient vocational training or capital (ibid.). In 1943, Stahmer came to a similar conclusion in retrospect: apparently, many unemployed young men had started their own business running a *Fischbratküche* and expected it to be an easy way to earn a secure living, even though they possessed neither sufficient capital nor professional skills (Stahmer 1943, 277).

Whether hygienic standards in Germany were in fact so much higher than in Britain may be questionable, but otherwise these authors have most likely correctly identified the shortcomings of the German fried fish trade.

However, these factors alone do not sufficiently explain the failure of *Fischbratküchen*, as a comparison with the British fried fish trade and with later examples of foreign food in Germany, which flourished under quiet similar conditions, will show. In the early twentieth century, fish and chips was not yet cherished as the national dish and symbol of Britishness in its homeland. On the contrary, the British fried fish trade was often perceived as a health hazard because of appalling smells from unrefined frying media, visibly defective hygiene and occasional, well-publicized prosecutions for the sale of spoiled fish. In fact, until 1940, the authorities officially classified fish and chip shops as an offensive trade (Walton 1992, 13).

The economic background of the British shops was not so different from the German case, either. The shops were mostly small, family-run businesses, and the owners derived from the ranks of skilled labor, but immigrants were also well represented in the trade. In any case the fryers had no background in the fish trade or the fishing industry. Much as in Germany, individual shops often had to close down soon after being established (Panayi 2008, 78; Walton 1992, 52–71). Nevertheless, the fried fish trade—if not necessarily the individual shops—did well in Great Britain.

The main difference between the fried fish trades on either shore of the North Sea lay instead in the market they served. In Britain, the unique position of fish and chips had evolved slowly and in tandem with its urban working class market. In this way, fried fish became deeply rooted in the British working-class culture. In Germany, however, this market segment was already occupied by the time the *Fischbratküche* tried to copy the British model, and fried fish faced competition supported by strong traditions. In the German case, workers ate at canteens or had their lunch prepared at home and took it to work in a lunchbox—a *Henkelmann*—or in the form of cold sandwiches (a *Butterbrot* or *Stulle*). Additionally, public soup kitchens and a wide range of bars, booths and small restaurants catered to a less affluent clientele (Allen 2002b, 15–22; Allen 2002a, 8–14; Teuteberg and Wiegelmann 1972, 286–7).

One of the newspaper articles on *Fischbratküchen* from 1928 inadvertently pointed out the competition fried fish shops had to face by explaining that fried fish shops were as popular in England as booths selling sausages, *Knackwurststände*, were in Germany (anon. 1928a). Therefore, history in this case might be fitting national stereotypes, and the German sausage—or rather its traditional significance within German alimentation—might be one of the reasons for the failure of *Fischbratküchen*.

Contemporary ideas of gender and domesticity probably also played a role. As previously mentioned, advocates of fried fish shops in Germany and Britain also advertised this form of catering as a partial replacement for meals prepared at home. As such they considered fried fish shops a great help to women shouldering the double burden of waged work and household responsibilities. According to Walton, fish and chips in this way actually was beneficial to working-class households. However, at least prior to WWII, the British middle class disdained these shops for this very reason and associated them with bad housekeeping and secondary poverty. Fried fish shops threatened the ideal of domesticity that stigmatized women's work outside the home and valued time-consuming food preparation by housewives as a symbol of family unity and maternal affection (Walton 1992, 155–64). Similar attitudes prevailed in Germany, too, and they did much to curtail the development of charitable soup kitchens around the turn of the century. It was preferred instead to train girls in housekeeping and cooking (Allen 2002a, 8, 21–2). Such middle-class values had little influence on the British working class, but if they were more influential in Germany than in Britain, they might have contributed to the difficulties of German fried fish shops.

Fried Fish and Other 'Travelling Food'

The classic examples of 'travelling food' Germans have wholeheartedly appropriated are Italian dishes like pizza and pasta, and the Turkish *doner kebab*. Italian restaurants and ice cream parlors boomed in West Germany from the mid-1960s to the mid-1970s and spearheaded the development of foreign gastronomy, but forerunners in larger towns were already present in the nineteenth century (Möhring 2007a, 72; Teuteberg and Wiegelmann 1972, 245). According to Maren Möhring, the success of the Italian restaurants in West Germany cannot be ascribed solely to the food they served. Rather, the customers also consumed an atmosphere created by the restaurant's interior decoration and staff. Just like a German tourist in Italy, a guest in such a restaurant hoped—if only for an evening—to participate in the stereotypical light-hearted Italian way of life and escape from her or his dull everyday life in the Federal Republic (Möhring 2007a, 81–2). Other foreign cuisines like hamburgers or Chinese food also benefited from attractive images associated with the 'American way-of-life' or the 'exotic far-east.'

One might object that these examples are from affluent post-war West Germany, a time which cannot be compared to the 1920s. However, the charm of the foreign and a kind of 'ethnic marketing' played no small role, even at the end of the nineteenth century. An example is found in the case of Aschinger, a Berlin-based chain of beer halls and fast casual restaurants, founded in 1892, which came to operate more than 50 branches between the turn of the century and WWII. Aschinger's success was based on the combination of a very modern concept of catering and Bavarian-style decorations. In the eyes of Aschinger's customers in Berlin, Bavaria stood for tradition and coziness and was sufficiently far from Berlin to be exotic, and still close enough to be considered as a holiday destination (Allen 2002b, 95–113).

The *Fischbratküchen*, by contrast, had little to offer in the way of atmosphere or exotic allure. In Germany, the argument for fried fish shops was always pragmatic and conveyed nothing about creating a culturally alluring image, and the industry's British origin was no help in this regard. Remarkably however, only a few years after WWI it did not pose any problems either: the advocates of fried fish in Germany did nothing to hide its British origin, and instead emphasized the success and unique status of the British fish and chip shops in almost every article. Even during the Nazi period, fried fish shops were discussed at times as a way to raise fish consumption, and authors referred to the unfulfilled expectations of the 1920s without concealing the industry's British origin (Mosolff 1938, 35–6; Stahmer 1943, 276–7). The German fishing industry always saw in Britain a model during this period. On the other hand, the designation *Friedfisch* (see above), used in early articles from 1924 to 1926, was probably too close to its British inspiration to be successful.

The origins of fried fish are not only British; its history contains a strong Jewish element. Even though its exact origins are obscure, the British fried fish trade likely evolved out of Jewish traditions (Walton 1992, 24). Certainly, in the nineteenth and early twentieth century, a high percentage of the fish fryers in London and other British towns were Eastern European Jews. Partly this was because fish frying had a poor reputation, and as such it was an occupation open to the latest group of immigrants. Over the course of the twentieth century, it passed from continental Jews to Italians and later to Cypriots, Chinese and Indo-Pakistanis (Priestland 1972, 20, 82; Walton 1992, 2, 64; Panayi 2008, 17, 78).

After the National Socialists seized power, Hans Lübbert lost his job at the Hamburg state fishing authority, his editorships and other positions because his father's background defined him as a Jew (Watermann 1992, 126–9). Nonetheless, publications from the Nazi period never used the Jewish elements in the history of the British fried fish trade—possibly nobody was aware of it in Germany at the time—or Lübbert's family background to label the concept of *Fischbratküchen* as 'Jewish,' nor is there any indication that Lübbert's contemporaries perceived the fried fish trade as such. It is therefore safe to assume that anti-Semitism played no role in the failure of the German fried fish trade.

Certain forms of foreign food began to thrive in West Germany in the 1960s not only because of the cultural images associated with them, but also because they had been brought by sizeable groups of immigrants who had the necessary knowledge. Often they first established a restaurant in order to cater to their countrymen, and in many cases the labor market offered them few opportunities other than to start their own business in the restaurant and catering industry. Therefore, they stayed in the trade, even if their success was limited at first and they had to accept low incomes. But this in turn gave them a price advantage. This is true for Italian or Yugoslav restaurants; but a case in point is the Turkish *doner kebab* shop, which first arose in West Berlin when unemployment rates rose at the beginning of the 1970s. *Doner kebab* can therefore be described as an economic survival strategy (Möhring 2007b, 88–9).

Nothing comparable can be found in the case of the German fried fish shops of the 1920s. Certainly many young men who started a *Fischbratküche* in the 1920s sought to escape from the troubled labor market by opening their own shops, but there was no specific group of people predestined or restricted to this industry. Once it became apparent that the concept of the *Fischbratküche* would not live up to expectations, novice fish fryers probably left the trade as quickly as they had entered it and went looking for something else.

Probably, the attempt to transfer the fried fish trade from Great Britain to Germany was bound to fail from the outset, because it was devised from the supply side only. Primarily it was conceived as a way to solve the trawler fleet's pressing overcapacity problem by creating a demand for fish. Its advocates were to be found among state fishing authorities and the fishing industry. Hamburg's daily newspapers devoted extensive and benevolent coverage to the nascent German fried fish trade because fishing and fish processing were an important sector of the city-state's economy. The demand side was not examined thoroughly; it was just presumed that there would be demand in Germany because there was demand in Britain.

Conclusion

As one contemporary observer pointed out, it is very difficult to transfer to any one country methods of food preparation and catering thriving under the specific conditions in another (Stahmer 1925, 160). Obviously, consumers in Germany never embraced fried fish as British consumers had, but the reasons for consumers' preferences or disinclinations are difficult to identify. In 1986 the historian Hans-Jürgen Teuteberg admitted that, while we do know what people do eat and should eat, we do not know why they eat it (1986, 2). Why people eat what they eat remains a question of taste, and while there are manifold determinants of taste, it is beyond the scope of this article to reconstruct these, assuming it would even be possible to do so. Clearly, cultural appropriation cannot be taken for granted, initiated at will or predicted.

Nevertheless, based on this negative case study, a number of preconditions for the appropriation of a 'travelling food' can be identified; these, if met at least partially, may increase its chances. First, the new food or style of consumption must find a market niche, meeting a demand not fully covered by existing foods or kinds of catering. Second, it must evoke a certain image in a wider context and thereby enable its consumers to distinguish themselves from others simply by consuming it. Third, the outcome depends on the agent or the set of agents who initiate the transfer and push the new food variety, be it a large multinational such as an American fast-food chain, with the means to finance a long introductory period and absorb initial losses, or an immigrant group who sticks to the business precisely because it lacks financial power. When the labor market has little to offer them, immigrant groups, as a last resort, often find or carve out a niche in the catering trade, even though profits to be made in this way are often very low.

In the case of the *Fischbratküchen* none of these preconditions was met. By the 1920s, the demand for fast-food or low-cost casual restaurants in Germany was already well covered. Fried fish, furthermore, did not evoke any (positive) images and had no broader associative meanings to make it attractive to customers. Last, the fishing industry and related authorities—outside of a few seaports where the fried fish trade had more lasting success—were weak agents.

Notes

1 Interestingly, the terms *braten* (to roast, to fry) and *backen* (to bake) were used synonymously in this context even though it always referred to the process of deep-frying the fish in oil or fat.

2 "Viele Haushaltungen wissen sich den Nutzen der werthvollen Fische, namentlich der Seefische, noch nicht anzueignen. Die Fische erscheinen auf dem Markte fast wie eine fremde Ware, der man nicht traut"; my translation.

3 The term 'whitefish' refers to those species mostly caught by the trawler fleet like cod, haddock, whiting and pollock and excludes herring.

4 Fish fillet that spared the housewives the hassle with the fishbone, skin and fins was only introduced on the German market in 1926, but did not become common until the late 1930s (Heidbrink 2006, 141; anon. 1926e).

5 Numbers also depended on the definition used, because not only dedicated *Fischbratküchen* offered fried fish but some restaurants, canteens and fishmonger's shops did so as well.

References

Articles from daily newspapers were taken from a collection of newspaper clippings available at the Staatsarchiv Hamburg under this call-number: StAHH Best. Nr. 135–1 I–IV, Staatliche Pressestelle I–IV, Sign. 7339.

Allen, Keith R. (2002a). Von der Volksküche zum fast food. *WerkstattGeschichte*, 31, 5–25.

Allen, Keith R. (2002b). *Hungrige Metropole. Essen, Wohlfahrt und Kommerz in Berlin.* Hamburg: Ergebnisse-Verlag.

anon. (1926a). Die Bedeutung des Bratfischhandels. *Hamburger Nachrichten*, January 30.

anon. (1926b). Die Bedeutung des Bratfischhandels. *Hamburger Fremdenblatt*, April 30.

anon. (1926c). Bratfischhandel in Großbritannien und Deutschland. *Hamburger Echo*, May 1.

anon. (1926d). Fischbratküchen in Hamburg. *Hamburger Nachrichten*, July 28.

anon. (1926e). Gründung der Fisch-Filet, G.m.b.H., und der Tütenfisch, A.G. in Wesermünde-F. *Die Fischwirtschaft*, 2, 76.

anon. (1927a). Fischbratküchen. *Die Fischwirtschaft*, 3, 28.

anon. (1927b). Fischbratküchen und Konzessionen. *Die Fischwirtschaft*, 3, 61.

anon. (1928a). Über Bratfischküchen in Hamburg und im Rheinland. *Hamburger Nachrichten*, 223, May 13.

anon. (1928b). Bratfischküchen im Rheinland und in Hamburg. *Hamburger Fremdenblatt*, May 15, 135.

anon. (1933). Schafft fachliche Fortbildungsmöglichkeiten für den Fischkleinhandel. *Deutsche Fischerei-Rundschau*, March 29, 152–3.

bg. (1928). Ein englischer Sachverständiger über die deutschen Fischbratküchen. *Hamburger Anzeiger*, May 11, 110.

Biegler, Peter (1932). Einweihung eines Fischbratrestaurants. *Fische und Fischwaren*, March 5, 67–8.

Brandes, Wilfried (1998). Einführung. In Wilfried Brandes (ed.). *»Nordsee« Geschichten über die größte deutsche Fischdampfer-Reederei*, 9–20. Bremen: Edition Temmen.

Brockmann, Roland (2009). Die Fischvergolder. *Mare*, 76, 72–3.

Ehrenbaum, Ernst (1936). *Naturgeschichte und wirtschaftliche Bedeutung der Seefische Nordeuropas*. Stuttgart: Schweizerbart.

F. (1927). Unterrichtskurse für Fischbrater. *Mitteilungen des Deutschen Seefischerei-Vereins*, 43, 21.

Fischmarkt Cuxhaven GmbH (1926). *Die Fischbratküche*. Cuxhaven: Cuxhavener Volksblatt.

h. (1926). Der Seefisch als Volksnahrung. *Hamburger Fremdenblatt*, July 28.

H., W. (1926). Zur Steigerung des Fischkonsums. *Der Naturalist*, 47, 8.

Heidbrink, Ingo (2004). *"Deutschlands einzige Kolonie ist das Meer." Die deutsche Hochseefischerei und die Fischereikonflikte des 20. Jahrhunderts*. Hamburg: Convent-Verlag.

Heidbrink, Ingo (2006). Creating a Demand: The Marketing Activities of the German Fishing Industry, c. 1880–1990. In David J. Starkey and James E. Candow (eds.). *The North Atlantic Fisheries: Supply, Marketing and Consumption, 1560–1990*, 136–52. Hull: North Atlantic Fisheries Association.

Hellmann, Kai-Uwe (2003). *Soziologie der Marke*. Frankfurt/Main: Suhrkamp.

Huth, Friedrich (1926). Die Friedfisch-Produktion. *Der Materialist*, 47, 6.

Kaelble, Hartmut (2006). Herausforderungen an die Transfergeschichte. *Comparativ*, 16, 3, 7–12.

Keune, Hanns A., and Wilhelm Ziegelmayer (1939). *Handbuch über Fische und Fischwaren für die Gemeinschaftsverpflegung*. Berlin: Verlag Das Fischnetz.

Loftas, William (1926). *Die Bedeutung des Bratfischhandels. Vorschläge eines Praktikers über praktische Fragen der Fischverwertung*. Blankenese: Kröger.

Loftas, William (1931). *Bratfischhandel in Großbritannien*. Stuttgart: Schweizerbart. (=*Handbuch der Seefischerei Nord-Europas*, 9, 3/1)

Lübbert, Hans (1924). Was sind Bratfischläden? *Hamburgischer Correspondent*, March 30.

Möhring, Maren (2007a). Gastronomie in Bewegung. Migration, kulinarischer Transfer und die Internationalisierung der Ernährung in der Bundesrepublik. *Comparativ*, 17, 3, 68–85.

Möhring, Maren (2007b). TransLokal. Ausländische Gaststätten in der Bundesrepublik Deutschland. *Traverse*, 3, 85–96.

Mosolff, Hans (1938). *Die deutsche Fischwirtschaft im Vierjahresplan. Steigerung der deutschen Seefischversorgung und ihre Grundlagen.* Berlin: Haude & Spener.

Panayi, Panikos (2008). *Spicing up Britain: The Multicultural History of British Food.* London: Reaktion.

Priestland, Gerald (1972). *Frying Tonight: The Saga of Fish and Chips.* London: Gentry Books.

Sarrazin, Jenny (2002). War, Public Intervention and Structural Changes in the German Fishing Industry, 1914-1930. In Randi Ertesvåg et al. (eds.). *Maritime Industries and Public Intervention. The Fourth North Sea History Conference*, 137–55. Stavanger: Maritime Museum.

Siebs (1927). Tagung der deutschen Fischbäcker. *Hamburger Fremdenblatt*, January 28.

Schmidt, Cornelius (1925/26). Die Volkswirtschaftliche Bedeutung der Fischbratküche. *Die Volksernährung*, 1, 341–2.

Schmidt, Cornelius (1926). Die Entwicklung der Fischbratküchen. *Hamburger Fremdenblatt*, August 31.

Schnakenbeck, Werner (1928). *Die Nordseefischerei.* Stuttgart: Schweizerbart. (=*Handbuch der Seefischerei Nord-Europas*, 9, 5/1)

st. (1926). Bratfische. *Hamburgischer Correspondent*, April 30.

st. (1928). Die Fischbratküchen in Deutschland. *Hamburgischer Correspondent*, May 12, 221.

Stahmer, Max (1925). *Fischhandel und Fischindustrie*, 2nd ed. Stuttgart: Enke.

Stahmer, Max (1943). *Fischhandel und Fischindustrie*, 3rd ed. Hamburg: Keune.

Sterner, E. (1924). Friedfisch in Deutschland. *Der Fischerbote*, 16, 3–5.

Struve (1926). Bratfischhandel in Großbritannien und Deutschland. *Die Fischwirtschaft*, 2, 84–8.

Teuteberg, Hans Jürgen, and Günter Wiegelmann (1972). *Der Wandel der Nahrungsgewohnheiten unter dem Einfluß der Industrialisierung.* Göttingen: Vandenhoeck & Ruprecht.

Teuteberg, Hans Jürgen (1986). Die Ernährung als psychosoziales Phänomen: Überlegungen zu einem verhaltenstheoretischen Bezugsrahmen. In Hans Jürgen Teuteberg and Günter Wiegelmann (eds.). *Unsere tägliche Kost. Geschichte und regionale Prägung*, 1-19. Münster: Coppenrath.

Teuteberg, Hans Jürgen (2008). Hochseefischerei, Fischhandel und Fischkonservierung in der deutschen Hochindustrialisierung, 1885–1930. *Vierteljahrschrift für Sozial- und Wirtschaftsgeschichte*, 95, 135–56.

Valten, F. (1933). Hat die deutsche Fischbratküche noch eine Zukunft? *Deutsche Fischerei-Rundschau*, April 26, 200–1.

Walter, Wolfgang (1999). *Deutsche Fischdampfer: Technik, Entwicklung, Einsatz, Schiffsregister.* Reinbek: Carlsen.

Walton, John K. (1992). *Fish and Chips and the British Working Class, 1870-1940.* Leicester: Leicester University Press.

Watermann, Burkard (1992). Zum Schicksal einiger Meeresbiologen im Nationalsozialismus. *Historisch-Meereskundliches Jahrbuch*, 1, 126–9.
Westdeutscher Fischerei-Verband (1896). *Anleitung zur Bereitung von Fischgerichten.* Hannover: Göhmann. [Facsimile 1996. Rostock: Hinstorff.]

German Sausage for the British Cuisine: Migration and Cultural Appropriation

Margrit Schulte Beerbühl

The globalization of foods and food consumption habits has played a distinct role in the history of mankind. The appropriation of foreign, exotic food and its integration into daily meals is often understood in terms of globalization and has led, at least to a certain extent, to what has been called *McDonaldization*, implying a worldwide homogenization of products (Nützenadel 2008; Teuteberg 1997). It is often assumed that the growing adaptation of foreign foods leads to a disappearance of regional or national cuisines. From an historical perspective, however, as Maren Möhring, Panikos Panayi and others have pointed out, regional and national cuisine is an invention of the nineteenth century, an answer to the growing interconnectedness of the European and non-European world through commerce and the modernization of transport systems at that time (Möhring 2008; Panayi 2006).

The impact of migration on people's dietary habits has been taken up as a research topic by social scientists and historians only in recent decades. The majority of studies focuses on the second half of the twentieth century. However, dietary changes should not be regarded as a new phenomenon. In prehistoric times, before man became sedentary, people were already moving in search of food, and even in modern times scarcity of food drives people to distant places. A vital relationship between migration and food has existed from the beginning of mankind. Without food man cannot subsist. The search for basic foods, as well as for luxury products like spices, has been an essential engine of mobility.

The emergence of mass tourism, as well as the forced or voluntary migration waves following WWII, has certainly caused traditional eating habits to change more quickly and profoundly than in former times. Aspects such as the spread of ethnic food by immigrants through restaurants and the availability of foreign food in specialty shops have been widely discussed (Nützenadel 2008; Panayi 2008; Kershen 2002). The introduction of foreign food by immigrants certainly cannot be seen as a one-way process or as simple adoption; it is a complex process of appropriation, which implies partial rejection of the original composition of the food and its adaptation to local taste preferences and habits. The crucial interface is the household (Silverstone 1992), where food is incorporated and transformed into a part of everyday life. Moreover, the availability and price of foreign ingredients both for the immigrant as well as for the native also influences the process of appropriation.[1] These are decisive factors in assigning objects to social groups and conveying meaning and value. Many studies have concentrated on the impact of ethnic food on the societies hosting them, whereas the influence of migration and social network patterns on the diffusion and appropriation of new food has hardly been touched.

In the centuries before the two World Wars, mass migrations of Europeans to the New World had a big impact on the culinary habits of Americans. The United States has been called a melting pot of different nationalities, but it has been a 'culinary melting pot' too: the Italians brought their pastas and pizzas with them, the Germans introduced *Sauerkraut* and *Würstchen*, the Spanish their *tapas* (Diner 2001). Given the slowness of transportation systems and the comparatively low migration levels before the nineteenth century, earlier dietary changes occurred at a slower pace, and the impact of foreign food on local or regional habits varied greatly. However, profound changes had been taking place even before the nineteenth century. The introduction of new colonial drinks like coffee, tea and chocolate, as well as of sugar and other solid foods like potatoes, not only influenced the early modern eating habits of Europeans but revolutionized their social and cultural life. It brought about new communication cultures like the coffee houses, the *Kaffeekränzchen* or afternoon tea. A rich historical literature exists on the influence of the new colonial drinks on the traditional European culture.[2] Most historians have approached this history from a cultural point of view. The relationship between the spread of these new hot drinks and migration, however, has hardly been looked into. It must be pointed out that the high mobility of early modern food pedlars and food producers contributed to the diffusion of these foods across Europe and among various social classes. The orange and lemon sellers from Alpine regions, the sugar bakers or confectioners of Graubünden, the *cioccolatieri* from Ticino and the Italian ice-cream makers from Beluno and Emilia Romagna left their homes regularly to sell their goods in distant markets, only to return home at the end of the season.[3]

Through the end of WWII Britain's food history could hardly be associated with the introduction of foreign food, the above-mentioned colonial drinks excepted. British cuisine was, and to some extent still is, regarded as plain and flavourless (Oddy 2003). New culinary cultures were introduced by the unprecedentedly massive migration of Afro-Caribbeans and Asians to post-war Britain. Today any given restaurant in London is probably more likely to serve foreign food than traditional English food.

Although people have been immigrating to Britain since the late Middle Ages, little is known about the culinary impact of the mass immigration of religious, political or economic refugees since the sixteenth century. Economic and social historians of the late nineteenth and early twentieth centuries, investigating the mass immigration of religious refugees, occasionally mention the introduction of new drinks and vegetables by migrants. Two examples are the introduction of beer brewing by Dutch and Germans, or the introduction of salads and vegetables by the Dutch in the sixteenth century (Cunningham 1897; Lipson 1947). More recently Lien Bich Luu has highlighted the contribution of religious immigrants to the British diet (Luu 2002; Schulte Beerbühl 1995).

Panikos Panayi has examined food's role in defining and redefining ethnic relations since the Victorian age, but his main focus is on changes ensuing from the mass immigration of non-European immigrants after WWII (Panayi 2008, 9). Occasionally, he refers to the consumption of German meat and bakery products; he claims that food did not play as important a role among the German community as it did among other ethnic groups, and that the consumption of German pork delicacies was confined to London (ibid., 56–7). However, he underestimates the impact of German food in the transformation of meat consumption in Britain. In order to understand how German meat products came to dominate a market niche, this article examines the migration and network patterns of Germans in Britain and the circulation of knowledge within these networks. The following questions are addressed: when and from which region did the German pork butchers come? Where in Britain did they settle? Where did they find niches for their products, and who consumed them?

Immigration Routes and Migration Patterns of German Pork Butchers

In eighteenth- and nineteenth-century Britain Germans could be seen in a variety of occupations: in commerce, in academia (as teachers and governesses) and in the trades. Their number was especially high in the catering trades (waiters) and in some branches of the food processing industries such as sugar refining. They were often butchers or bakers. German pork butchers were one of the largest groups among the immigrants working in the food processing industries before WWI.

The overwhelming majority of these German pork butchers came from Hohenlohe, a rather poor agricultural region in the southwest of Germany. Hohenlohe was originally not a geographical term, but the name of a dynasty; only later did it come to refer to a region in Baden-Württemberg. Most of the butchers came from small villages like Niederstetten, Ingelfingen or Künzelsau, situated loosely in the triangle formed by Würzburg in the north, Heilbronn in the southwest and Nürnberg in the east.

While the pioneer migrants were probably skilled butchers, the majority of later migrants were not trained as such. They were agricultural labourers or *Heuerlinge* (day labourers) who, in Germany, had no prospect either of social advancement or of starting a family. Many of them had some basic knowledge of slaughtering and sausage making, because during the dull winter months, when work in the fields had stopped, peasants would turn to butchery. For many, their actual training in the butcher's trade took place in England.

In the eighteenth and nineteenth centuries many inhabitants of Baden-Württemberg left their homes in search of work or a better life. Britain was not their country of first choice; the large majority went to America. However, the United States was not an option for all. Where the migrants eventually found a new home depended on chance, opportunity, the availability of transportation and communication structures, and on money. The example of one John Jacob Shum may illustrate how opportunity and chance led him to settle in Bath. After his apprenticeship he left home and travelled through France searching for work before he happened to go to London. According to records, he became acquainted with someone from Walthamstow and, because he had some basic knowledge of French, his new acquaintance asked that he accompany him in his travels, first to Paris and then to Bath, where he eventually settled and opened a shop (M. S. W. 1893).

We do not exactly know when the first German pork butchers arrived in Britain. The number of German immigrants had been increasing continuously since the beginning of the eighteenth century. The majority of Germans settled in London, and here the first German pork butchers can be found. Among them were two brothers, John Adam and Schweikhert [sic] Schweikhert. They came from Gemmrigheim on the Neckar. John Adam

Schweikhert arrived in England in 1786, followed by his brother two years later (TNA, HO 5/24). They started a butcher's shop in Westminster and within a couple of years opened branches in Southwark and Whitechapel. Only a few years later Walther Seyzinger came to London. He was born in Stuttgart in 1767 and married an Englishwoman. In 1817 he applied for British citizenship (ibid.). At about the same time, German pork butchers could already be found outside the capital. A comparatively large group had settled in Bath, a spa popular among the prosperous classes. Among them were the five Shum brothers from Niederstetten. Four of them worked as butchers while the fifth was a confectioner.

One of the first German butchers to settle in Birmingham was Christian Schriber. He came from Villingen in the Black Forest and arrived in England in 1792. For four years after his arrival he worked as a butcher in Bristol, but then moved to Birmingham, where he finally settled. The first recorded butcher in Sheffield is Johann Michael Ebert from Württemberg. He came to Sheffield in 1791 and was joined by several other family members and kin in the following decades.[4] In Hull, German pork butchers had opened shops by the 1830s at the latest.[5] Migration to Liverpool began somewhat later, not before the middle of the century. By that time German pork butchers could be found in many towns of the industrial Midlands, in Hull, in Liverpool and as far north as Glasgow and Edinburgh.

After the middle of the nineteenth century the number of German pork butchers increased rapidly, rising from about 244 in England and Wales in 1861 to 1,251 in 1891. The butchers were one of the largest occupational groups among German immigrants; their number was exceeded only by the bakers, servants/waiters and tailors.[6] The number of pork butchers was particularly high in Sheffield and Liverpool (Schuster 1908, 107–8; Newton 1993, 82; Hennings 1923, 134). The improvement and mechanization of the transportation systems, and a significant decrease in transit fares, facilitated mobility decisively.

A sophisticated transportation and agency system, as had evolved beginning in the eighteenth century for transporting emigrants to the New World, did not exist for travel to England (Wokeck 1999; Hoerder 1993). Many of the poorer sorts among German migrants were supported by relatives either in Germany or in England. An interesting anecdote about this concerns the previously mentioned Shum brothers. As it goes, by the time John Michael Shum had finished his apprenticeship, three of his brothers were already working in Bath. Despite disapproving parents, John Michael and his cousin Caspar Shum decided to leave for England. Because they did not have enough money, they became stranded in Rotterdam, penniless. They sent a letter to the Shum brothers in Bath and asked for money. Thanks to the generosity of a Dutch landlord, they were allowed accommodation until the eldest brother arrived from Bath to take them to England. While Caspar found a position in London, John Michael settled with his brothers in Bath (M. S. W. 1893).

The German pork butchers' shops were family businesses, and a continuous migration of family and kin was characteristic for the group. Mobility within the transnational networks was kept vigorous by a more or less permanent flow of migrants spanning more than a century. The Shums, the Dimlers and Egners in Liverpool, like the Hohenreins in Hull, were joined by family members over succeeding generations. The chain migration resulted in a dense network of ties between Hohenlohe and the emigrants in England. A closer look at the pattern of migration reveals particular relationships between individual towns and villages in Hohenlohe and towns in England. In Sheffield the majority of German pork butchers came from Ingelfingen, while in Liverpool they came from the area around Künzelsau.

The pioneer migrants were predominantly young, unmarried men. But later when they settled and opened shops, they often sent for family members and kin, young and old and of both sexes, asking for help. Some did not come alone, like the smallholder George Bohm (Böhm) from Steinkirchen. He arrived with his wife and daughter in Liverpool.[7] Young German immigrant women, already working in England as servants, also found employment in the German shops. The assistance of family and of young female immigrants saved wage costs that could then be re-invested in the shops. The head of the household frequently accommodated young assistants or newly arrived immigrants from home, not least because their room and board was an additional source of income (Rössler and Schulte Beerbühl 2002, 183).

The flow of migration was not unidirectional. The German pork butchers were a highly mobile group. They would visit Germany from time to time or would return home, after a successful career in England, to spend their retirement years among family and friends. Houses built in the English style in Hohenlohe are evidence of wealth acquired in England (Wüstner n. d.). This migration pattern facilitated the spread of information about chances and opportunities.

Although England was not the most favoured destination, it had several advantages besides its proximity to the continent. Since the eighteenth century at the latest, people in England had been enjoying economic and social liberties the German emigrants did not have at home. Travellers praised England for its 'spirit of freedom' and 'equality.' Upward social mobility, i.e. from dishwasher to millionaire, was also possible in England (Rössler and Schulte Beerbühl 2002, 165). In 1798, Jakob Burckhardt, the pastor of the German Lutheran Church Savoy in London, could already remark: "People from Lower Saxony, Wurttemberg, and from Switzerland seem to have been especially successful [...]: taylors, furriers, shoemakers, bakers and butchers have earned so much that they could retire and live independently from the interest on their fortunes."[8]

Many pork butchers prospered in England. They acquired a fortune they could never have achieved in their country of birth. John Adam Schweikhert, mentioned previously, possessed several houses in London that were worth at least 2400 pounds in 1826, and by that time he had retired to a country seat in Kilvington, Essex. Walther Seyzinger, of Stuttgart, owned freehold estates consisting of fourteen houses in Bishopsgate, Middlesex and Kent in 1817.[9] An impression of the imposing wealth of a German pork butcher can be gained from the photograph of the Dimler house in Liverpool (fig. 1).

Fig. 1: Dimler house
(source: http://litherland-digital.co.uk/album_5/pages/seaview_house.html)

Throughout the nineteenth century the prospects of economic and social advancement continued to be good. Shortly after the turn of the century, Wilhelm Schuster, the pastor of the German Church in Liverpool and head of the *Seemannsmission* stated:

"Wages and incomes, especially in the butcher's trade, and opportunities for self-employment, were much greater than in Germany about 30 or 40 years ago—that was appealing, [as was the fact] that even the *Verschlagene,* i.e. those who were determined or forced to emigrate by adverse and unlucky circumstances at home, whatever their previous occupation had been, could enter the butcher's trade soon after they had arrived in England and learned of the promising circumstances. They start either as assistants or journeymen in the shops of already established German butchers."[10] (1908, 192–3)

The immigrants' early years in England were frequently a time of high mobility for them. They would take any job offered them after their arrival in England. George Smith for example came to London at the age of 22. After two years of residence in London he went for a time to Newfoundland, and after his return to Britain he worked, first in sugar refineries in Bristol and Gloucester, before deciding to go live with his brother, who owned a butcher's shop in Sheffield. He worked there for some years, and at the age of 29, he finally opened a new butcher's shop in Leeds.

The surviving records of George Smith describe another interesting migration pattern. He applied for naturalization together with his nephew John Christopher Smith in 1830 (TNA, HO 5/25). John Christopher was 28 years old, and he had come to England at the age of 14. He began an apprenticeship with his uncle John Smith in Hull and later on became his assistant. Then he moved to Leeds, where he worked with his uncle George Smith for two years. After that he found employment in Sheffield and in London, where he worked again in the shops of two German pork butchers. He finally settled in Leeds and opened his own shop. His career was characteristic of that of many other Germans who entered the butcher's business. After their arrival in England, they would be trained and then move in German immigrant circles, acquiring the necessary knowledge, learning about the local dietary habits, consumption preferences and working conditions, and looking for market opportunities. John Friedrich Egner, the first German pork butcher in Liverpool, had worked in several English towns and "by chance, he travelled through Liverpool and, seeing the big and flourishing town, he decided to open a shop"[11] (Rosenkranz 1921, 57). That was in 1857. He was born in Hohenlohe in 1831 and initiated a chain migration to Liverpool.[12] The high-mobility search for market opportunities resulted in German butchery businesses opening all over England, in Scotland and in Ireland.[13]

The Culinary Niches

The successful establishment of the German butcheries can only be explained by the niches they found unfilled in Britain. According to the *Newcastle Daily Journal* of 1897, the Germans created their business in Britain, and "the German porkmen cannot be said to compete with Englishmen, seeing that there are no English pork butchers" (qtd. after Gibbons 2001, 31). Evidently they had transferred from Germany new production methods, as well as new types of sausage and ham which had not been produced before in Britain, because the same article goes on to claim that a German pork butcher "can cure swine's flesh as none other can cure it, make sausages as none other make them." (ibid.)

At first, the immigrant butchers undoubtedly served the needs of their own ethnic community. Eating habits and food preferences emerge early in life. They play an important role in the development of people's identities. For obvious reasons, immigrants bring their eating habits with them. Moreover, people's memory of their accustomed foodways links them to their place of birth and may even become part of the collective memory of later generations (Diner 2001, xvi). Since the eighteenth century, London had been home to a large German community, and the first German pork butchers certainly were responding to the demand of the expatriates. Given the geographical location of the first German butchers' shops in London and Bath, it seems they catered to different social groups among the immigrants. The wealthier ones lived in Westminster and in other respectable parts of London, like Denmark Hill, or the fashionable spa of Bath, while the poorer ones lived in the boroughs of Southwark and Whitechapel, which was crowded with a particularly high number of the poorer sort of German. It was the leading centre of the English sugar refining industry at that time, and sugar refining was more or less exclusively done by German immigrants.

However, the long lasting success of German butcheries cannot be attributed to demand in the immigrant community alone. Towns like Manchester, Hull and Liverpool had German communities large enough to sustain butcheries serving only that segment of the population, but demand went beyond those communities. German butchers had also settled in many smaller places. German sausage evidently filled a market gap in England. At the beginning of the twentieth century, Wilhelm Schuster, mentioned previously, remarked that German sausage had gained a "certain reputation among the English people; many of them prefer the German butcher's wares to the English butcher's"[14] (1908, 192). The reputation of German sausage was such that English butchers started to employ Germans to make sausage and to teach sausage making to Englishmen (Oxley 1943, 20).

Fig. 2: Fr. Schmidt (source: Anglo-German Publishing Company (ed.), 1913, 119)

Besides butcher's shops, German immigrants also opened delicatessens which imported and sold a broad variety of German products, including sausage and other meat products. They would offer delicacies such as, for example, Westphalian or Brunswick ham, Hamburg smoked meat, Sauerkraut, or dark bread. Some of these delicatessen shops became successful enterprises. Rühmann Brothers in Tottenham Court Road, as well as Hermann Appenrodt's delicatessens and restaurant, emerged as giants.

Hermann Appenrodt came to London in 1886 (at the age of 19) and opened a small corner shop. By 1909 his firm was, according to *The Times*, "one of the most catering concerns of present-day London" with ten establishments, mostly in the West End, and a branch in Paris (Oct 20, 1909, col. f). Besides the shops, he owned a bakery and a sausage and canning factory on

Charlotte Street just before WWI (Panayi 2008, 57–8). He offered all kinds of continental delicatessens and confectionary. German bread and meat products ranked high among his offerings, e.g. "Appenrodt's ham sausages," "Viennise and Frankfurt sausages" and "Thüringen blood and tongue sausages." (*The Times*, Dec 15, 1913, col. f, and his price list, *The Times*, Oct 20, 1909, col. e)

The success of these German delicatessen firms in London should not lead us to exaggerate the general opinion of German food among the upper classes in Britain, especially in London. German food had certainly gained some popularity, but French and Italian food was much more popular. The number of nineteenth-century cookbooks providing recipes for French and Italian dishes was high, while only a few give German recipes. The number of German cookbooks was, correspondingly, low.[15] Charles Elmé Francatelli's cookbooks were among the most popular and most widely read in the nineteenth century, but only occasionally do they furnish a recipe for a German dish. In his *Modern Cook* there is just one recipe for Westphalian ham (1848, 223–4).[16] Accordingly, Appenrodt sold not only German food, but a broad variety of continental dishes. German sausage and food were just two specialties among many other foreign products in his store. His shops had gained less of a specifically German reputation than one of, according to *The Times*, "London's Most Cosmopolitan Stores and Café-Restaurant." (Oct 20, 1909, col. f)

German sausage also found customers among the working classes. During the nineteenth century working hours were long and wages were low. The average workingman could hardly afford English beef or lamb. Women and children worked overlong hours in order to earn a bare living, and women did not have time to prepare and cook a proper meal. Moreover, few working class households had a cooking stove. Meat—if affordable at all—and some potatoes or a pudding would all be put into one dish and taken to the bake house to be 'baked' in the baker's oven, which would still be warm after the bread was finished (Picard 2005, 182).

Sausage, in preparation, had several advantages over meat. It was already cooked and could easily be consumed after work or during breaks. Moreover it could be bought in very small portions, which made it affordable to poorer people. Thus German sausage filled a gap in the English working class diet. It was a cheap, early form of ready-meal and take-away. Moreover sausage could be stored longer than meat, which also made it attractive to the navy and army. At the beginning of the twentieth century, German sausage was included in the supplies of the military divisions (*The Times*, Oct 10, 1899, col. d).

Certainly, another factor in the success of German pork butchers' shops was that they adapted the sausage to local and regional taste preferences. As Wilhelm Schuster mentions in his previously cited article, "many Englishmen do not like sausage prepared in the German fashion"[17] (1908, 192). Even today, the multinational food companies adapt big brands to local and regional taste preferences, even though those products have the same name in different markets. Customers usually remain unaware of this practice. In absence of research or of surviving records, we do not know to what extent, or in what way, German pork butchers adapted the recipes to local tastes.

With the outbreak of WWI, a difficult time began for the German pork butchers. Anti-German riots broke out everywhere in Britain, and many German butchers' shops were attacked and raided. After the sinking of the Lusitania in Mai 1915 by a German submarine, more than 200 German pork butchers' shops and homes were attacked and destroyed in Liverpool (Bourke 2008; Newton 1993, 82–101). Many German pork butchers were interned or forced to leave the country during the war. After the war, some of the shops, such as the Dimlers' in Liverpool, reopened. Many did so under new, English names, as for example the Hohenreins, who changed their name to Ross.[18] A few pork butchers' businesses of German origin, like that of the Haffners, still exist today.

Conclusion

From the early eighteenth century until WWI a continuous stream of German immigrants came to Britain. Beside their presence in sugar refining and in the bakery business, the immigrants were particularly prominent in the butchery trade. The pork butchers came from Hohenlohe, an agricultural area in Baden-Württemberg. Through migration and a high degree of mobility within Britain, they created both an extensive, dense transnational network linking their country of origin to Britain as well as a regional network within Britain. Both networks were sustained for more than a century and a half by a constant flow of migrants. Through these networks, one immigrant transferred to the next the skills and knowledge of sausage making, which had been unknown in Britain before, and which contributed to the reputation of their trade. German sausage became so popular that English butchers hired Germans to produce it in their shops, and English butchers were instructed in the German ways of making it. Thus, sausage production became a specialized field of training in the butchery business.

Food plays a multiplicity of roles in the economic, social and cultural lives of individuals: among migrants food is a key to their maintaining their identities. The first shops obviously served the needs of immigrants, but they increasingly found a profitable market among the native population. Food also recreates bonds of family and friendship abroad and maintains links to immigrants' homelands and to their ancestors. Among Britons both the prosperous and the poorer classes were attracted to the novelty, quality, and low cost of the products, as well as to the neat adaptation of the German sausage to local taste preferences.

Because the German butchers' shops were family-run businesses, production costs remained low. Having family members process and sell meat and sausage allowed the immigrant pork butchers to strive for, and achieve, upward economic and social mobility. Panikos Panayi believes that the most important impact of migrants lies in the innovations they introduced into the culinary culture of Britain (2008, 215). Like the Italian ice-cream makers or pizza bakers, German pork butchers certainly had a considerable impact on the English diet, because they influenced meat consumption among all classes.

Notes

1 See the articles of Hans Peter Hahn, Stefan Bauernschmidt, Christian Huck and Sonja Weishaupt in this volume.

2 See Cowan (2005), Coe (2000) or Mintz (1985), to name only a few.

3 For the confectioners of Graubünden see Kaiser (1988); for the *cioccolatieri* see Rossfeld (2007); Rossfeld (2003); Schulte Beerbühl (*forthcoming* 2012). One reason for the relative paucity of historical research is the lack of records. This is not to say that these merchants left no recorded trace; but because of the high mobility of this group, and because they seldom kept any business papers, such information is hard to locate. The same holds true of food migrants in continental Europe and in Britain.

4 The Eberts were joined by the Auer, Hamm, Koerner, Leonhardt, Nissler families and others. They were all more or less related (cf. Newton 1993, 82–3). I would like to thank Mr. Koerner, Sheffield, for sending me this information.

5 For Hull see Sheila Dixon, *The Hohenrein Family of Hull* (Hull History Centre, L DBHR, Papers of the Hohenrein family and related papers).

6 According to an estimate by the Board of Trade from 1887, about half of the four thousand master bakers in London were German (Panayi 1995, 120).

7 Cf. Registers of the German Lutheran Church in Liverpool.

8 "besonders scheinen die Niedersachsen, die Württemberger und die Schweitzer in England ihr Glück gemacht zu haben. [...] Schneider, Kürschner, Schumacher, Bäcker und Fleischhauer [hätten] so viel erworben, dass sie ihre Geschäfte aufgeben und unabhängig von den Interessen ihres gemachten Vermögens leben können"; my translation

9 Sun Insurance Records (GL) MSS 11936, vol. 506, No. 1051607; for Seyzinger TNA, HO 1/13; also his will TNA Prob. 11/1604.

10 "Löhnungen und Verdienste, besonders auch im Fleischergewerbe, und die Möglichkeiten sich selbständig zu machen, [sind] viel größer in England als vor 30 oder 20 Jahren in Deutschland—das lockte" and "dass selbst auch Verschlagene, d. h. durch ungünstige und unglückliche Heimatsverhältnisse zum Auswandern bestimmte oder gezwungene Deutsche, wenn sie auch bisher allen möglichen anderen Erwerbszweigen angehört haben, doch sofort zur Metzgerei greifen, sobald ihr Fuß Englands Boden betreten hat und sie sich nur einigermaßen über die dort vorhandenen Sachlage klar geworden sind. Sie treten dann als Gesellen und Gehülfen in die shop's der deutschen, bereits ansässigen Metzger ein"; my translation.

11 "zufällig auf einer Reise durch Liverpool gekommen und beim Anblick der großen und aufblühenden Stadt habe er den Entschluß gefaßt, es mit der Eröffnung eines Ladens zu versuchen"; my translation.

12 Among the emigrants were Johann Deeg, George Dimler, George Michael Happold, and Friedrich Egner from Hohenlohe, and several members of the Jaags family from Kocherstetten, Künzelsau.

13 A similar pattern of chain and family migration might be found among the German bakers. The bakeries were also family-run businesses. Unlike the butchers though, the bakers came predominantly from Hessen.

14 "gewisses Ansehen in den Augen des Engländers; die deutsche Fleischerware hat für diesen a priori einen Vorzug vor der Englischen"; my translation.

15 Two books are known: anon. (1873). *German National Cookery for English Kitchens*; Howe, Robin (1911). *German Cooking.*

16 German sausage is mentioned several times, but no recipe is given for making it. It is only referred to as an ingredient for preparing certain other dishes, e.g. *Black Game à la Suedoise* or braized ox-cheek with stewed cabbage (Francatelli 1848, 256, 285).

17 "[dass] nicht wenige Engländer wiederum speziell die deutschen, nach unserer besonderen Methode zubreiteten Wurstsorten nicht essen mögen"; my translation.

18 John Markham, Pictures and Pork Sausages; The Hohenrein Family (Hull History Centre L DBHR papers of the Hohenrein Family and related papers).

References

anon. (1873). *German National Cookery for English Kitchens.* London: Chapman & Hall.

Bade, Klaus (1994). *Homo Migrans: Wanderungen aus und nach Deutschland. Erfahrungen und Fragen.* Essen: Klartext Verlag.

Bourke, Joanna (2008). Another Battle Front. *The Guardian,* First World War section, November 11, 5.

Burckhardt, Johann Gottlieb (1798). *Kirchen-Geschichte der Deutschen Gemeinden in London.* Tübingen: Ludwig Friedrich Fues.

Cunningham, William (1897). *Alien Immigrants to England.* Swan: Sonnenschein.

Coe, Sophie, and Michael D. Coe (2000). *The True History of Chocolate.* London: Thames and Hudson.

Cowan, Brian (2005). *The Social Life of Coffee. The Emergence of the British Coffeehouse.* New Haven: Yale University Press.

Davies, Margaret L. (ed.). (1931). *Life as we have known it.* London: Hogarth Press.

Diner, Hasia R. (2001). *Hungering for America: Italian, Irish and Jewish Foodways in the Age of Migration.* Cambridge, MA: Harvard University Press.

Fischler, Claude (1999). The McDonaldization of Culture. In J. L. Flandrin and M. Montari (eds.). *Food: A Culinary History from Antiquity to the Present,* 530–47. New York: Columbia Press.

Francatelli, Charles Elmé (1848). *The Modern Cook: A Practical Guide to the Culinary Art in All its Branches.* London: Longman.

Gibbons, Sue (2001). *German Pork Butchers in Britain.* Maidenhead: Anglo-German History Society Publications.

Hennings, C. R. (1923). *Deutsche in England.* Stuttgart: Ausland und Heimat Verlags-Aktiengesellschaft.

Hoerder, Dirk (1993). The Traffic of Emigration via Bremen/Bremerhaven: Merchants' Interest, Protective Legislation and Migrants' Experience. *Journal of American Ethnic History,* 13, 68–101.

Howe, Robin (1911). *German Cooking.* London.

Kaiser, Dolf (1988). *Fast ein Volk von Zuckerbäckern? Bündner Konditoren, Cafetiers und Hoteliers in europäischen Landen bis zum Ersten Weltkrieg.* Zürich: Verlag Neue Zürcher Zeitung.

Kershen, Anne J. (ed.). (2002). *Food in the Migrant Experience.* Aldershot: Ashgate Publishing.

Luu, Lien Bich (2002). Dutch and their Beer Brewing in England 1400-1700. In Anne J. Kershen (ed.). *Food in the Migrant Experience,* 101–33. Aldershot: Ashgate Publishing.

Mintz, Sidney W. (1985). *Sweetness and Power: The Place of Sugar in Modern History.* London et al.: Penguin.

Möhring, Maren (2008). Transnational Food Migration and the Internationalization of Food Consumption. In Alexander Nützenadel and Frank Trentman (eds.).

Food and Globalization. Consumption, Markets and Politics in the Modern World, 129–50. Oxford: Berg.

M. S. W. (1893). The Story of the Schumm family. *The Methodist Recorder*, December.

Newton, Gerald (1993). Germans in Sheffield 1817–1918. *German Life and Letters*, 46, 82–101.

Nützenadel, Alexander, and Frank Trentmann (eds.). (2008). *Food and Globalization. Consumption, Markets and Politics in the Modern World.* Oxford: Berg.

Oddy, Derek (2003). *From Plain Fare to Fusion Food. British Diet from the 1890s to the 1980s.* Woodbridge: Boydell.

Oxley, Walter George (1943). *Bumpkin Came to Town.* London: R. Ackrill.

Panayi, Panikos (1995). *German Immigrants in Britain during the 19th Century, 1815-1914.* Oxford: Berg.

Panayi, Panikos (2006). Immigration and Food in 20th-Century Britain. Exchange and Ethnicity. *Journal for the Study of British Cultures*, 13, 7–20.

Panayi, Panikos (2008). *Spicing Up Britain. The Multi-Cultural History of British Food.* London: Reaktion Books.

Picard, Liza (2005). *Victorian London. The Life of a City, 1840–1870.* London: Phoenix.

Ritzer, George (1993). *The McDonaldization of Society: An Investigation into the Changing Character of Contemporary Social Life.* Thousand Oaks: Pine Forge Press.

Rosenkranz, Albert E. (1921). *Geschichte der deutschen evangelischen Kirche zu Liverpool.* Stuttgart: Ausland und Heimat Verlags-Aktiengesellschaft.

Rössler, Horst, and Margrit Schulte Beerbühl (2002). Auf ins gelobte Land—Aspekte der deutschen Englandwanderung im 18. und 19. Jahrhundert. *Archiv für Familiengeschichtsforschung*, 6, 165–86.

Rossfeld, Roman (2003). Mit Stillstand zum Fortschritt. Über Handel, Verarbeitung und Konsum von Schokolade in der Schweiz bis 1800. *Mitteilungen Internationaler Arbeitskreis für Kulturforschung des Essens*, 11, 24–35.

Rossfeld, Roman (2007). *Schweizer Schokolade. Industrielle Produktion und kulturelle Konstruktion eines nationalen Symbols, 1860–1920.* Baden: Hier und Jetzt Verlag.

Schulte Beerbühl, Margrit (*forthcoming* 2012). Süße Verlockungen. Von wandernden Zuckerbäckern, Konditoren und Eismachern (17.–20. Jahrhundert). In Matthias Beer and Dittmar Dahlmann (eds.). *Migration und Ernährung.* Essen: Klartext.

Schulte Beerbühl, Margrit (1995). War England ein Sonderfall der Industrialisierung? Der ökonomische Einfluss der protestantischen Immigranten auf die Entwicklung der englischen Wirtschaft vor der Industrialisierung. *Geschichte und Gesellschaft*, 21, 479–505.

Schuster, Wilhelm (1908). Unsere Schwaben in England. *Deutsch-Evangelisch im Ausland*, 7, 191–212.

Silverstone, Roger, and Eric Hirsch (eds.). (1992). *Consuming Technologies. Media and Information in Domestic Spaces.* London, New York: Routledge.

Sponza, Lucio (2002). Italian Penny-Ice in Victorian London. In Anne J. Kershen (ed.). *Food in the Migrant Experience*, 17–41. Aldershot: Ashgate Publishing.

Teuteberg, Hans J., et al. (eds.). (1997). *Essen und kulturelle Identität: Europäische Perspektiven.* Berlin: Akademie-Verlag.
Wokeck, Marianne S. (1999). *Trade in Strangers. The Beginnings of Mass Migration to North America.* University Park, PA: Pennsylvania State University Press.
Wüstner Karl-Heinz. *New Light on the German Pork Butchers in Britain, 1850–1950.* [n. d., privately circulated].

Institutional Archives

Dixon, Sheila. *The Hohenrein Family of Hull* (Hull History Centre, L DBHR, Papers of the Hohenrein family and related papers).
Home Office Papers 1/13, Memorial, April 12, 1817 (The National Archives, Kew).
Registers of the German Church in Liverpool (German Lutheran Church, Liverpool).
Probate Records 11/1604 (The National Archives, Kew[TNA]).
Sun Insurance Records (Guildhall Library [GL], London, MSS11936, vol. 506, No 1051607).

Newspapers

The Times

Appropriating Books

Introduction

Susanne Scholz

In his famous essay *Unpacking my Library* Walter Benjamin introduces the constitutive difference between a book collector and a student and avid reader of books (1992, 64). While the student is merely interested in the wisdom or information contained in the book, the collector establishes a very personal relationship to the object of his desire: "Dates, place names, formats, previous owners, bindings, and the like: all these details must tell him something, not as dry, isolated facts, but as a harmonious whole; from the quality and intensity of this harmony he must be able to recognize whether a book is for him or not." (ibid., 65) Admittedly, collectors are a special type of owner, and the value of an object for them observes specific, not always market compatible, rules. Yet despite the fact that a collector's piece is not, in the strict sense, a commercial good, the collector's position is revealing when it comes to determining the value—be it personal, monetary, cultural, or otherwise—of books.

Books are a special type of good, comparable only to other cultural products such as paintings, recorded music, or DVDs. At once material objects and containers of meaning, they participate in two distinct economies, that of the product and that of the sign. Book lovers and collectors value a book for the way it was made, its binding, paper, lettering and cover. A book can be a precious object even if its owner is not interested in or able to read what it contains. Gutenberg bibles, early editions of the classics, or first folios of canonical authors are usually not esteemed for the value of their contents, but for their value as outstanding examples of the art of bookmaking. Their price in a market economy is established in consideration of their rarity and the skills that went into making them. It usually does not take into account the cultural value of their contents or usefulness. In any case, Benjamin's collector deems questions of the 'use value' of books eminently wrongly posed. He refers to Anatole France, who, asked whether he had read all of his books, responded: "Not one-tenth of them. I don't suppose you use your Sèvres-china every day?" (ibid., 64)

Most people, however, value books for different reasons. Readers, whether reading leisurely or for academic purposes, are more interested in what is between the covers, they want to understand the inside rather than look at the outside of the book: they want to learn something, to experience aesthetic pleasure or simply be entertained. For them, the book is merely the material form of the text they are interested in. As of recently, the object side of the book can be dispensed with more or less completely: in the age of digitalization, a universal container—the Kindle—can hold all kinds of (textual) content.

Nonetheless, books are not just texts but also goods. Goods do something for and with their owners: they confer prestige, signal belonging to a social or cultural group, and distinguish the connoisseurs from the *hoi polloi*. In the case of books, some of these points need to be rephrased in light of the specificity of the 'literary capital' the book confers.[1]

Ownership, for example, acquires a new dimension when one speaks of things stored not on a shelf but in the mind. In legal terms, two kinds of ownership apply to the commodity 'book.' The first refers to the book as a material possession. The second, much more complicated, refers to its content. As recent debates have shown, copyright, the right to possess and market one's own intellectual property, is a highly contested issue—as is its appropriation (Hahn in this volume).

In many cases, the capital of the book lies not only in the (monetary) worth of the (material) object itself but in the cultural value attributed to its contents. Judging the 'literary capital' of books necessarily involves both. Specifically, in Bourdieu's terms, the book is a container and a sign of cultural capital in that texts, stored in books, have cultural value, and to have knowledge of them confers social prestige to the consumer/reader.[2] While the monetary value of a Penguin paperback edition of a Virginia Woolf novel might be way below that of a hardcover edition of a new Dan Brown bestseller, the cultural value ascribed to the Woolf novel can contribute more to the reader's symbolic capital than Brown's. On the other hand, the first edition of Brown's book will probably never appreciate, nor is a leather-bound folio of his works ever likely to appear. The canon of a culture—congealed in the books it treasures—tells us much about the (moral, aesthetic etc.) values this culture, or its dominant institutions, has consented to promote, uphold and teach to its members. At the same time, these cultural values largely determine the monetary value of the good 'book.'

The economic capital of the 'book' as a good, just like the cultural capital of literature, is grounded in the specific status of the written word in Western cultures. Since the meaning of the textual content is conveyed through the medium of language, specific skills are necessary to access this meaning. Reading—a precondition for any expert handling of the object 'book'—is a cultural technique that grants access to education and in turn confers higher social prestige and better social positions on those who possess it. Books are integral to education, so unavoidably, they are a means of acculturation, of indoctrination at worst and of participation at best. But books and their contents also travel: they leave the confines of one culture and enter the next.

What happens, then, when books migrate from one cultural context to another? What is transported, appropriated or transformed when a book travels from one country, one culture, one language to another? How do specificities of genre, style and ideology fare? How does context inflect on the content, value or influence of a book? For better or worse, books have an impact on culture, so the transfer of their content, texts, is a precarious issue. From the point of view of the receiving culture, book content must be policed so as not to threaten its cultural values. For the individual reader, content might be alien and so must be familiarized, translated and acculturated. Adaptation to a new cultural context can be achieved, for instance, by making the commodity in question appealing in the new culture, by locating it within its value system. Due to the double nature of the book both as object and container of meaning, the transcultural appropriation of books poses problems. Language is certainly one of them.

The mediation of content through translation from one language to another is always a precarious venture. Entering a new cultural space, the translated text must familiarize what might be too alien for the new set of readers to understand. At the same time, and especially when it comes to literary texts, a translation is also supposed to be true to the original, a prescription that limits the adaptability of the content to new contexts. Also, because of the imperative to sell books, translation is not only about faithfully, and, ideally, poetically rendering the text in another language but also about making it fit for the new market in the process. On the author's side, translation can also mean success, and here it ties in, again, with Casanova's notion of 'literary capital': in the international literary scene, translation confers prestige (and thus literary capital) on the author, because it signals his departure from the provinciality of a national or regional 'literary space' (Casanova 135–46 and *passim*).

As *Frederike Felcht* points out in her article in this volume, literature at once both reflects and actively participates in processes of cultural appropriation. Dealing with the travelogues of Hans Christian Andersen, her article foregrounds the special, self-reflexive ability of travel literature to comment on travelling literature. Travelogues appropriate foreign countries for the imagination of their readers while at the same time inserting themselves, by translation and adaptation, into a market economy where they successfully cater to a desire for both cultural knowledge and cultural appropriation.

When it comes to cultural appropriation, adaptation to context is not always easily accomplished. Apart from the 'constructive' potential of the text itself to comment on and shape its adaptation, other actors need to be taken into account whose agency in redesigning contexts, and in re-establishing the meaning and/or the value of goods, can vary considerably. In the case of books, with their 'ideological' charge and their load of cultural capital, adaptation is fraught with potential conflicts. Not only what is lost in translation, but what readers make of the translated text, can lead to serious intercultural friction. *Olivia Anne M. Habana's* article on the deployment of American school primers in the context of the colonial Philippines shows what can happen if the 'cultural knowledge' transferred through the book is incompatible with the real experience of its readers. Especially schoolbooks, with their blatantly didactic goals of acculturation, have designs on their readers' imaginations, self-esteem and collective self-awareness; the cultural technique of reading itself cannot be separated from the content the books teach. So on a fundamental level, this content, with its associated world view and ideologies, gets deeply rooted in the colonial imaginary.

Even if they are not compulsory reading, or at all a means of learning how to read, 'foreign' books can be regarded as containers of potentially dangerous meaning. *Christian Huck's* article in this volume deals with literature which certainly cannot claim a high score in terms of literary or cultural capital: the dime novel. In this case, the high popularity of the books among a broad and possibly manipulable reading public alerts the guardians of public morality to the books' potentially corrupting contents. Here we witness the bottom-up transculturation of a good that resists, for a long time, all efforts to police its entry into a new cultural context. Even so, its entry into the new culture is not naturally smooth. Here, two significant agents in the process of cultural appropriation are poised opposite one another. Publishers, not in the least concerned about moral degradation, are willing to please their reading audience by adapting the 'foreign' protagonists to the new cultural audience—without, however, destroying their attractiveness. Here, foreign can be sexy and as such an asset in the marketing process. Faithful translation is not an issue here, nor is cultural knowledge. In a globalized economy, transculturation means fashioning a mass product from one culture into a product that is similarly attractive in another culture and that, ideally, whets the consumer's appetite for more of the same. Opposed to the interests of the publishers are the guardians of cultural 'purity,' who, fearing the appeal of the foreign, stigmatize the product as corrupting of adolescent readers. At the same time, its affordability adds to its attractiveness before a mass audience and makes its distribution almost impossible to control.

As they participate in two different economies, books function as both objects and subjects of cultural appropriation. In the context of a globalizing commodity culture, they mediate cultural knowledge through adaptation, translation and contextualization with an eye both to their individual readership and the market. In light of this, the following section explores questions of the mobility of meaning, desires and values, the trade in cultural capital, the adaptability of texts to contexts, and the possibilities and opportunities of a transnational readership.

Notes

1 Pascale Casanova, following Bourdieu, describes as "literary capital" the book's capacity to confer prestige on both its readers and its author (Casanova 2004). For a more detailed account of Casanova's concept cf. the article by Frederike Felcht (in this volume).

2 On the concepts of symbolic and cultural capital cf. Bourdieu (1984).

References

Benjamin, Walter (1992). Unpacking my Library. A Talk about Book Collecting. In *Illuminations*, 61–9. London: Fontana.

Bourdieu, Pierre (1984). *Distinction. A Social Critique of the Judgment of Taste*. London: Routledge.

Casanova, Pascale (2004). *The World Republic of Letters*. Cambridge, MA: Harvard University Press.

American Dime Novels on the German Market: the Role of Gatekeepers

Christian Huck

The following contribution deals with the adaptation of the American dime novel to the German market in the early years of the twentieth century. Dime novels had been an enormously successful genre, economically that is, on the American market since the mid-nineteenth century. By the turn of the century, such print products, now known by the German name *Groschenhefte*, entered the German market. Analyzing the forces that shaped this entry, I will focus on German publishers on the one hand, and cultural critics on the other, as what I call *gatekeepers* in the process of introducing a cultural product with a distinctively foreign provenance. While the publishers tried to open a market for the new product, the critics tried to keep the door shut. While the publishers *appropriated* the typically American genre to the German market, librarians, teachers and others campaigned against the proclaimed *inappropriateness* of such publications for the German reader.

My analysis will proceed in three steps: first, I will introduce the sociological model of gatekeeping and suggest why this theory could be useful in analyzing the transcultural appropriation of foreign goods; second, I will present the success story of the dime novel in the USA and show how German publishers adapted the genre as *Groschenhefte* to make it suitable to the German market; third, I will look at public utterances decrying the reading of dime novels, and the subsequent development of the product on the German market.

Gatekeeping and the Mobility of Goods

Gatekeepers, according to Gordon Marshall's *Oxford Dictionary of Sociology*, are "individuals or groups in crucial positions from which they can control access to goods, services, or information" (1994, 195). "In other words a gatekeeper in a social system decides which [...] commodity [...] may enter the system." (anon. 2010) The gatekeeping model was first applied to the study of news broadcasting; here, editors decide what news is disseminated to the audience, and in what form. In its classical version as developed by David Manning White (1964, 160–72), the process can be visualized as in fig. 1.

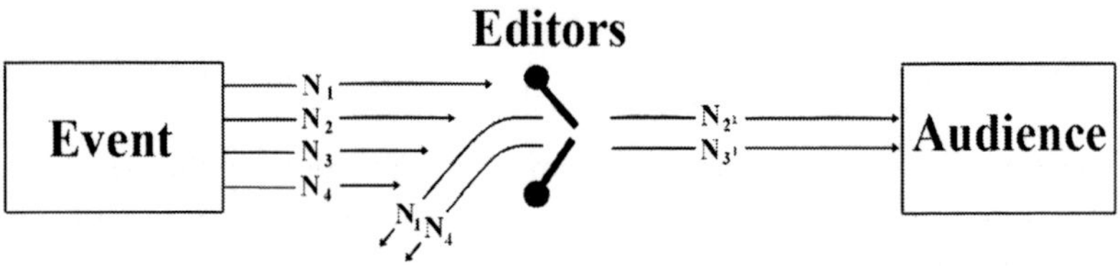

Fig. 1: The process of gatekeeping (N = news item) (cf. anon. 2010)

Of all available news items, some are discarded, while others are selected and forwarded to the audience. The model can, as I want to suggest, be applied to more general questions of cultural transfer as well (cf. Hirsch 1972, 639–59), and, as Takeshi Matsui (2009) has shown in his analysis of Japanese Manga comics in the USA, in particular to the introduction of foreign print products.

Matsui focuses on publishers' behavior as gatekeepers when a cultural product originally created in one culture is introduced into another (Peterson 1994, 163–89). The publishers *localize* the product, to use Matsui's term, by giving it a place within the value system of the new culture. This is accomplished by attributing meanings to the good that are relevant to the new culture. The publishers select and discard certain features of the good and sometimes create new features in order to make the transformed product appealing to the new audience. The publishers, however, I want to add, are not the only ones trying to control the introduction of foreign cultural products—they are not the only gatekeepers.

In a more or less free market, control over the dissemination of goods is a matter of controlling the value, monetary as well as social, of those goods. And the value of products is determined, although not exclusively, by what they mean to consumers. Grant McCracken's theory of how cultural meanings are attributed to goods distinguishes between two general forces.

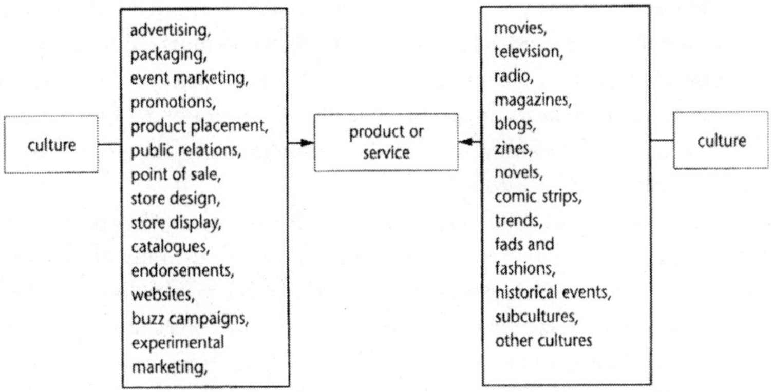

Fig. 2: Transferring cultural meaning to products (source: McCracken 2005, 178)

On the left (fig. 2), we find all those mechanisms and techniques available to the producers and distributors of a product, that is, in our case, the publishers. Via such marketing means as advertising or product design, they can try to attach specific values and meanings available within a certain culture to their good.

However, the publishers are not the only ones who contribute to the meaning of a good. On the right hand of McCracken's chart, we find a much less specific list of determinants enumerating all kinds of cultural forces that contribute to forming cultural values. However much they might try, the producers of consumer goods do not control all of these venues. The magazines, texts and audio-visual programs listed here report about goods and attach meanings to them by the way they report about them. Films and novels may feature specific cars or food products and thereby insert the good into a cultural map of meanings. Subcultures and celebrities may use certain products and add new meaning to these, or alter existing meanings (McCracken 1991, 79–83). Long before individual consumers appropriate goods to fit their household needs, a cultural appropriation has taken place; the consumers, however, are the ones who decide whether the process of appropriation will be a success.

The attribution of meaning is normally a constant, ongoing process, but it becomes especially salient when a new consumer good, having entered a culture, does not yet have a fixed place within the map of values and meanings that make up that culture. If the consumer good is a completely new invention, its cultural meanings have to be deduced from its practical functions, its relation to other goods and the cultural capital of first adopters. If the consumer good is not really new, but has originated in another culture, as in our case, the meanings and values attached to the good in its culture of origin have to be adapted: they are selected, discarded, transformed and reimagined by the gatekeepers so as to fit the new culture. As an example of such a process of transcultural meaning making, I want to look at the transformation of dime novels into *Groschenhefte*.

As we will see in the following, however, information management is not the only work of the gatekeeper, and books do not consist only of meaning. *Groschenhefte*, as any other books, are media that use materiality to present meaning. While McCracken's chart (fig. 2) lists those forces involved in the attribution of meaning to consumer goods, other forces try, not to influence the meaning of a good, but to limit the access to the material medium itself—even in a liberal consumer market.

From the US Dime Novel to the German *Groschenheft*

The term 'dime novel' was introduced by the publishers Irwin and Erastus Beadle in 1860, when they began publishing their *Beadle's Dime Novel* series. While the Beadle brothers were not the first to offer "cheap, paper-covered, sensational literature" (Johannsen 1950, 3), they were the first to issue such reading material "in continuous series and at a fixed price of ten cents [i.e. a dime], instead of issuing them sporadically" (ibid.). Soon, the term 'dime novel' was attributed to publications of other publishing houses and sold at different prices. "Popularly," Albert Johannsen writes in his extensive study of the dime novel in nineteenth-century USA, "the term had little reference to the price at which the booklets were sold, but it was applied especially to any sensational detective or blood-and-thunder novel in pamphlet form." (ibid.)

The booklets were published in various material forms. "The original *Beadle's Dime Novels* [...] were small booklets [of] approximately 100 pages, with clear type and with orange wrappers upon which was printed a stirring woodcut in black." (ibid., 4) Later publications were published without a wrapper, and they were larger. They were "printed in small type, two or three columns to the quarto page [31 by 24 cm]" (ibid.), had a length of 16–32 pages, and a picture inserted on the front page. By the turn of the century, most booklets had brightly colored covers and were between 32 and 64 pages long. They were between 25 and 29 cm high, and 18 to 22 cm wide. By now, curiously enough, most dime novels sold for a nickel, i.e. five cents.

Fig. 3: Development of dime novel design

Between 1860 and 1880, most booklets told frontier and western stories, but some contained adventures at sea, either often infused with romance. Their success was immediate: a contemporary reviewer estimates that Beadle sold five million books in the first five years alone (Everett 1864, 303–9). After the American Civil War, the Reconstruction Era brought to the fore increased literacy levels and an interest in decidedly American topics. The new railway system made it possible to distribute the products of the new printing and papermaking machines, and a competitive publishing market filled the station bookstalls. In these early years, the culturally defining experience of frontier life was still current to some and a recent memory to most. When urbanity became the leading lifestyle towards the end of the century, urban crime became a central topic, and the detective replaced the cowboy.[1] All in all, the dime novels brought everyday topics, in a more or less sensationalized form, to a general reading public.

From the very beginning of the new genre, however, many commentators, most of them coming from a more refined background, feared that reading about *common*, meaning general or shared, topics would make readers *common*, meaning ordinary or lewd (cf. Webster 1876). As early as 1847 (May 22), the *Western Literary Messenger* writes: "Riding on the cars through Michigan today, we have been half amused and half pained to see with what avidity 'yellow covered literature' is here as elsewhere, devoured by travelers

[…]. Numbers of well dressed and sensible looking ladies and gentlemen, with foreheads of respectable dimensions, have busied themselves for hours today […] in perusing, page by page, the contents of some shilling romance by […] some […] stale and insipid novelist." (qtd. in Johannsen 1950, 3) Wasting time (and money) with reading entertainment was considered a serious problem. In 1864, the *North American Review* claims: "Why these works are so popular is a problem quite as much for the moralist and the student of national character as for the critic." (Everett 1864, 308) Especially young readers were supposedly in danger of being adversely affected by what they read:

"The pernicious effect upon children of reading dime novels, and other literature of the yellow cover variety, has recently been illustrated by an occurrence in this city [Cleveland]. A number of young boys […] have been in the habit of reading these trashy works, to an unusual extent. One of them has expended $12 or $16 in the purchase of dime novels during the past summer […]. The boys of which we speak had gorged themselves with this class of literature so long, that they had contracted a morbid desire for adventure, which took a practical shape about two weeks ago. At this time five or six of them […] organized themselves into a 'band of robbers' […]. This would enable them to become practical Dick Turpins and Jack Shepards, about whom they had read in the dime novels." (anon. 1866)

However, the endless repetitions of such claims had little influence on the dissemination of dime novels: in 1893, the *Morning Oregonian* estimated that 10 million copies were being published alone in New York every year, which it characterized as a "flood" of the country (anon. 1893).

The press, in texts like this and many others, began to stigmatize the dime novel as an unrespectable waste of time and an adverse influence on young readers. Publishers, consequently, had to engage in what the sociologist Erving Goffman (1963) has termed *stigma management* (cf. Matsui 2009). In order to counter the accusation of subliterary standards, for example, publisher Beadle repeatedly circulated these guidelines, apparently handed out to prospective writers in order to prevent their *common* topics from becoming all *too* common:

"So much is said, and justly, against a considerable number of papers and libraries now on the market, that we beg leave to repeat the following announcement and long standing instructions to all contributors:

Authors who write for our consideration will bear in mind that

We prohibit all things offensive to good taste in expression and incident—

We prohibit subjects of characters that carry an immoral *taint*—

We prohibit the repetition of any occurrence which, though true, is yet better untold—

We prohibit what cannot be read with satisfaction by every right-minded—old and young alike—

We require your best work—

We require unquestioned originality—

We require pronounced strength of plot and high dramatic interest of story—

We require grace and precision of narrative, and correctness in composition. […] Those who fail to reach the standard here indicated cannot write acceptably for our several Libraries, or for any of our publications." (qtd. in Johannsen 1950, 4–5)

As in the USA, the forerunner of the dime novel in Germany was so-called railway fiction, a form of entertainment that was especially designed to counter the boredom encountered when travelling (Galle 2002, 29; cf. Haug 2007). The topics and forms of these publications were too diverse to be enumerated here. Similarly diverse were the subscription titles, which delivered long, meandering novels in short, weekly chunks. While most publications were still based on European traditions, by the end of the nineteenth century German publishers had begun to look to the USA for innovative formats.

One of the first to find these was Alwin Eichler, a young publisher who had done part of his apprenticeship in the USA. In 1903, he returned to Germany, but not without having acquired the copyright to such famous American dime novel series as *Buffalo Bill* and *Nick Carter* (Galle 1988, 53; Galle 2006, 44–52). In 1905, he began publishing German translations of these series, and translations into other European languages soon followed (LeBlanc 1991, 111–3). Because Eichler had also acquired the rights to the cover images, the German versions were very similar to the American ones, even in size (21.5cm x 27.5cm) and length (around 64 pages). Especially the Nick Carter series proved to be an immediate success, selling up to 80,000 copies a week.

As a paradigmatic example, let us stay for a moment with Nick Carter, who started investigating crimes in the late 1880s. In 1903, Street & Smith publishing house was already issuing No. 341 of the *Nick Carter Weekly* series, entitled *Nick Carter's Chemical Test, or, Animal Blood or Human*. The *Nick Carter Weekly* was already the second series featuring *Nick Carter*; the first series, the *Nick Carter Library*, had grown to some 282 issues since its inception in 1891; the *Library*-series, however, was of the black and white type described above. The Eichler publishing house in Dresden published the *Chemical Test*-story as No. 111 of their series *Nick Carter: Amerika's grösster Detektiv* with the title *Die künstliche Blutspur*.

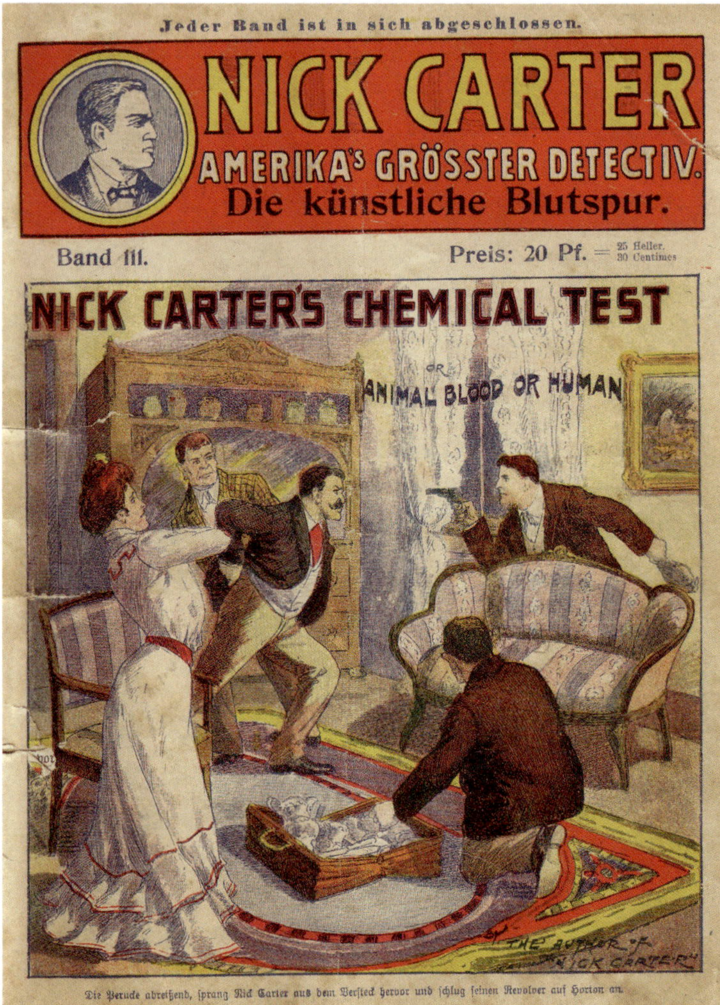

Fig. 4: Nick Carter, vol. 111: Die künstliche Blutspur

All in all, Eichler published 375 issues of the 819 original stories—using, as fig. 4 shows, the original American covers with the English title still on it. The translations are often quite free, adapting the American narrative style of abrupt beginnings and uninterrupted dialogues into a somewhat more descriptive form of narration; the storylines and figures remained largely unaltered, however. Indeed, Nick Carter seems to be an ideal candidate to travel from the USA to Germany. He has proved, throughout many stories, that he can investigate not only in all parts of the USA, but in virtually every corner of the world (cf. Huck *forthcoming*). On the back of the booklet Carter is introduced as 'America's Greatest Detective,' well-known and yet unknown: "There is no American that has never heard of Nick Carter—however, there seems not to be a single person in the United States who could claim to have seen the famous detective's face."[2] As such a ubiquitous, yet invisible figure—Nick Carter was the undisputed master of disguise—Nick Carter found its way into Germany.

In the wake of such successful translations, free adaptations of American and British originals spread; together these two forms dominated the market until WWI (Schmidtke 1981, 19–21). Nick Carter's success was quickly followed by a series on Nat Pinkerton, modeled after the real-life American detective Allan Pinkerton, and by some crude, newly invented adventures attributed to Sherlock Holmes. The next in line was Lord Lister, whose adventures were based on those of John C. Raffles, an invention of Arthur Conan Doyle's friend Ernest William Hornung. The German inventions of the time did not seem to be able to rival this success.

The situation changed after WWI. While the general anti-British and anti-American mood after the defeat was soon overcome, at least by the consumer population, the method of buying up copyrights, or simply appropriating existing characters, was not taken up again.[3] Instead of copies of American and British originals, a large number of German publishing houses, especially in Dresden and Berlin, started publishing their own series. Although these were written in the German language by German authors in Germany, they nonetheless continued to give the impression that they were of American provenance. After translating and adapting came *reimagining*.

Detective series dominated the interwar period (Galle 2006, 170). A quantitative analysis[4] of more than 9,000 crime-related titles published in interwar Germany reveals that actual translations of Edgar Wallace, Arthur Conan Doyle and others made up only about fifteen percent of the market, whereas titles that *pretended* to be American or British made up the majority of publications. (The statistics are based on the number of published titles and do not reflect the number of issues actually sold.) One series of 566 issues about the detective Tom Shark, for example, recounted adventures purportedly recorded by his sidekick Pitt Strong; in reality, they had been created by the German author Elisabeth von Aspern. Such pseudonyms were widespread: John Toward's real name is Eugen von Sass; Forest White is really Mathias Blank; Paul Oskar Ernst Erttmann assumes the pseudonym

Paul Pitt; and Peter Carr is known to his friends as Wilhelm Reinhard. Similarly, the protagonists were given an Anglo-American coloring (Marßolek 1996, 144–60): the most successful detectives on the *German* market of the interwar period were John Kling, Frank Allen, Harry Piel, Bill Cannon, Allan Scott, James Robertson, John Baxter, Ethel King, Allan Pinkerton, Ralph Garby, Fred Parker, Harry Hill, Hannibal Blunt, Harry Tyne, Will Morton, Jimmie Jackson, and, above all, Tom Shark. (And in rare cases where neither author nor hero claimed Anglo-American provenance, at least the setting of the story was either England or the USA.) Harald Harst is one of the few German detectives who works in Berlin and whose stories are openly written by a German author, Walter Kabel (Schmidtke 1981, 31); even here, however, many of the crime victims and the culprits have Anglo-American backgrounds. Wanda von Brannburg and Rolf Brand are other notable exceptions. Nonetheless: "Respectable Germans, at first at least, did not make for good business," Otto Kreiner comments. "Be it because admiration for the elegant West was great in dowdy Germany, or because the Germans granted the Anglo-Saxons the copyright to detective stories and, as connoisseurs of the authentic, dismissed imitations. From early on, however, attempts were made to transplant the American-English brand of detective into a German milieu." (Kreiner 1978, 267)[5]

Indeed, Tom Shark marks what seems to be the final step in the process of localizing an American genre, even though its provenance is still not completely obscured. The publisher proclaims on the back of one of the first issues that Tom Shark has turned his back on the North American lifestyle he experienced for most of his life and returned to the fold of his birthplace, Berlin. Here, he solves various crimes together with his friend Dr. Pitt Strong, who, mimicking the famous Dr. Watson of Sherlock Holmes, reports the adventures. He enjoys a German brandy called *Asbach Uralt*, but keeps his butler Bill, a 'mulatto,' as Dr. Strong lets us know. The stories are filled with references to local German geography, but Shark's demeanor remains American. The product now manages to cater to German demands and at the same time succeeds in conjuring up the appeal of the foreign without actually being it. Others followed suit: "Another whose name alone suggests sporty Americanness is 'Frank Allan, Avenger of the Dispossessed.' Behind the name, much of German provenance was hidden." (Kreiner 1978, 282)[6]

The *Schmutz-und-Schund* Campaign[7]

Like the dime novels in the USA, the *Groschenhefte* in Germany were not met with general acclaim. Like in the USA, literacy levels in Germany had risen tremendously throughout the nineteenth century. By the turn of the twentieth century, probably as much as ninety percent of the population was able to read simple texts. And these newly literate masses wanted to read—albeit not what the traditional literate classes (the clergy, the civil servants and teachers) wanted them to (Krieck 1930, v–viii). Instead, mass producing publishers catered to these new desires. Just when Alwin Eichler began to publish his Nick Carter stories, a campaign against *Schmutz und Schund* (i.e. 'filth and trash') was launched by some who thought they had to protect readers against such impulses (Schenda 1976, 91). After a number of state edicts and moralist publications, a touring exhibition was organized. It traveled through Germany in 1910/11 and sought to educate young and/or working class Germans (Epstein 1930, 4) about 'good,' i.e. *appropriate* literature. Finally, with the outbreak of WWI, laws for the protection of young people were passed including a list of nearly two hundred series that were no longer to be published, among them Nick Carter (Schmidtke 1981, 11).

The campaign against *Schmutz und Schund* has been analysed in some detail in recent years by the cultural anthropologist Kaspar Maase (2002a) and others, revealing the manifold pedagogical, ideological and sometimes downright economic (Schenda 1976, 94) motives behind trying to suppress the publications of Eichler and others. What I want to concentrate on here is the importance of the foreign provenance of the dime novel genre when it came to condemning them.

Karl Brunner, for example, was a consultant to Berlin police forces on questions of protecting minors. His pamphlet *Unser Volk in Gefahr! Ein Kampfruf gegen die Schundliteratur* ('A Danger to Our People! A Battle Cry against Trash Literature') was published by the same publisher who published ostensibly 'good' literature in his *Volkstümliche Bücherei*. In order to warn his readers, he also published a blacklist of novels not to buy. He begins with detective stories, which he seems to see as paradigmatic; here we find: 1. Nat Pinkerton; 2. Fritz Staggart; 3. Sherlock Holmes; 4. Nick Carter; 5. Ethel King; 6. Wanda von Brannburg; 7. John Wilson; 8. Bill Canon; 9. Minx; 10. a German Sherlock Holmes (Brunner 1909, 5–6).

One of the most avid and important campaigners against *Schundliteratur* was Dr. Ernst Schultze, director of public libraries in Hamburg and founder of the *Deutsche Dichter-Gedächtnis-Stiftung*. The aim of this 'Society for the Memory of German Writers' was to stop 'trash literature' and promote 'good literature,' which, as it seems, was primarily German literature. Members of the society, small-town public libraries and similar institutions, could subscribe to the house series for a small charge (Kostra 1998, 42–3); many similar societies were making comparable offers (Schenda 1976, 92–4).

In his public manifesto *Die Schundliteratur: Ihr Vordringen, ihre Folgen, ihre Bekämpfung* ('Trash Literature: Its Advance, Its Consequences, and the Fight to Stop It'), published in 1909, with a second edition only two years later, Schultze rehearses well-known arguments against every form of new media: they are a threat to young people in particular, they lead to crime and suicide, and consequently they are a detriment to the national economy. Schultze lists various ways of stopping the advance of dime novels in Germany. Three distinct strategies are to be differentiated, a legal, an economic and a moral one: one can (a) try to regulate dime novels by law, (b) offer a better alternative or (c) stigmatize dime novels. Whereas the society Schultze founded campaigned for what is popularly known as a "Lex-Nick Carter" (Galle 2006, 26), and also offered cheap alternatives, his book is an attempt to manage public taste, to give a bad name to dime novels, and to attribute a specific, unappealing meaning to the product—in short, to make it appear *inappropriate*. These strategies reflect the whole spectrum of influence a gatekeeper can exert, as they seek either to control the meaning of the medium or to make sure that *Groschenhefte* do not find their way onto the bookshelves of shops and libraries in the first place.

Schultze devotes a whole chapter to Nick Carter, whose name he uses as a synonym for all kinds of detective literature (Schultze 1909, 14). Similarly, Nick Carter is symbolic of the lowest form of literature for the early twentieth century literary scholars Heinrich Keiter and Tony Kellen (1912, 190). For Schultze, trash literature is an international problem: "We can see this from the fact that our most popular new trash literature collections have American titles (*Nick Carter*, *Nat Pinkerton*, *Buffalo Bill*, etc.). This is because they came over to us from the United States. To obtain translation rights, the German publishers of trash literature pay large sums to their American colleagues." (1909, 55)[8] The "cancer" (ibid., 58), which is how Schulze identifies the dime novels, is alien to the German people and has to be driven out of the German culture—to consume inappropriate goods damages the *Volkskörper*, as right-wing thinkers liked to suggest. The argument gets repeated when pulp magazines, which succeeded dime novels on the American market, eventually enter the German market: "It is telling that we have inherited these kinds of magazines from America," the secretary of another society is reported to have said in a talk on *Schund und Schmutz in ihren vielfachen Erscheinungsweisen* ('Trash and Filth in its Manifold Appearances') in 1926 (Galle 2006, 168).

After WWI, a more liberal climate made direct legal intervention more difficult. Most campaigners also realized that they had lost the economic battle against the publishing houses. Ernst Krieck, a right-wing educationist, comments: "Compared to the pedagogical antagonists of trash literature, the businessmen have no doubt emerged the stronger—maybe because their instinct or their experience gave them a better understanding of the primitive emotional desires of their customers." (1930, vi)[9] However, public discussion of the *Groschenhefte* continued—now on a purportedly scientific level, albeit with moral undertones. When, in 1926, an exhibition put on by the Berlin police force wanted to document the influence of crime fiction on young delinquents, the force commissioned a study by two psychologists who asked approximately one thousand pupils from vocational schools to write down the most fascinating crime story they knew of. Most students simply retold the adventures of Frank Allan, Percy Stuart, Tom Mix, Harry Peel and the rest of the Anglo-German detectives. Of course, the psychologists found the students to have been adversely influenced by what they read (Kelchner and Lau 1928).

Most publishers were well aware of the moral stigma attached to dime novels. Many responded to the anticipated concerns with appeasement tactics (Thole 2000, 51; Galle 1988, 30). The publishing house Sarrasani, for example, published a special issue full of praise for their own publications, compiled from letters by some of the most avid critics of *Schmutz und Schund* (Schmidtke 1981, 13). At the station bookstalls, stationary shops and tobacconists who distributed the dime novels, advertisements appeared in the form of postcards and leaflets trying to paint a brighter picture of dime novels. Advertisements in magazines by the same publishers presented the booklets as respectable publications. The most important space for advertising, however, was the booklets themselves, with their brightly colored front covers and editors' notes on the back. The covers became a sort of calling card, beckoning to the prospective host, i.e. the reader.

Often, publishers and writers would directly acknowledge the stigma and counter it in an attempt to reopen the gates the campaigners were trying to close. Robby Ix, later known as Robby King, is the protagonist of a dime novel series by the Dresden based publisher Freya (Kreiner 1978, 284–7). Robby, we learn, is the *nom de guerre* of a certain Robert von … (name not revealed); although of German origin, his operating area spans the whole globe: Paris, Chicago, New York, Yokohama. He is introduced in the very first issue as a "young man with good manners." The introduction of his character ends with a request to the reader to give this detective, who is obviously not as immoral as all the others, a chance: "Please, get to know him yourself! It will be rewarding, and he will surely not be an unpleasant companion!" The publishers seem to say: 'Please, open the gates and welcome him into your home.' And many readers did: a successful series would have had a circulation of up to 300,000 copies a week in the early 1930s (Schmidtke 1981, 49).

It was the Nazis who finally closed the door on the dime novel as we know it. In 1935, the *Reichsschrifttumskammer* placed many series on the index, and once the war began they forbade all Anglicized heroes (Galle 1988, 121): Jim Hoover (also known as Alaska-Jim) had to become Rolf Rauhaar; Patrick Button is turned into Hein Lemke; Tom Shark becomes Wolf Greif; his sidekick Pitt Strong becomes Peter Strunz; John Kling turns into Robert Ramm and is now assisted by Hans Kiekebusch (Galle 1988, 121; Schmidtke 1981, 36). But the publication even of these completely Germanized versions was halted in 1941, supposedly due to a shortage of paper (Schmidtke 1981, 16).

The Role of Gatekeepers in the Process of Appropriating Foreign Goods

The debate over dime novels was imported from the USA to Germany along with the genre. Even as the producers were advertising their material to a general audience, various types of cultural critics were denigrating the same material as being too trashy. In Germany, however, the distinction between popular and trivial became a nationally specific distinction: while German artists were producing folkloristic material deemed appropriate for the common people, American-style dime novels, deemed inappropriate, apparently made people *too* common.

Finally, the role of gatekeepers in the process of appropriating foreign goods seems to be twofold. On the one hand, publishers try to open the market for dime novels by transforming the good in such a way that it would appeal to a German audience. At the same time, cultural critics try to stop the dime novel from establishing itself in Germany by giving it a bad name, by offering cheaper alternatives or by simply making it illegal. Both gatekeepers, of course, the critics and the publishers, could not succeed without the backing of different segments of society. On the one hand, juvenile readers support the efforts of publishers by buying, reading, collecting and sharing the publications; only if these individuals appropriate the books can cultural appropriation be successful. According to contemporary sources, second-hand trading and swapping made up a huge portion of the market (Kelchner and Lau 1928, 2). On the other hand, teachers, librarians and parents take up the cause of the contrarian campaigners by confiscating publications, eradicating them from their repertoire and penalizing their consumption. As the publishers and readers *appropriated* the good to their culture, its opponents tried to hinder this process by pronouncing the good morally *inappropriate*. Together, these diverse forces lead to an appropriating transformation of the dime novel which, however, never completely negates its American provenance.

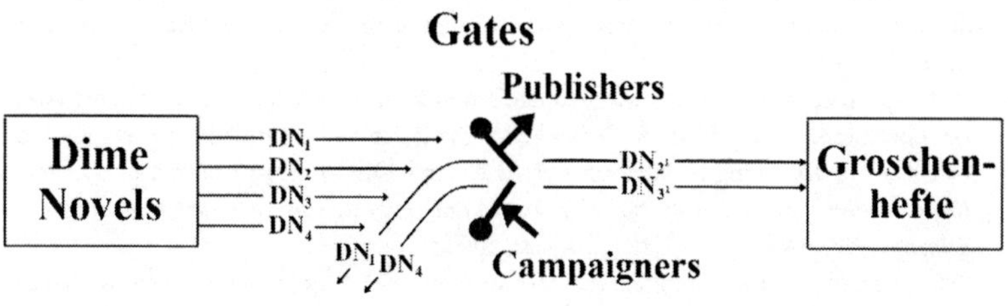

Fig. 5: Dime novels appropriated as Groschenhefte *(DN = dime novel)*

Notes

1 The development in Germany followed suit: "Während früher Indianer-, Seefahrer- und Goldgräbergeschichten von der Jugend verschlungen wurden, sind in neuester Zeit Räuber-, Kriminal- und Detektivgeschichten massenhaft unter die Jugend und das Volk gebracht worden. Ihre Helden sind die 'berühmten' Detektive Sherlock Holmes, Nick Carter, Pinkerton u. a." (Keiter and Kellen 1912, 190)

2 From the back cover of *Das Opfer des Giftmischers* (anon. n. d.): "Es gibt keinen Amerikaner, der nicht von Nick Carter gehört hätte—und trotzdem existiert in den Vereinigten Staaten wohl nicht ein Mann, der behaupten könnte, das Gesicht des berühmten Detektivs zu kennen"; my translation. (The issue at hand is probably a reprint from the 1930s.)

3 While there was a brief period dominated by reprints of pre-war successes, this ended when the publishing scene had gathered sufficient strength to publish their own creations.

4 The relevant data is extracted from Schädel (2006).

5 "Biedere Deutsche waren, wenigstens vorläufig, kein Geschäft. Sei es deshalb, weil die Bewunderung für den eleganten Westen im rauhen Deutschland groß war, sei es auch, daß man den Angelsachsen das Copyright für die Detektivgeschichte zugestand, und, als Genießer des Echten, Nachahmungen ablehnte. Immerhin begannen schon sehr früh Versuche, den amerikanisch-englischen Markenkriminalisten in das deutsche Milieu zu verpflanzen"; my translation.

6 "Sehr sportlich amerikanisch wirkte auch, schon vom Titel her, 'Frank Allan, der Rächer der Enterbten.' Unter dieser Äußerlichkeit verbarg sich viel Deutsches"; my translation.

7 Much of the following is based on Kaspar Maase's DFG-funded research on *Die soziale Konstruktion von Massenkultur: Die Auseinandersetzung um 'Schmutz und Schund' im deutschen Kaiserreich 1871–1918* (cf. Maase 2002b).

8 "Wir erkennen dies schon daran, dass unsere bekanntesten neuen Schundliteratur-Sammlungen (Nick Carter, Nat Pinkerton, Buffalo Bill usw.) amerikanische Titel tragen. Sie sind eben von den Vereinigten Staaten zu uns herübergekommen. Für die Übersetzungserlaubnis zahlen die deutschen Schundliteratur-Verleger an ihre amerikanischen Kollegen zum Teil sehr hohe Summen"; my translation.

9 "Gegenüber den pädagogischen Bekämpfern der Schundliteratur haben sich deren Unternehmer ohne Zweifel als die Stärkeren erwiesen—vielleicht, weil sie aus Instinkt oder aus Erfahrung eine bessere Kenntnis der primitiven seelischen Bedürfnisse ihrer Kundschaft besaßen"; my translation.

References

anon. (1866). A Youthful Band of Robbers. *Milwaukee Daily Sentinel*, Saturday, November 24, n. pag.

anon. (1893). The Nickel Novel. Old Sleuth and his competitors. *Morning Oregonian*, September 10, n. pag.

anon. (1931). *Das Opfer des Giftmischers*, Nick Carter: Amerikas Grösster Detektiv, vol. 11. Leipzig: Gustav Kühn Verlag.

anon. (2010). Gatekeeping. *University of Twente, Theorieënoverzicht TCW.* 15.06.2011 http://www.utwente.nl/cw/theorieenoverzicht/Theory%20clusters/Media%2C%20Culture%20and%20Society/gatekeeping.doc/.

Brunner, Karl (1909). *Unser Volk in Gefahr! Ein Kampfruf gegen die Schundliteratur*, 2nd ed. Pforzheim: Volkstümliche Bücherei.

Epstein, Hans (1930). *Der Detektivroman der Unterschicht. Die Frank Allan-Serie.* Frankfurt/Main: Neuer Frankfurter Verlag.

Everett, William (1864). Critical Notices: Beadle's Dime Books. *North American Review*, 99, 303–9.

Galle, Heinz J. (1988). *Groschenhefte. Die Geschichte der deutschen Trivialliteratur.* Frankfurt/Main: Ullstein.

Galle, Heinz J. (2002). *Populäre Lesestoffe. Groschenhefte, Dime Novels und Penny Dreadfuls aus den Jahren 1850 bis 1950.* Cologne: Kleine Schriften der Universitäts- und Stadtbibliothek Köln.

Galle, Heinz J. (2006). *Volksbücher und Heftromane*, Bd. 2: Vom Kaiserreich zum Dritten Reich—40 Jahre populäre Lesestoffe. Lüneburg: Dieter von Reeken.

Goffman, Erving (1963). *Stigma: Notes on the Management of Spoiled Identity.* Englewood Cliffs, NJ: Prentice-Hall.

Haug, Christine (2007). *Reisen und Lesen im Zeitalter der Industrialisierung. Die Geschichte des Bahnhofs- und Verkehrsbuchhandels in Deutschland von seinen Anfängen um 1850 bis zum Ende der Weimarer Republik.* Wiesbaden: Harrowitz.

Hirsch, Paul M. (1972). Processing Fads and Fashions: An Organization-Set Analysis of Cultural Industry Systems. *American Journal of Sociology*, 77, 4, 639–59.

Huck, Christian (*forthcoming*). The Total Mobility of the Dime Novel Detective.

Johannsen, Albert (1950). *The House of Beadle and Adams and its Dime and Nickel Novels: The Story of a Vanished Literature*, vol. I. Norman: University of Oklahoma Press.

Keiter, Heinrich, and Tony Kellen (1912). *Der Roman. Theorie und Technik des Romans und der erzählenden Dichtung, nebst einer geschichtlichen Einleitung*, 4th ed. Essen-Ruhr: Fredebeul & Koenen.

Kelchner, Mathilde, and Ernst Lau (1928). *Die Berliner Jugend und die Kriminalliteratur: Eine Untersuchung aufgrund von Aufsätzen Jugendlicher.* (=Beihefte zur Zeitschrift für angewandte Psychologie, vol. 42) Leipzig: Barth.

Kostra, Frank (1998). *Die Geschichte der Stadtbibliothek Minden von 1906–1945: Ein Beitrag zur Entwicklung der Literaturversorgung seit dem 18. Jahrhundert.* Marburg: Tectum.

Kreiner, Otto (1978). Die Deutschen Detektive. Hefterl-Literatur, retrospektiv. *Protokolle: Wiener Halbjahresschrift für Literatur, bildende Kunst und Musik,* 2, 265–92.

Krieck, Ernst (1930). Geleitwort. In Hans Epstein. *Der Detektivroman der Unterschicht: I. Die Frank Allen-Serie,* v–viii. Frankfurt/Main: Neuer Frankfurter Verlag.

LeBlanc, Edward T. (1991). American Dime Novel Reprints in Europe. *The Dime Novel Roundup*, December, 111–3.

Maase, Kaspar (2002a). Die soziale Bewegung gegen Schundliteratur im deutschen Kaiserreich. Ein Kapitel aus der Geschichte der Volkserziehung. *Internationales Archiv für Sozialgeschichte der deutschen Literatur,* 27, 2, 45–123.

Maase, Kaspar (2002b). Schundliteratur und Jugendschutz im Ersten Weltkrieg. Eine Fallstudie zur Kommunikationskontrolle in Deutschland. *kommunikation@gesellschaft*, 3, article 3. 05.06.2011 http://www.uni-frankfurt.de/fb03/K.G/B3_2002_Maase.pdf.

Marshall, Gordon (1994). *The Concise Oxford Dictionary of Sociology.* Oxford, New York: Oxford University Press.

Marßolek, Inge (1996). Internationalität und kulturelle Klischees am Beispiel der John-Kling-Heftromane der 1920er und 1930er Jahre. In Alf Lüdtke et al. (eds.). *Amerikanisierung: Traum und Alptraum im Deutschland des 20. Jahrhunderts,* 144–60. Stuttgart: Franz Steiner.

Matsui, Takeshi (2009). The Diffusion of Foreign Cultural Products: The Case Analysis of Japanese Comics (Manga) Market in the US. *Princeton University: Center for Arts and Cultural Policy Studies, Working Paper Series,* 37. 05.06.2011 http://www.princeton.edu/~artspol/workpap/WP37-Matsui.pdf.

McCracken, Grant (1991). *Culture and Consumption: New Approaches to the Symbolic Character of Consumer Goods and Activities.* Bloomington: Indiana University Press.

McCracken, Grant (2005). *Culture and Consumption II: Markets, Meaning, and Brand Management.* Bloomington: Indiana University Press.

Peterson, Richard A. (1994). The Production Perspective. In Diane Crane (ed.). *The Sociology of Culture: Emerging Theoretical Perspectives,* 163–89. Cambridge, MA: Blackwell.

Schädel, Mirko (2006). *Illustrierte Bibliographie der Kriminalliteratur, 1796–1945, im deutschen Sprachraum*, 2 vols. Butjadingen: Achilla.

Schenda, Rudolf (1976). *Die Lesestoffe der kleinen Leute: Studien zu populären Literatur im 19. und 20. Jahrhundert.* Munich: Beck.

Schmidtke, Werner G. (1981). Sherlock Holmes auf der Hintertreppe: Die Kriminalerzählung im deutschen Heftroman. In Armin Arnold (ed.). *Sherlock Holmes auf der Hintertreppe*, 7–81. Bonn: Bouvier.

Schultze, Ernst (1909). *Die Schundliteratur: Ihr Vordringen, ihre Folgen, ihre Bekämpfung.* Halle: Verlag der Buchhandlung des Waisenhauses.
Thole, Werner (2000). *Kinder- und Jugendarbeit: Eine Einführung.* Weinheim & Munich: Juventa.
Webster's Dictionary. Authorized and Unabridged Edition (1876). London: George Bell & Sons.
White, David M. (1964). The Gatekeeper: A Case Study in the Selection of News. In Lewis A. Dexter and David M. White (eds.). *People, Society and Mass Communications,* 160–72. New York: Free Press.

Appropriating America? American Schoolbooks in Philippine Classrooms, 1900–1912

Olivia Anne M. Habana

In the first decade of the American period in the Philippines, a paramount concern of the colonial administration was English language instruction in public primary schools. This paper relates how the Americans tried to achieve this with the use of American schoolbooks in Philippine classrooms in the early years of the colonial period, i.e. from 1900 to 1912. In particular, the paper will investigate the role of the *Baldwin Primer* that was widely used in the American public school system in the Philippines. The *Baldwin Primers* were a series of English reading and language textbooks originally devised to be used in primary schools in the United States. The language and content of these books were foreign to Filipinos, yet they were used for the social project of creating America's 'little brown brothers.' Although technically not a consumer good, the widespread and mandatory use of the textbook and the meanings it acquired make it an interesting object for inquiry within the context of this collection.

This paper will investigate the *Baldwin Primer* in the cultural context of the colonial Philippines. In particular, this paper will look at two aspects of learning that American colonial officials hoped the texts would address: English language and American ideals and institutions. Historical research and analysis on the period under study will provide historical context for the paper, while textual analysis of the source schoolbooks will be used to interrogate the cultural meanings attached to them. The paper will further attempt to investigate and interpret how Filipino children reacted to these new cultural artifacts through an analysis of diaries, memoirs and correspondences of American teachers and education officials. Did the Filipino school children imbibe the lessons and values in the primers and spread them to the rest of society, as the Americans hoped, or did they appropriate them for their own ends and create their own meanings?

American Colonial Rule in the Philippines

The Philippines was an American colony from 1898 to 1946, and it is commonly perceived that one of the major contributions of the American period was education, specifically free public primary education, which had not been widely available during the Spanish period. The American colonial era in the Philippines was envisioned as an experiment in democratic tutelage, with Filipinos as pupils and Americans as teachers. United States President William McKinley coined the phrase 'benevolent assimilation' to describe the American vision and goal for the Philippines; on a practical level this meant transforming the Filipinos into America's 'little brown brothers,' in the famous words of William Howard Taft, a colonial official in the Philippines and future President of the United States. To the Americans' dismay however, Filipinos proved to be less than grateful, continuing military and other forms of resistance that undermined American notions of a 'benevolent' colonialism. American officials, however, found hope in an apparently more malleable element of the Filipino population: the Filipino primary schoolchildren.

This view was shared by the American military, which also used education as a means to pacify people. As with most aspects of military social reform, this had a "strong element of enlightened self-interest: education offered the best opportunity to Americanize the people and explain to them their obligations as subjects of the United States" (Linn 2000, 258). First Lieutenant Russell G. Langdon believed that "the problem of amalgamation of natives of the islands as American citizens can best be solved by promptly and properly taking hold of the children" (Atkinson 1902b, 1324). Fred Atkinson, an early Bureau of Education official, agreed. "We must begin with the child. You cannot make Americans out of adult Filipinos—we may make of the child what we choose." (Atkinson, 1902a, 382)

American military and civic officials believed that the 'little brown brother' could be created through education in the English language, which was also expected to Americanize Filipinos by imparting such American ideals as democratic government and self-reliance. The objective of Americanizing the Filipino child through education would involve a process in which the Filipino child was to be alienated from Filipino society and instead made to identify with the United States, but where the child would still be aware that s/he was not on par with the Americans. The child would thus occupy a liminal space between Filipino and American: the ideal 'little brown brother.'

The hope was that the child would then bring this attitude to the rest of his family and the larger community.

Educational Policy in the Philippines

The transition from military to civilian hands was completed on May 5, 1900, when Dr. Fred W. Atkinson, a high school principal from Massachusetts with a PhD from the University of Leipzig, was appointed General Superintendent of Public Instruction. Atkinson drafted an education bill that was enacted into law as Act No. 74, or the Education Legislation Act, on January 21, 1901. It provided for the establishment of the Department of Public Instruction in charge of financial support for a system of public primary schools, and for the training of teachers, construction of schoolhouses, and the prescription of a school curriculum. The law also specified English as the language of instruction and compulsory education for children ages six to twelve. Based on the Massachusetts school system, the curriculum for each year included reading, language, spelling, arithmetic, geography, nature study, drawing, sewing, physical training, hygiene, music, writing, rhetoric and the history of the United States. This was carried out in the schools despite the fact that students and teachers had little knowledge or familiarity with the English language.

To achieve this, Atkinson made use of the readily available *Baldwin Primer*, a primary school textbook devised by May Kirk, which had been used in the United States since 1899. Although these were written for and used in American public schools, they would now be used for the same purpose in the Philippines. In addition, one thousand American teachers were hired for the Philippine primary school system. They arrived in several batches; the largest one being the contingent on the transport ship USS Thomas that arrived in Manila on August 21, 1901, with 368 male and 141 female teachers on board. These teachers were briefed and sent off on assignments throughout the archipelago. They would become the face of American education in the Philippines and be known as the 'Thomasites.'

Fig. 1: Igorot children of the Northern Philippines
(source: American Historical Collection, Rizal Library, Ateneo de Manila University)

The Philippine public school system was to be based on that of the American system and would use English as the sole language of instruction (Report of the Taft Philippine Commission 1901, 31–2). The old Spanish-era municipal and convent schools had to be replaced with schools that met the American standards of "a non-sectarian graded school with a prescribed course of study and definite standards each year, under charge of trained teachers and in suitable buildings. Common schools must be established everywhere and as a minimum standard every child must be taught arithmetic and to read and write the English language" (ibid., 108). Atkinson also believed that the education suited to Filipinos should be "an agricultural and industrial one, after the pattern of our Tuskegee Institute at home," since a higher education would "[unfit] the Filipino for practical work" (qtd. in May 1980, 93). This suggests that the goal was a Filipino school system to serve the American need for an English-speaking labor force that accepted American norms and values.

Atkinson's performance, however, was not up to par, and in 1903 he was replaced as Head of the Bureau of Education by David Prescott Barrows, who held the position from 1903 to 1909. An anthropologist, Barrows arrived in the Philippines in 1900 and after briefly serving as superintendent of schools in Manila became the head of the Bureau of Non-Christian Tribes. In his view, the principal aim of the American educational system in the Philippines was an ideological one: the "destruction of *caciquismo* [=bossism], and the first step in that direction was to extend the system of education to the *barrios* [=neighborhoods]." He believed in the Jeffersonian ideal that "universal education was the necessary precondition for the success of popular government [...] to break down class barriers, [and] to create an educated, independent yeomanry" (May 1980, 98). This statement clearly reveals the expectation that education would impart these American ideals into Filipino society.

Barrows reduced the primary course to three years; he put Filipino teachers in charge of primary education and American teachers in charge of supervising school districts and teaching secondary school; and he simplified the curricula (Barrows 1904, 214–6). In all primary schools children were to be taught the English language, elementary arithmetic, geography of the Philippines, music, drawing, games and body development, gardening, sewing, along with housekeeping instruction for older girls. In this way, Barrows hoped to provide education to more children, especially those in the rural areas whom he felt were most vulnerable to abuse by the Filipino elite. Barrows envisioned that after three years of primary school, three years of intermediate school and two to four years of secondary school or high school, the Filipino child would have thrown off the yoke of dependence and indebtedness and come to realize the importance of freedom and democracy.

In 1909, W. Cameron Forbes, who had consistently opposed Barrows' educational vision, became Governor General of the Philippines. Barrows resigned his post, and Forbes appointed Frank R. White, who had held various positions in the Bureau of Education since 1901, to replace him. Under the Forbes-White tandem, there again was a radical shift in educational policy from one that would create literate and democratic-minded Filipinos to one that would harness their productive manual labor. "The aim of education in the Philippine Islands must for many years be in large part utilitarian; the boys and girls must be taught that manual labor is honorable and be equipped for some occupation, trade or profession upon which they can enter at the conclusion of their studies." (Report of the Philippine Commission 1912, 227) This was a radical turn away from the earlier policies; White immediately established a department to take charge of industrial education and revised the primary curriculum to include more industrial work. For grade one, this would be daily classes in weaving, gardening, woodworking, clay-modeling and sewing. Embroidery, basket making, loom weaving, and poultry raising would be introduced in succeeding grades. At the end of the third grade, students were expected to produce a useful and marketable product (May 1980, 117).

Learning English with the Baldwin Primers

Despite the changes in overall policy, the main tool for achieving the goals of American colonial education remained the same: the *Baldwin Primer*. This reader was seen as a tool not only for teaching English but also American ideals of democracy, popular government and individualism, as indicated in the Bureau of Education's policies. The central role of the English language may be seen from the very beginning of American colonial rule, when the Philippine Commission, faced with about a hundred indigenous languages, decided that the Filipinos needed a common language. Spanish was rejected because it was spoken only by a small minority, while Filipino languages were deemed uncivilized.

"None of these dialects possess any literature of consequence, and to give instruction in any of them would simply perpetuate the provincialism of the people [...]. What the people require, if any scheme of ultimate independence is to be realized, is the unifying influence of a common language." (Williams 1913, 132)

English was also touted by American military and civil officials as the key to the democratic tutelage envisioned by the insular government for the Philippines, although it was not clear how exactly these values were to be transmitted and imbibed by the mere teaching of English.

"The knowledge of English which public schools offer to the youth of the islands will contribute materially to the emancipation of the dependent classes and the development of personal independence which at present is almost entirely wanting in the great masses of the people." (Moses 1902, 881)

Many pro-American Filipinos enthusiastically supported this idea. Trinidad Pardo de Tavera, a leader of the pro-United States Federalist party in the Philippines, was "hopeful that the Filipinos would adopt the values as well as the language of the Americans" (qtd. in May 1980, 84).

"After peace is established all our efforts will be directed to Americanizing ourselves; to cause a knowledge of the English language to be extended [...] in the Philippines, in order that through its agency the American spirit may take possession of us and that we may so adopt its principles, its political customs and its peculiar civilization that our redemption may be complete and radical." (qtd. in May 1980, 84)

The Spanish *caton* and *doctrina* texts[1] could not apply to teaching English and were discarded immediately. In 1900, Atkinson ordered for the Philippine public school system 50,000 copies of *Baldwin's Primers*, 10,000 copies of *Baldwin's First Readers*, and 25,000 copies of *Baldwin's Second Readers*, in addition to Wentworth's *Elementary Arithmetics*, Montgomery's *History of the United States* and others (Atkinson 1902b, 1334).

The content of these books was designed for American schools and was thus unfamiliar to Filipinos, who had no experience of such things as snow and were unaware of the symbolic meanings of autumn leaves and Jack Frost. This would have been doubly difficult for the children since they were not only expected to learn a new language but also a whole new culture and way of life. They had never seen acorns or sleds and had no idea of the cultural significances of Santa Claus and Thanksgiving turkey. The result was that although there was a prescribed curriculum, most of the school day was instead devoted to rudimentary English lessons. Early American teachers record that they would often have to improvise learning methods by pointing at objects and making pupils recite the English terms for them. This was simple enough for common everyday objects like chairs and clothes but would become difficult with unfamiliar realities such as the seasons of the year and the highly contextual meanings of American heroes. Atkinson believed that teaching the lives of former American presidents such as "Washington, Lincoln, [and] McKinley [...] can be made living realities to the child [...] and will serve as the basis for lessons on patriotism." (qtd. in May 1980, 88)

In 1902, Atkinson decided that in the face of the difficulties of teachers and students alike, textbooks prepared specifically for Filipinos would have to be used. Thus was born the Philippine edition of the *Baldwin Primer*, written for Filipino children by American and Filipino teachers. Instead of simply learning the words 'apple' or 'bat,' the children also read their Filipino or Spanish counterparts like 'mansana' and 'palopalo,' often with illustrations to aid understanding. However, the use of direct translations may not have addressed the problem of unfamiliarity and irrelevance to Philippine realities, since the lesson on trees mentions "maple, elm and oak," while that on flowers mentions "red poppies, buttercups and forget-me nots," none of which are found in the Philippines.

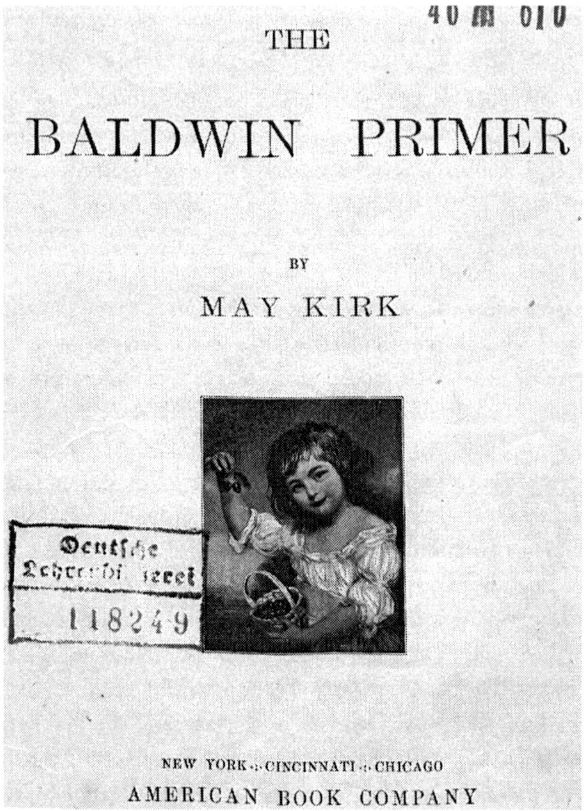

THE

BALDWIN PRIMER

BY

MAY KIRK

NEW YORK · CINCINNATI · CHICAGO
AMERICAN BOOK COMPANY

Fig. 2: The Baldwin Primer

The rhyme entitled "Five Little Chickadees" was translated as "Limang Mumunting Chickadees" (Kirk 1902, 23) and must still have been strange to a Filipino child who had never seen a chickadee. The poem "Winter is Here," translated as "Naito ang Invierno," still portrayed a world alien to the little Filipino with its "Snow and Ice are on the ground" translated as "Nieve at hielo ay nanga sa lupa" (ibid., 96), revealing a further complication in the use of Spanish words where native Tagalog words were non-existent. It is thus evident that the use of the *Baldwin Primer* did not have a one-way effect on the Filipino children by teaching them English. American colonial officials also had to adapt these readers to fit Philippine multilingual realities as well. The translators were local Filipino teachers, and alterations in meaning and nuance may well be traced to the agency of this group.

The *Baldwin Primer* was also seen as a tool to impart desired American modes of behavior to Filipino children and, by extension, to their families and communities. The book contained rules of conduct to be memorized and disseminated to the students' families and communities (May 1993, 101–2). Subsequent texts went into greater detail with admonitions such as: "look directly at the questioner. Do not hang your head as if ashamed" (McVenn 1918, 210). Moral lessons were intended to correct perceived character flaws of the Filipino race. Filipino children were thus introduced to American icons such as George Washington and Abraham Lincoln, who embodied certain American social ideals such as self-control, rational thinking, consistent reasoning, fearlessness, truth telling, punctuality, self-respect, order, and overcoming obstacles (Fuller 1917, 207–8). This was perhaps due to the well-known story of George Washington's honesty when he admitted chopping down a cherry tree without permission and to Abraham Lincoln's struggle to get an education and rise to become President of the United States.

Perhaps the 'character flaw' that received the most attention in the primers would be the Filipino attitude towards manual labor. Many Filipinos had a lukewarm reception to vocational or industrial training in the program of the public schools. Although its primacy in American educational policy fluctuated over the years, it was never totally removed from public education. William H. Taft, Secretary of War in 1908, writes that industrial education will "fit young men to be good farmers, good mechanics, good skilled laborers, and shall teach them the dignity of labor and that it is no disgrace for the son of a good family to learn his trade and to earn his living by it." (Taft and Dickinson 1919, 81)

Early education officials noted that the Filipinos in general had an aversion to manual labor. It is probably more accurate to say that the parents had an aversion to manual labor for their children, even if many of the parents were engaged in manual or agricultural labor themselves and were willing and capable of working hard. For many parents, the point of schooling may have been to allow their children to transcend the back-breaking labor which was their lot. Filipinos had an idea of what education was supposed to obtain for them, and it certainly was not more work in the fields. As such, there was a gap between the American and Filipino ideas of the goal of education. Various teachers and officials such as William Freer narrated anecdotes of Filipino children showing up for industrial classes with relatives or servants in tow to perform the manual labor expected of them, despite admonitions on the dignity of labor in the *Baldwin Primers* (Pecson and Racelis 1959, 41).

Contesting and Transforming the Baldwin Primer

The *Baldwin Primers* were perceived by Filipinos as tools for achievement and emancipation in the context of colonial society. This was especially true given the fact that in the previous Spanish colonial era, speaking Spanish meant entry into a privileged world. In fact, the *ilustrados* or educated upper class clamored for the teaching of Spanish in municipal schools as a means of social emancipation. Conservatives in colonial society, especially religious conservatives, considered learning Spanish unsuitable and unnecessary for *indios*. The result was a situation in which the existing schools (usually run by clergy) did not teach the one thing that the populace asked for: the Spanish language. The American colonizers on the other hand were teaching their language to all and sundry. It is no wonder that many ordinary Filipinos seized the opportunity to learn English, because it, too, was perceived as a tool for achievement and emancipation.

English was also perceived as the language of the elite and the learned. As such, it was prestigious for parents to raise an English-speaking child. But at the same time, Filipino parents took a very pragmatic view of English. Most children stayed in school just long enough to obtain a rudimentary knowledge of the language. This is borne out by the dropout rate after about two to three years in primary school, as reported by the school officials all over the country. It concluded that most of the primary school years were spent acquiring a basic grasp of the language, after which the child was deemed fit enough to get a job with the American bureaucracy or private business, or at the very least to navigate colonial bureaucracy. Director of Education David Barrows himself conceded this and stated that most Filipinos saw education not as a means towards democracy and enlightenment but in the very prosaic manner of acquiring skills and well-paid jobs (Barrows 1909, 805).

While the Americans wanted to prepare the Filipinos to become good English-speaking colonial subjects prepared to do manual labor, the Filipinos perceived that learning the language of the colonizer would give them entry into a privileged world. Americans thought that Filipinos should concentrate on manual work, while in Filipino eyes education was supposed to enable a person to move away from it. The *Baldwin Primers* were thus viewed similarly by both Americans and Filipinos, as a tool to learn English. The ends, however, were quite different. Whereas the Americans wanted this for their colonial purposes, most Filipinos felt that it was a way to navigate in the new colonial world, one in which power lay in the knowledge of the American language and familiarity with American images and things proper to its idiom, such as apples, robins, autumn leaves and winter snow.

The American strategy was to teach democracy and American ideals hand in hand with the English language. However, Filipino tactics were centered around learning just enough English to deal with the colonial world. Thus we see the phenomenon of Filipinos who had never seen snow or autumn leaves writing poetry about the beauty of falling maple leaves and the chill of winter. Filipino school children played baseball because it was the game of the colonizers. They shook hands and gazed directly at authorities, because these had been indicated as the 'right' manners. Away from the colonial gaze, however, they continued to play native games and act according to Filipino norms in their own communities. There was also no apparent contradiction in learning English while preserving nationalist feeling. General Vicente Lukban, head of the revolutionary forces in Samar and Leyte, had left his children in the care of his brother as he waged a bitter war against the American forces. Even while being pursued by the Americans in Samar, he instructed his brother that his children be made to learn and become fluent in English because it would be "the language of the century" (Guerrero 1998, 228). Apparently, many Filipinos, used to a colonial setting, were not bothered by this inconsistency. To the American colonial officials, the primers were symbols of their 'benevolent' mission that carried the belief that they could change a people simply by teaching American English. But to many Filipinos, the primers represented modernization and a dichotomized lifestyle.

Appropriating American Culture and Language

In the opening essay to this volume, Hans Peter Hahn states that cultural appropriation refers to "actors and the agency of those who redesign contexts and re-establish meanings of specific things" (in this volume, 21–2). This is evident in the case of the *Baldwin Primers* in the American-era Philippines, which can be used to depict different levels of appropriation. The Filipino teachers and students were important agents in the transformation of the textbook from a simple English teaching tool to one that taught literacy in English, Tagalog and Spanish. Unknown Filipino teachers were instrumental in revising the texts into the Philippine editions. They translated and edited the texts to be more suitable, and in the process added nuances and changed meanings as well. This may be seen in the use of Spanish words, retention of certain English words, and the inclusion of indigenous stories and heroes.

A further aspect of appropriation is evident in the adaptation of the teaching method. Primers using methods identical to those of the *Baldwin Primers* would be utilized in teaching literacy in English and Tagalog or in other indigenous languages to adults. This was seen in the *The People's Readers,* authored by Camilo Osias, who used the primers as templates and transformed and adapted them to specific needs. In his words, "consideration has to be given to the fact that the needs of adults beginning to read are different from those of children" (1921, 5). This may be seen as an instance in which "the powerless use cultural appropriation as a tactic to engage in decision making processes from which they would otherwise be excluded." (Hahn in this volume, 29)

The use of the schoolbooks and the learning of English allowed powerless, marginal Filipinos entry into a world formerly reserved for the Spanish-speaking elite. The abrupt change in colonizing power put the old elite, *mestizo* Spanish speakers on the same level as their former social inferiors, the non-Spanish speakers. Everyone had to begin from scratch to learn English. This leveling of Filipino society was indeed one of the targets of American education. However, many Filipinos stopped school in the third or fourth grade once they had achieved a functional knowledge of English. Clearly, just learning English was not enough to change the deep-seated social structures of Philippine society, despite American expectations that it would do so.

On the level of English language teaching itself, American teachers lamented not only the lack of ideological appropriation of their students but also their inability to speak with correct American accents. The way Filipinos spoke was comically described as 'carabao English' and has come to connote ungrammatical English spoken with a Filipino accent. Anna Donaldson, a Thomasite assigned to Nueva Caceres in the Bicol region, humorously describes how a student recited an English rhyme in a native accent.

"I lub de name of Washington
I lub my country too
I lub de plag, de dear old plag
Of red and white and blue." (qtd. in Racelis and Ick 2001, 267)

Fig. 3: From the 1899 editon of the Baldwin Primer

Donaldson complained that no amount of correction could remove the Filipino pronunciation. Perhaps unknown to Donaldson, Filipino children who spoke with an American accent might have been subject to teasing, mimicry and other forms of social disapproval.

English words and phrases from the primer also found their way into Filipino games and rhymes through the agency of the schoolchildren themselves. A good example is the *habulan* (=tag) rhyme that goes:

Pen pen de sarapen
Kuchillo de almacen
How how the carabao
Batuten

This may be loosely translated as: "pen pen de sarapen, knife of warehouse, how how the carabao, stinky." Essentially a nonsense rhyme, it jumbles together Tagalog, Spanish and English words more for the sound than the sense that they made.

Some teachers reported with glee the fact that their students adopted games from stories or poems found in the *Baldwin Primers*. Although taken directly from the books, they were also transformed to suit local realities. A favorite was to play 'William Tell' by shooting an arrow at a mango or other local fruit in place of the apple. Organized athletic games such as basketball and baseball also gained in popularity. American teacher Mary Fee described in detail a baseball game that was scarcely recognizable as such because of the use of local fruits and boards instead of balls and bats, as well as very different rules to accommodate the cramped playing area, lack of equipment, and number of players (Fee 1912, 284–5). William Freer observed in 1906 that a child had taken the rhyme "Cherries Ripe" from the *Baldwin Reader* and used it to call out his wares (banana fritters or *sinaput*) by singing "Sinaput, sinaput, who will buy my sinaput?" (106)

The mixing up of three different languages was not limited to Filipinos but was also done by Americans, especially those who associated closely with Filipinos. This is evident in songs sung by the American soldiers in the country, an excerpt of which is as follows:

"His daddy un beun [sic] Filipino
Who never mixed tubig with bino
Said, 'I am no insurrecto, no got gun or bolo,'
Yet used both to kill a vecino […].

He once owned a bulic manoc
With a haughty and valorous look,
Which lost him a name, y mil pesos tambien,
So he changed to Monte for luck." (Military Order of the Carabao 1913, 133–4)

Conclusion

As such, the use of the *Baldwin Primers* in Philippine public schools during the first few years of the American era reveals different sides of the phenomena of cultural appropriation. The texts were not consumer goods purchased by choice but were instead imposed and supplied from above by the colonial authorities. A study of American education policy suggests that the colonial authorities actually wanted Filipinos not only to learn English but also to adopt American ideals, institutions, and modes of behavior from the books.

Filipino children proved to be eager learners, and the *Baldwin Primer* became a symbol of modernity and learning. However, it was evident that the primers posed certain problems not only to students but to teachers as well. In 1902, the colonial administration revised the books with the help of Filipino teachers, and these Philippine editions now included Tagalog and Spanish words as well as stories of Filipino heroes like Jose Rizal. Later, the methodology of the *Baldwin Primers* was employed by Filipino teachers to teach literacy in native languages to adult students, as seen in the *Philippine Primers* of Camilo Osias.

On a different level, school children who had used these books appropriated the words, phrases, and stories and incorporated them into their own games and rhymes. In so doing, these marginal, seemingly powerless elements of colonial society were active agents not only in learning the English language and appropriating its stories, phrases and words, but also in using these out of their original context and for their own purposes. The *Baldwin Primer* was thus more than just a simple English language textbook but became a site of negotiation, appropriation, and transformation in the colonial setting of the American-era Philippines.

Notes

1 The *caton* is a Spanish-period primary text for teaching letters of the alphabet to children; *Doctrina* refers to the *Doctrina Christiana* which was used in the Spanish colonial period to teach Catholic prayers and the catechism.

References

Atkinson, Fred W. (1902a). Education in the Philippines. *The Outlook,* 70, April 5, 832–40.

Atkinson, Fred W. (1902b). The Present Educational Movement in the Philippines. In *Report of the Philippine Commission,* 1317–440. Washington: Government Printing Office.

Barrows, David P. (1904). *Courses for Instruction for the Public Schools of the Philippine Islands Prescribed by the General Superintendent of Education.* Manila: Bureau of Public Printing.

Barrows, David P. (1909). *Report of the Director of Education, 1908.* Washington: Government Printing Office.

Fee, Mary H. (1912). *A Woman's Impressions of the Philippines.* Chicago: A. C. McClurg & Company.

Freer, William B. (1906). *The Philippine Experiences of an American School Teacher.* New York: Charles Scribner's Sons.

Fuller, Alice M. (1917). *Housekeeping: A Textbook for Girls in the Public Intermediate Schools of the Philippines.* Manila: Bureau of Printing.

Guerrero, Milagros C. (1998). *The Story of the Filipino People. Vol. 6. Under Stars and Stripes.* Hongkong: Asia Publishing Company Limited.

Kirk, May (1899). *The Baldwin Primer.* New York et al.: American Book Company.

Kirk, May (1902). *The Baldwin Primer, Tagalog Edition.* New York et al.: American Book Company.

Linn, Brian McAllister (2000). *The Philippine War: 1899–1902.* Lawrence: The University Press of Kansas.

May, Glenn (1980). *Social Engineering in the Philippines: The Aims, Execution and Impact of American Colonial Policy.* Westport, London: Greenwood Press.

McVenn, Gertrude E. (1918/1919). *Good Manners and Right Conduct.* Boston: D. C. Heath & Co., Publishers.

Military Order of the Carabao (1913). *Historical Sketch, Constitution and Register of the Military Order of the Carabao, Together with songs that have been Sung at "Wallows" in Various Places.* Washington: W. F. Roberts.

Moses, Bernard (1902). First Annual Report of the Secretary of Public Instruction, Year Ending Oct. 15, 1902. In *Report of the Philippine Commission*, 867–902. Washington: Government Printing Office.

Osias, Camilo (1921). *Barrio Life and Barrio Education.* New York: World Book Company.

Pecson, Geronima T., and Maria Racelis (1959). *Tales of the American Teachers in the Philippines.* Manila: Carmelo & Bauermann, Inc.

Racelis, Mary, and Judy Celine Ick (2001). *Bearers of Benevolence: The Thomasites and Public Education in the Philippines.* Quezon City: Anvil Publishing Incorporated.

Report of the Taft Philippine Commission, 1900 (1901). Washington: Government Printing Office.

Report of the Philippine Commission, 1912 (1913). Washington: Government Printing Office.

Taft, William H., and J. M. Dickinson (1919). *Special Reports on the Philippines*. Washington: Government Printing Office.

Williams, Daniel R. (1913). *The Odyssey of the Philippine Commission*. Chicago: A. C. McClurg & Co.

Network of Texts: H. C. Andersen and the Transnationalization of Literature

Frederike Felcht

Hans Christian Andersen is one of the most translated authors in the world. Fairy tales such as *Prindsessen paa Ærten (The Princess on the Pea)* (1835), *Den grimme Ælling (The Ugly Duckling)* (1844) or *Den lille Pige med Svovlstikkerne (The Little Match Girl)* (1845) are read all over the world. The transnational history of Andersen's texts offers rich material for research on cultural appropriation.[1]

This article traces the spread and reception of Andersen's texts in the nineteenth century and thereby analyzes structures of literary exchange. Furthermore, it reveals how the texts themselves deal with and contribute to processes of cultural appropriation. The article shows correspondences between the material history of the texts and the stories these texts tell; it thus combines an external view of the texts with the internal perspective on these. In this context, cultural appropriation is understood not only as a reciprocal relationship between producers and consumers,[2] but also as one between human beings and texts. Texts establish the relationship between producers and consumers, and they develop their own dynamics in such exchange processes.

These dynamics are part of a more comprehensive historical development of the nineteenth century, namely, the rise of a global commodity culture including an enormous increase in the number of things in everyday life (Böhme 2006, 17–9). Approaching commodity culture from a perspective of appropriation helps grasp the complex interplay between uniformization and heterogenization that characterizes global processes. The differences in the ways Andersen's texts were appropriated prove that the globalization of literary structures does not inevitably lead to their homogenization. Thus, Hans Peter Hahn's (in this volume) emphasis on the persistence of cultural differences in a globalizing world proves true in the field of literature.

Literature has a specific character in processes of appropriation. As appropriated objects, Andersen's texts not only form part of the spread of a global commodity culture; they participate actively in processes of appropriation themselves and reflect them. They exhibit a high degree of agency, i.e. the ability to participate in chains of events and influence their outcomes. The concept of agency in this article is informed by actor-network-theory (Böhme 2006, 72–94; Latour 2007, 76–88, 122–5). Employing actor-network-theory in observing cultural appropriation can help us grasp the complex interplay between textual and non-textual realities.

In the second half of this contribution, the travelogue *I Spanien (In Spain)* (1863) serves as an example of the textual dynamics of appropriation. The travelogue is both an object and a subject of appropriation. It is distributed in its material form, read and understood in various ways, and it is an act of appropriation itself: travelogues appropriate other texts and foreign countries for the imagination of their readers.

Navigating in World Literary Space: the Spread and Appropriation of Andersen's Texts

Andersen's publishing strategy was transnational from the early years of his career. Even for successful authors, it was difficult to earn enough money in the Danish literary market because it was so small. Since international laws for copyright protection did not exist (Seville 2009, 8–9), Andersen did not receive any money for the early translations of his works. However, he was compensated later through contracts with German, English, and American publishers that secured his authorship rights. Andersen published some of his works in Germany first, then in Denmark in the 1840s; later on, he signed contracts with British or American publishers and sent them his manuscripts for translation before the Danish edition appeared. This way he was able to avoid pirated editions.

In Andersen's autobiographies, economic details were not omitted. For example, the narrator of *Mit Livs Eventyr (The Fairy Tale of My Life)* (1855) reports having received a sum of money for a German edition of his writings thanks to German friends who had arranged business contacts for him (Andersen 2007a, 319).[3] By telling stories about sales, the text reflects on its own status as a commodity.

However, economic concerns were not the only reason for Andersen's transnational publishing strategy—he was grateful for the early, unpaid translations as well. In order to understand why, it is helpful to consult Pascale

Casanova's Bourdieu-inspired study *The World Republic of Letters* (2004), which describes the implicit laws that govern the transnational literary field. According to Casanova, literature produces a specific form of value, separate from its economic value, which allows 'literary capital' to accumulate. Literary capital is a specific form of prestige national literatures possess,[4] and in some cases it is transferred to authors who publish in these literatures. According to Casanova, literary capital is, first of all, composed of texts in their material form. The age of a literature is one of the central qualities of literary capital. Also, literary prestige depends on the existence of a professional milieu, a cultivated public, a specialized press, and of sought-after publishers in a competitive field. Literary capital concentrates in centers of power, and these centers form the international space of literature. Translators and critics are important actors in the international space of literature (ibid., 12–23, 135–46).

Casanova distinguishes between national and international authors. The latter "find themselves so at odds with the norms of their native literary space and, by contrast, so at home with norms current in the centers of international space that they are able to make their way only outside their homeland" (ibid., 110). Norms of the international space include cosmopolitanism and the autonomy of literature. The international space consecrates innovative texts that do not conform to traditional norms, and it favors authors that promote openness to other literatures rather than national narrow-mindedness (ibid., 85–7, 113–5). Local color may be used as part of the marketing strategy, but it is always directed towards a transnational audience. Constructing an observably international authorship is especially important for innovative authors from peripheral literatures such as Danish literature.

Many of Andersen's texts conform to the norms of the international space. In order to gain recognition, Andersen had to find his way into the international space. His reward was a long-term accumulation of literary capital. Andersen's publishing strategy respected the implicit laws of the 'world republic of letters' and thus contributed to his transnational success. In the nineteenth century, a system of national literatures developed, and literary value circulated among these literatures (ibid., 75–81, 103–15). Whereas Casanova (ibid., 23–40, 67–100) emphasizes the centrality of France in the world literary system, the centers of translation and popularization of Andersen's texts were England and Germany.

Germany has traditionally been a mediator of Danish literature because of Denmark's close linguistic and cultural connection to Germany, a connection that weakened during the nationalization that took place over the course of the nineteenth century (Winge 1992, 185–334). German literature had a central position in the literary system of the nineteenth century. It had industrialized book production and was a big market (Wittmann 1982, 111–5); it had successfully constructed a literary tradition and had a recognized professional milieu. In the construction of a German literary tradition the translation of ancient Greek, Roman and other classical authors had played an important role. As a result, German literature was relatively open to foreign influences (Kauffmann 2002, 117–30), and it was attractive to international authors because of its central position in the international space.

Andersen's reception in Great Britain was mediated by German translations (Bredsdorff 1954, 489, 495–6, 503; Hjørnager Pedersen 2004, 18–20, 84, 103, 116, 128, 154–5, 170, 226). Translations of translations were quite common in the nineteenth century despite the poor quality of translations produced this way. England's position in the world republic of letters was central, too, and for successful authors it was one of the most lucrative markets.

The reception of Andersen's texts varies with its context. Critics in Denmark tended to judge the young author's stylistic and poetic innovations as errors of literary convention because the critics still had Andersen's proletarian background in mind. According to Helge Topsøe-Jensen (1934, 178–81) and Erling Nielsen (1990, 123–7), Andersen's autobiographies exaggerate the Danish critics' disregard for his writing. Surprisingly, this exaggeration helped him accumulate literary capital. Andersen's autobiographies suggest that negative reviews ought to be explained by the provinciality of Denmark's literary scene, and they use Andersen's positive reception in Germany and England to demonstrate the true value of his work. Foreign critics accept this line of argumentation, as a review from Sweden, cited in the 1855 autobiography (Andersen 2007a, 201), demonstrates. In this review Danish enviousness is set against a superior European view praising Andersen as a European writer. Thus, the autobiography presents Andersen as an international author in Casanova's (2004, 108–15) sense: he obtains his literary prestige through translations and distances himself from national provinciality. As a part of the dialogue with critics, the autobiography develops agency in processes of appropriation.

Germany welcomed Andersen, a seemingly naive genius who made his way from a poor childhood in a Danish province to become a member of the European artists' elite. The popularity of Andersen's texts is closely connected to the biographical narratives of the genius, the social climber, and the childlike fairy tale hero, as Ivy York Möller-Christensen (1992, 104–13, 268–75 and *passim*) has shown. The German appreciation for Andersen's 'naivety' should be seen in the context of a German emphasis on values like "'authenticity'" and an "'immediately popular'" quality of poetry (Casanova 2004, 76). The positive reception of Andersen's work can also be traced back to the hostility of conservative German criticism toward the contemporary politicization of German and French literature (Möller-Christensen 1992, 98–113). Because of their anti-liberal point of view, German critics appreciated Andersen's novels as affirmative texts, whereas according to the Danish critics, they had revolutionary tendencies: it was quite unusual in Denmark in the 1830s to write novels about the everyday lives of people of different classes in unpretentious prose (Mortensen 2008, 361, 377–9). Depending on the national literary and political field, the critics' appropriation of Andersen's texts varied considerably. Even though most of the German and Danish critics shared a conservative attitude, they pursued different strategies in maintaining the status quo. German critics stressed the non-political traits of Andersen's texts and the author's naive charm, and so appreciated his writings; Danish critics pointed to the unconventional form of the texts and criticized their disregard of traditional literary standards and moral conventions.

Andersen's biographical background was used to create a positive image in Great Britain as well (Bredsdorff 1954, 431–5). Andersen and his publishers aided in the construction of these myths by disseminating his image (J. Andersen 2005, 289), and they used modern technologies for their aims as soon as they could: Andersen is one of the most photographed authors of the nineteenth century (Thage 2007, 25). Another strategy that strengthened the link between author and literary text were public readings and many tours during which Andersen met the cultural elites of Europe. His travelogues arose from these journeys.

The autobiographies distinguish between the critical and the popular reception of Andersen's texts. They report that Andersen's texts were popular in Denmark too, despite negative reviews. This claim is supported by the sales volume of Andersen's texts. In the nineteenth century, several editions of his novels, fairy tales and collected works were published.[5] But even though there is no difference in the national popularity of the texts among Denmark, Germany or England, the reception certainly differed: whereas Andersen's original texts are full of irony and wit (and thus aroused the Danish critics' distrust), translators often erased sexual allusions or black humor in consideration of the moral standards of their culture (Butts 1995, 97; Jones 1993).

Fig. 1: Portrait of H. C. Andersen (source: Thage 2007, 178)

Furthermore, since Andersen's humor is based on his virtuosic use of the Danish language, it is partly untranslatable (Anz 2005, 36; Brandes 1902, 120).

But these variations in understanding were less important for Andersen. Whereas the autobiographies group the professional milieus by nation, they treat the non-professional readers as a global entity, not divided into national parts. The divergence of the professional reception is employed to create literary value, and the hierarchy among national literary milieus contributes to the accumulation of literary capital. The non-professional reception of the texts is judged differently from the professional reception: every act of appropriation is appreciated in the autobiographies. This appreciation expresses respect for the popular appropriation of the texts. Pascale Casanova's theory focuses on professional appropriation and cannot explain adequately Andersen's respect for the popular appropriation of his texts, but Michel de Certeau's (1988, 85–92) concept of tactics is helpful at this point. Unlike professional appropriation, tactics are not rule-bound or based on specific knowledge, and their motivation and goals vary considerably. Tactics do not control the field of action; they operate within given structures and withstand the requested paths of action. Initially defined by lack of power, they can subvert power relations and change existing structures (Hahn in this volume). In Andersen's case, the consistent popularity of his texts contributed to their gradual recognition by Danish critics. His appreciation of every act of non-professional appropriation can be understood in this way. Coming from a poor family environment, Andersen was not familiar with the conventions of the Danish literary scene at the beginning of his career, but he was aware of consumers' influence on the success of products and producers.

In 1835, the first collection of Andersen's fairy tales was published in Denmark. The critics' reactions were somewhat restrained, but the fairy tales soon became the most important genre in Andersen's transnational commercial success. In 1839, they strengthened his popularity in Germany. The first German edition of his collected works began to appear in 1847 and was published years before the Danish edition. Andersen's popularity in England soared in the 1840s with the publication of his novels and fairy tales in English translation (Bredsdorff 1954, 438). A breakthrough in the United States followed soon thereafter. Dennis Butts (2010, 16–22) sees the success of Andersen's fairy tales in the context of a changing English society whose increasing distress at the negative sides of capitalism produced a tendency toward intellectual escapism and critical realism. Andersen's texts suited both tastes, and they contributed to the substantial change in standards of children's literature that took place in England between 1820 and 1850 (ibid., 12).

The illustrations of the fairy tales also added to their popularity. Andersen's German publisher offered an illustrated edition of the fairy tales in 1848.[6] Vilhelm Pedersen, a Danish naval officer and illustrator, provided the pictures for the illustrated edition. The successful book design of the German version was used in the Danish edition of 1850. Over the course of the nineteenth century, German children's literature became more entertaining and also began to address smaller children. Increasing readership encouraged industrial modes of production and new illustration techniques (Petri 1988, 35–6). The German appropriation of the fairy tales led to changes in their Danish mode of production, so the appropriation of Andersen's books was multidirectional and as such is consistent with Hahn's (in this volume) characterization of appropriation. The illustrations by Vilhelm Pedersen are still popular today (see e.g. Andersen 2005).

Fig. 2: The Steadfast Tin Soldier

The Transnationalization of Culture and the Agency of Texts

The contents of Andersen's autobiographies, travelogues and, in some cases, of his fairy tales reflect the emergence of a transnational textual culture closely connected to material innovations such as the mass production of printed media and the expansion of communication networks.

There are fetishistic elements in this textual culture; people develop emotional ties to texts in their material form, and texts gain social power. In addition to the previously mentioned photographs, the collection of autographs, letters and books is a recurring subject in Andersen's texts. In the autobiographies and travelogues, texts stabilize or even generate relationships such as the author's personal contacts to readers and publishers. The texts circulate and through their circulation provide the author with the financial means to travel.

The differences in the reception of Andersen's work show that texts develop their own dynamics: neither the author's nor the critics' nor the readers' intentions control their movements. Instead, a network of human beings and things spreads, and in this development texts play an active role. From the perspective of thing theory, texts have agency, i.e. they are active elements in the network of relations (Böhme 2006, 72–94; Latour 2007, 76–88, 122–5). They are not only able to diverge from intended paths of reception, but they can also influence the self-conception of their producers and consumers. For example, Andersen's biographical narratives heavily influenced his self-understanding and his relationships with other people. Andersen's self-portrayal as a naive fairy tale hero, the charming illustrations accompanying his works, and the censured translations contributed not only to his commercial success, but also to the classification of Andersen as a children's author, a classification that did not correspond to his intentions.

The spread of literary texts forms part of a more comprehensive development. Mass production, transnational trade in connection with local variations in the marketing and appropriation of goods, and the fetishistic power of things are characteristic traits of a globalizing commodity culture. In the following sections, the travelogue *In Spain* exemplifies the textual dynamics in processes of appropriation and the complex interplay between producer, consumer and text.

In Spain: Ways of a Book

The American version of Andersen's autobiography (Andersen 2007b, 250, 444) reveals that it was his publisher's handsome offer for the second edition of his illustrated fairy tales that allowed him to travel to Spain in 1862. Thus, the American autobiography, itself a 'travelling text,' comments on the financing of the trip on which the travelogue ultimately is based. The illustrations of this second edition of the fairy tales were taken from the German edition.

During his trip to Spain, Andersen sent several poems and letters to Danish newspapers like *Illustreret Tidende*, an illustrated magazine, and they published his texts. The complete travelogue was published in Denmark in November 1863. A month earlier, Andersen had already sent the manuscript to his English publisher (Andersen 2006, 553–4).[7] In 1864, the travelogue appeared in print in England and Germany, and was published in 1870 in New York (Schovsbo 2004, 246). The Danish critics wrote benevolent reviews (ibid., 241). *The Spectator*, an English magazine, gave the German version very positive reviews. The English version that appeared shortly afterwards did not attract as much attention (Bredsdorff 1954, 478–9). The exchange between the literary markets had already reached a considerable pace.

The market-based dissemination of the book was joined by distribution through personal channels. Andersen's diaries reveal that he gave the travelogue as a present to friends in Denmark. He also sent his book to King George in Greece in 1863 and gave it to a Portuguese friend upon his visit to Lisbon in 1866. He presented a Spanish singer who visited Denmark in 1867 with a German version along with a portrait of himself, this in exchange for two portraits of the singer.[8] These gifts demonstrate that Andersen often used books to strengthen or establish personal relationships, which often transcended national borders.

In the American version of Andersen's autobiography, *The Story of My Life* (1871), the first-person narrator answers a letter from an English woman who wants him to correct a misleading detail from *In Spain* concerning the description of a place in Malaga (Andersen 2007b, 256–7). Thus, the autobiography forms part of a dialogue starting with the woman's reading of *In Spain*, a text that she reads as a factual report despite its highly poetic structure. The answer to the letter addresses the readership of the autobiography instead of the English woman, which changes the communicative structure of the dialogue significantly.

The public correction of the misleading detail takes into account that the travelogue might influence the movements of later travelers. The growing number of travelers and the development of tourism in the nineteenth century (Hachtmann 2007, 9–17, 48–97) led to an increased use of guides. The ambiguity of the term 'guide,' particularly its dual reference to books and human beings, reveals parallels between human and textual agency in modern ensembles of action such as tourism. Still, the response to a personal letter in *The Story of My Life* blurs the distinction between the personality of the author and the narrator of the autobiography. The autobiography and the travelogue thereby attain an authentic character, and they contribute to the construction of Andersen's persona.

Such feedback loops are typical of Andersen's texts, in which letters, books and humans communicate, and thus the texts blur the distinction between author and narrator and between textual and non-textual reality. For example, in *In Spain*, a young German is delighted to meet the famous author while the two are on a boat trip. The German is anxious to make him comfortable; he wraps his woolen shawl around the narrator's throat and lays his cloak over his feet (Andersen 2006, 242). Thus the texts reflect the social power of texts, which had grown during the nineteenth century as the networks of texts expanded and connected more and more people. Andersen became an international celebrity, and his books popularized the story of his life throughout Europe and North America.

The Travelogue as an Act of Cultural Appropriation: the Example of *In Spain*

Travelogues are nodes of different forms of cultural appropriation. On the one hand, *In Spain* is embedded in the expansion of a transnational literary system and is appropriated by readers of English, German, or Danish books, even if they live in Portugal or Greece. On the other hand, travelogues are themselves acts of cultural appropriation. They appropriate other texts, and they appropriate countries for the imagination of their readers.

As Manfred Pfister (1993, 109–32) has shown, the travel genre is highly intertextual; this observation is valid for *In Spain*, too. The travelogue includes references to Danish and Spanish history and literature. Biographical studies demonstrate that Andersen read other travelogues in preparation for his tour

(Schovsbo 2004, 226, 230–9). On an intertextual level, *In Spain* crossfades between Danish and Spanish history, and it takes up a motif from the autobiography to stress the home-like character of Spain: the narrator's first visit to Spain occurs on the anniversary of his arrival in Copenhagen and, previously, in Italy (Andersen 2006, 226, 562; Felcht 2011, 53). The travelogue even ironizes its own intertextual character: after referring to the history of Tangier, it notes that this information can be found in any "Conversations-Lexicon" (Andersen 2006, 341), i.e. encyclopedia.

Since the appropriation of countries for the imagination of readers has a very complex character in *In Spain*, my commentary will be limited to providing general information on the nineteenth century conception of Spain in order to present some characteristics of the travelogue and to demonstrate the role of texts in it.[9] Spain's image was rather negative at the beginning of the nineteenth century; it was considered an unsafe and corrupt country and was feared because of the inquisition, not permanently abolished until 1834. With the advent of Romanticism, its image improved, but in the 1860s it still was not receiving many visitors (Zimmermann 2003, 54–9). In Andersen's travelogue, the representation of Spanish women is often highly eroticized. Because of this, Christian von Zimmermann (ibid., 61) interprets *In Spain* as a reaction to the removal of passion from the domain of the self and its relegation to the realm of the exotic other.

Although it shows distinct traits of 'othering,' the character of the travelogue is determined by something else. Focusing on the world of things and texts in the travelogue, instead of on interpersonal relationships, gives a different picture of the appropriation of foreign countries for the reader's imagination. This focus is justifiable, since in *In Spain* material infrastructures are represented extensively, and interpersonal relationships remain mostly superficial.

From this standpoint, Spain is presented instead as a hybrid country of modern cities and underdeveloped areas. This hybridity is reflected in descriptions of the infrastructure for travelling. Throughout *In Spain*, the means of transportation shift constantly among modern railway systems, steamers, diligences, and small walking tours. Thus, the narrator's appropriation of Spain is characterized by diversity. Spain is both foreign and familiar, not a homogeneous entity, but a multifaceted country. According to Klaus Müller-Wille (*forthcoming*) the stylistic heterogeneity of the travelogue—its oscillation between poems, journalistic description, and lyrical prose—corresponds to the fragmentation or upheaval of Spanish culture. It mediates the narrator's contrasting impressions.

The architecture of Spain embodies its historical connection to Africa, whereas its landscapes remind the narrator of Denmark, Italy and Africa. Using Danish landscape images that had attained national significance, e.g. the coast of Jutland or the rocks of Möen, the travelogue refers to the cartographic and literary construction of Danish nationality in the nineteenth century (Behschnitt 2006, 277–340), but it delocalizes its stereotypes and brings the countries closer together in the reader's imagination (Felcht 2011, 22–4).

The narrator travels from France through Spain (via Gibraltar) to Morocco and all the way back. His first encounter with African people upon arriving in Tangier reflects European orientalist fears. "[H]alf-naked sunburnt Moors" are "screaming and making signs"; Moroccan Jews carry the narrator's luggage without him asking them to: "it was like a regular work of plunder." At customs, every bag is searched until the narrator says the "magic words—'the English Ambassador!'", and is "permitted to depart, which we did guided, or rather accompanied, by a score of half-naked barbarians. Were we not on the coast of the barbarians, in the country from which, in olden times, pirates went forth, as they did from Tunis, Algiers, and Tripoli, for the purposes of rapine and murder?" (Andersen 1864, 177–8) The idea of the uncivilized Other, the barbarian without manners and discipline, is pervasive. The customs officer obeys magic words instead of legal procedures. But the following description of Africa answers the narrator's question—"Were we not on the coast of the barbarians?"—in an unexpected way. The Pasha of Morocco welcomes the ambassador and the narrator "with much cordiality and European politeness" (Andersen 2006, 346; my translation),[10] and the narrator's encounters with African people proceed without complications. Even more significant for the de-alienation of Africa is the description of its material culture. Africa is integrated into a global universe of commodities. For example, the house of the English ambassador provides European comfort; its living room could have been a Danish room, as the narrator states (ibid., 339). European souvenirs are imported and sold in Tangier to European tourists (ibid., 341). Texts participate in this network of commodities, too. Andersen's host possesses "a not insignificant library" (Andersen 1864, 190), and his daughters know Andersen's fairy tales from an English translation. The narrator receives letters and newspapers from Denmark, and it takes only eight days for them to arrive at their destination (Andersen 2006, 347). Thus, Africa is no mere outpost of civilization.

The narrator presents a Genevan edition of the fairy tale *Dynd-Kongens Datter (The Marsh King's Daughter)* (1858), a fairy tale set between Africa and Denmark, to his host's daughters. He writes a dedication for his gift and cites it in the travelogue:

"From Denmark's shore these bouquets came,
With Danish mem'ries fraught they are;
Two dear young friends, say, may I claim
On Africa's bright coast afar?" (Andersen 1864, 184)

The fairy tale, the dedication and the reference to them in the travelogue establish a reciprocal relationship between Africa and Denmark, connecting the Danish author with his readers in Africa. The relationship is stabilized in the material form of books. It thus includes other European countries like Switzerland, where the Genevan book was produced.

The chapter on Africa indicates feelings of strangeness, but they soon dissolve. The expectation of barbaric wilderness, perhaps based on the reading of orientalist texts and shared by the readers of the travelogue, proves false. Africa surprises the narrator and the readers of the travelogue with the many familiarities of its material culture. This approximation does not exclude critical perspectives on differences between Africa and Europe. A key scene of the chapter on Africa depicts the narrator smoking a cigar and telling its production story (Andersen 2006, 337–8), one that reveals the connection between slavery and luxury goods, between the exploitation of African people and European pleasures.

Conclusion

Combining actor-network-theory with research on cultural appropriation allows an exploration of the interplay between textual and non-textual realities. This is particularly helpful in Andersen's case, since his texts form feedback circles in which letters, books and humans communicate, and thus they blur the distinction between author and narrator. With its strong concepts of authorship and of the intentionality of human actions, research on Andersen often neglects these interdependencies between human and non-human actions. This article takes a different position.

Andersen's texts travel between different cultures. According to Casanova, two poles define the spread of literature in the nineteenth century: the national and the international space of literature. Andersen is an international author; other literatures appropriated his texts. This article has highlighted some instances of the appropriation process. Depending on the literary and political background, reception of the texts varies considerably. Although a homogenization of the means of production occurs, the appropriation of the texts is ultimately characterized by cultural differences. Furthermore, differences exist between professional and non-professional appropriation. Andersen's texts reflect on the differences in processes of appropriation, e.g. they quote reviews and comment on them and thus influence new processes of appropriation. In this way, they develop agency in these processes of appropriation.

The agency of literature in processes of appropriation is not limited to aspects of the production and consumption of literary texts. Literary texts cause movements of people and influence or even establish human relationships. The term 'guide,' with its reference to books and human beings, served as an example of parallels between human and textual agency. The English woman's criticism of a misleading detail in *In Spain* shows that travelogues can play a role similar to that of a guide. The article has also presented correspondences between the external and the internal perspective on the travelogue: *In Spain* is an appropriated text and one that appropriates other texts and foreign countries for the imagination of its readers.

Andersen's texts reveal a high degree of awareness of aspects connecting different countries, and they participate actively in the process of connecting them. The transnationalization of literature is, as the industrialized modes of production and the development of marketing strategies indicate, part of the globalization of a commodified culture. It is this commodified culture that Andersen's texts observe and analyze, and they themselves form a part of it.

Notes

1 I would like to thank Gabriel Cooper for critical reading.
2 The present research data is such that these consumers are predominantly professional readers.
3 The meeting is mentioned in both the German (Andersen 1847a, 123–4) and the English (Andersen 1847b, 262) translations of the autobiography, too, but financial questions are not addressed in as much detail as in the Danish version.
4 Casanova's definition of the boundaries between literatures oscillates; nonetheless, it is helpful to think of national literatures in our case.
5 See www.andersen.sdu.dk (accessed September 12, 2011); heading "Søg & Sidemap" search term "oplag."
6 http://www.andersen.sdu.dk/rundtom/faq/index.html?emne=bogudg&oph=1 (accessed September 13, 2011).
7 See H. C. Andersen's diaries: http://www2.kb.dk/elib/mss/hcadag//index.htm (accessed September 19, 2011); October 31, 1863.
8 See H. C. Andersen's diaries: http://www2.kb.dk/elib/mss/hcadag//index.htm (accessed September 19, 2011); November 23, 1863; May 12, 1866; April 10, 1867
9 A more detailed account with a different thematic scope is given in Felcht 2011.
10 Bushby's English version (Andersen 1864, 202) translates the Danish original ("med meget Hjertelighed og europæisk Belevenhed") inexactly ("not only with cordiality, but with European good breeding").

References

Andersen, Hans Christian (1847a). *Das Märchen meines Lebens ohne Dichtung. Eine Skizze.* Leipzig: Carl B. Lorck.

Andersen, Hans Christian (1847b). *The True Story of My Life. A Sketch.* London: Longman, Brown, Green, and Longmans.

Andersen, Hans Christian (1864). *In Spain.* London: Richard Bentley.

Andersen, Hans Christian (2005). *Sämtliche Märchen.* Ed. Heinrich Detering. Zürich: Artemis & Winkler.

Andersen, Hans Christian (2006). *H. C. Andersens Samlede Værker. Vol. 15. Rejseskildringer II.* Ed. Det Danske Sprog- og Litteraturselskab. Kopenhagen: Gyldendal.

Andersen, Hans Christian (2007a). *H. C. Andersens Samlede Værker. Vol. 17. Selvbiografier II.* Ed. Det Danske Sprog- og Litteraturselskab. Kopenhagen: Gyldendal.

Andersen, Hans Christian (2007b). *H. C. Andersens Samlede Værker. Vol. 18. Selvbiografier III.* Ed. Det Danske Sprog- og Litteraturselskab. Kopenhagen: Gyldendal.

Andersen, Jens (2005). *Hans Christian Andersen. Eine Biographie.* Frankfurt/Main: Insel.

Anz, Heinrich (2005). "Aber das war ja gar kein Märchen!" Überlegungen zu Hans Christian Andersens Märchenpoetik. In Svenja Blume and Sebastian Kürschner (eds.). *Hans Christian Andersen zum 200. Geburtstag: "Mein Leben ist ein schönes Märchen, so reich und glücklich!"*, 35–55. Hamburg: Kovač.

Behschnitt, Wolfgang (2006). *Wanderungen mit der Wünschelrute: landesbeschreibende Literatur und die vorgestellte Geographie Deutschlands und Dänemarks im 19. Jahrhundert.* Würzburg: Ergon.

Böhme, Hartmut (2006). *Fetischismus und Kultur. Eine andere Theorie der Moderne.* Reinbek: Rowohlt.

Brandes, Georg (1902). *Gesammelte Schriften. Deutsche Original-Ausgabe. Vol. 3. Skandinavische Persönlichkeiten. Zweiter Teil.* Munich: Albert Langen.

Bredsdorff, Elias (1954). *H. C. Andersen og England.* Kopenhagen: Rosenkilde & Bagger.

Butts, Dennis (1995). The Beginnings of Victorianism (c.1820–1850). In Peter Hunt (ed.). *Children's Literature. An Illustrated History*, 77–101. Oxford: Oxford University Press.

Butts, Dennis (2010). *Children's Literature and Social Change: Some Case Studies from Barbara Hofland to Philip Pullman.* Cambridge: Lutterworth Press.

Casanova, Pascale (2004). *The World Republic of Letters.* Cambridge, MA: Harvard University Press.

Certeau, Michel de (1988). *Kunst des Handelns.* Berlin: Merve.

Felcht, Frederike (2011). On the topography of H. C. Andersen's travelogue *I Spanien* (1863, *In Spain*). *DESHIMA. Revue d'histoire globale des pays du Nord*, 5, 17–29.

Jones, W. Glyn (1993). Andersen in English—A Feasibility Study I. In Johan de Mylius et al. (eds.). *Andersen og Verden. Indlæg fra den første internationale H. C. Andersen-konference*, 85–99. Odense: Odense Universitetsforlag.

Hachtmann, Rüdiger (2007). *Tourismus-Geschichte.* Göttingen: Vandenhoeck & Ruprecht.

Hjørnager Pedersen, Viggo (2004). *Ugly Ducklings? Studies in the Translations of Hans Christian Andersen's Tales and Stories.* Odense: University Press of Southern Denmark.

Kauffmann, Kai (2002). Kulturelle Aneignung und Ausschließung. Die Funktion der Übersetzung für die nationale Identitätsbildung in Deutschland um 1800 und 1900. In Michael Böhler and Hans Otto Horch (eds.). *Kulturtopographie deutschsprachiger Literaturen. Perspektivierungen im Spannungsfeld von Integration und Differenz*, 117–37. Tübingen: Max Niemeyer.

Latour, Bruno (2007). *Eine neue Soziologie für eine neue Gesellschaft. Einführung in die Akteur-Netzwerk-Theorie.* Frankfurt/Main: Suhrkamp.

Möller-Christensen, Ivy York (1992). *Den gyldne trekant. H. C. Andersens gennembrud i Tyskland 1831-1850.* Odense: Odense Universitetsforlag.

Mortensen, Klaus Peter (2008). Fortællingens mange former—H. C. Andersen. In Sune Auken et al. (eds.). *Dansk Litteraturs Historie. Vol. 2. 1800–1870*, 361–409. Kopenhagen: Gyldendal.

Müller-Wille, Klaus (*forthcoming*). Hispanomanie—Dänische Spanienreisen und die Konzeption einer anderen Moderne. In Thomas Seiler and Frithjof Strauss (eds.). *Skandinavisch-ibero(amerika)nische Kulturkontakte*. Basel: A. Francke.

Nielsen, Erling (1990). Eventyrenes modtagelseskritik. In Erik Dal (ed.). *H. C. Andersens eventyr. Vol. 6. H. C. Andersen: Bemærkninger m. m. Erik Dal: Textkritikken. Erling Nielsen: Modtagelseskritikken*, 121–230. Kopenhagen: C. A. Reitzel.

Petri, Angelika (1988). Neunzehntes Jahrhundert. In Albert Schug (ed.). *Die Bilderwelt im Kinderbuch. Kinder- und Jugendbücher aus fünf Jahrhunderten. Katalog zur Ausstellung der Kunst- und Museumsbibliothek und des Rheinischen Bildarchivs der Stadt Köln*, 35–7. Cologne: Stadt Köln.

Pfister, Manfred (1993). Intertextuelles Reisen, oder: Der Reisebericht als Intertext. In Herbert Foltinek et al. (eds.). *Tales and "their telling difference." Festschrift für Franz K. Stanzel*, 109–32. Heidelberg: Universitätsverlag C. Winter.

Schovsbo, Henrik (2004). Efterskrift. In Hans Christian Andersen. *I Spanien*. Ed. Erik Dal, 223–48. Kopenhagen: Det Danske Sprog- og Litteraturselskab/Borgen.

Seville, Catherine (2009). *The Internationalisation of Copyright Law. Books, Buccaneers and the Black Flag in the Nineteenth Century*. Cambridge: Cambridge University Press.

Thage, Tove (2007). *Fotografiernes H. C. Andersen. En Ikonografi*. Kopenhagen: Høst & Søn.

Topsøe-Jensen, Helge (1934). Mit Livs Eventyr. In Svend Norrild et al. (eds.). *Festskrift til Vilhelm Andersen fra Kolleger og Disciple*, 155–81. Kopenhagen: Gyldendalske Boghandel/Nordisk Forlag.

Winge, Vibeke (1992). *Dänische Deutsche—deutsche Dänen. Geschichte der deutschen Sprache in Dänemark 1300–1800 mit einem Ausblick auf das 19. Jahrhundert*. Heidelberg: Carl Winter Universitätsverlag.

Wittmann, Reinhard (1982). *Buchmarkt und Lektüre im 18. und 19. Jahrhundert. Beiträge zum literarischen Leben 1750–1880*. Tübingen: Niemeyer.

Zimmermann, Christian von (2003). "die Inquisition ist in Spanien ja nun abgeschafft." Stationen der Spanienbilder bis zu Hans Christian Andersen. *Hispanorama: Zeitschrift des deutschen Spanischlehrerverbandes*, 102, 54–64.

Appropriating Machines

Introduction

Carsten Schinko

A machine is "an apparatus using or applying mechanical power and having several parts, each with a definite function and together performing a particular task." This basic definition, offered by my computer's built-in dictionary, is supplemented by a more straightforwardly technical definition: "any device that transmits a force or directs its application." Definitions like these by and large confirm our everyday understanding of a tool made to serve our (human) purposes. There is hardly ambiguity in such instrumentalist notions: a machine might be broken, but, once fixed, it will serve the same purpose again. Moreover, these definitions suggest that a machine will have the same effects, anywhere, anytime.

If we are inclined to accept the lack of complexity of a reference book, my *New Oxford American Dictionary* provides a third, figurative sense: 'machine' can also denote "an efficient and well-organized group of powerful people." In this last, metaphorical entry, there emerges an acknowledgement of the cross-effects and repercussions of mechanization as a *cultural* phenomenon. What we may well adore in a machine—its unceasing energy, its repetitious reliability—is transferred to people surrounded by machines to such a degree that the metaphor (man = machine) becomes intelligible. Although efficiency and organizational skills may sound like positive attributes at first, these same traits only slightly modified can also have a familiar, negative ring. It resonates in key Romantic texts: "Men are grown mechanical in head and in heart, as well as in hand," reasoned Carlyle (2010, 63) in his influential *Signs of the Times* (1831). He was most concerned with the overall effects of what he called the grasp of "industrialism" on a society and its individuals. To the Romantic critic Carlyle—who was not blind to the pleasant conditions afforded by the advent of new technologies—a label like the "Mechanical Age" was more than a metaphor. It may be a figural use of language to speak of the "Machine of Society" in order to chastise the apparent dehumanization of modern life and its institutions, "but here, as in so many other cases, the foam hardens into a shell, and the shadow we have wantonly evoked stands terrible before us and will not depart at our bidding" (Carlyle 2010, 66). Culture, it appears, seems detrimental to the deterministic instrumentalism of the machine.

It is safe to say that the dangers inherent in the ensuing encounters of man and machine have triggered a rich set of semantics, from Romantic alienation topoi like the above, to Adorno and Horkheimer's critique of modern rationalization in the *Dialectic of Enlightenment* (1947), to the neo-Luddite criticism of the digital age. It is a semantic repertoire that has never really dissipated; on the contrary it has been reaffirmed and actualized from generation to generation, from one technological innovation to the next. Almost as a rule, most innovations are met with twin reactions of dystopian fantasies and ecstatic embrace.

However, once we adduce an understanding of specific instances of appropriation, i.e. of the definitions assigned by various (groups of) people who use or are affected by machines, things get trickier, and cultural differences will always already have crept in. The same applies when we analyze these people's specific relationship to discourses that help embed an innovation or travelling technology in a cultural fabric. One good example is the range of transnational difference between the respective imaginaries of Great Britain and America, discussed in great detail by Leo Marx in *The Machine in the Garden* (2000). If Carlyle, the Scotsman, gave voice to the individual's losses in the process of modernization and mechanization, the American ideology of a 'middle landscape' has done much to soften these feelings of loss. Popularized by, among others, Thomas Jefferson and Ralph Waldo Emerson, the 'middle landscape' is a (successful) reconciliation of the thrust of technology with the pastoral ideal of domesticated nature. Jefferson's fascination with a steam mill near Blackfriars Bridge in London is a particularly interesting example. Even as he was thrilled with the prospects of bringing the machine's force to the young American republic, it "did not occur to Jefferson that the factory system was a necessary part of technological progress" (Marx 2000, 146). One of the reasons for this surprising intellectual lapse can be found in America's economic realities: "At the time industrialization scarcely had begun in America," Marx reminds us, and "there was nothing comparable to Soho [Matthew Boulton's famous factory near Birmingham], nor would there be for a long time." (2000, 147) Indeed, "the very notion of 'technology' as an agent of change scarcely existed" (ibid., 149). Jefferson's rural ideal—the yeoman farmer and the plot of land—went unscathed, at least according to the way he envisaged the travelling machine: "Once the machine is removed from the dark, crowded, grimy cities of Europe, he assumes that it will blend harmoniously into the open countryside of his native land." (ibid., 150) And even if later thinkers understood what Jefferson could or would not understand, the pastoral ideal proved to be a stubborn one that persisted in mythical self-descriptions of Americans. The machine, it appears here, does not at all have the same effects in all places and at all times.

Works by such scholars of myth and symbol as Leo Marx can seem overly holistic in this age of hybridity and creolization, and they are hardly elaborate enough to meet today's theoretical requirements; but even though the interest in representative cultural symbols has been justifiably criticized for its exclusionary drift, such symbols still help us understand the role of semantic repertoires and cultural discourses as we study travelling machines. Even if we become conscious of "the common misapprehension that technologies are composed chiefly, if not exclusively, of things" and are consequently careful not "to invest the history of technology with its own quasi-autonomous, internal logic" (Marx 1996, 144), serious scholarship on the cultural appropriation of machines requires us to be keenly aware not only of these material aspects, but also of a whole array of interrelated elements. Some of these are the agency of individuals and groups, distributive networks, and the actual routes taken by the travelling machines. With varying emphasis and conceptual hierarchies, this section's contributions all meet this challenge.

A set of Americanisms (and anti-Americanisms) inform the first two essays of this section. *Stefan Bauernschmidt* traces the internationalization of Ford from local car manufacturer to global enterprise. On German soil, he argues, the appropriation of Ford cars is a process best understood through the effects of visual registers. His contribution opens with a suggestive ekphrasis of an advertisement for an anti-theft device and subsequently sketches a recurring image of a hand or claw as an affective 'pathos formula' that had surprising repercussions. This image returns, slightly altered, in various domains, and it aids Bauernschmidt in establishing the strong contrast between civilization and barbarism—one whose currency in contemporary discussions of Ford's attempt to find a foreign niche, and later in a cultural discourse about a notion called Fordism, was great. As this cultural discourse reveals a strong anti-American sentiment, which—not only then—was part and parcel of Germany's cultural imaginary, these transatlantic moods are seminal for an understanding of the cultural appropriation at work. Bauernschmidt traces the effects of this 'pathos formula' at the interactional, organizational, and societal levels and thereby shows how an air of intimidation fed into German self-descriptions at large, which, in turn, shaped the Germans' sense of belonging in opposition to an American other. The Fordman and his mass-produced, mechanical selfhood threatened to eradicate what was considered to be the German soul. Appropriation, according to Bauernschmidt, cannot be disentangled from the intricate processes of creating meaning and forming identity. Given the nature of these social phenomena, there will always be a political (or at least proto-political) dimension to acts of cultural appropriation.

The political implications of acts of appropriation are abundantly evident in *Patricia Irene Dacudao's* discussion of the mechanization of Davao, a region in the southernmost Philippine islands. A wild territory waiting to be tamed by both Filipinos and the American colonizers, who considered this part of the foreign country to be nothing short of the "last American frontier," Davao became the site of a conflict of values, because, removed to Southeast Asia, the rugged individualism of the American frontier encountered the collectivist notions of and the "communal cooperation practiced in Asian societies." By tracing the intricate, knotty, and multicultural history of the *hagotan*, a hemp-stripping machine suitable for producing the regional abaca fiber, Dacudao demonstrates how cultural values that clash become reorganized. The quest for the innovative machine is determined by social, economic and physical realities such as labor scarcity and the time-consuming quality of raising the local plants on a particular soil type. The machine sought had to be portable, affordable, and efficient in stripping quality hemp beyond the capacity of manual labor. The story of the *hagotan* is located in the in-between of industrialization and agriculture, modernization and tradition, Western and Asian, etc.—and it is determined by the appropriation and transformation work on both a physical and a psychological level.

In Bauernschmidt's example, the car as a material entity crossing the Atlantic is unaltered, and its semantic repertoire is most decisive in producing meaning and forging national identity. Dacudao presents a quest in which the machine is a vision of the future, an emergent reality shaped by interrelated physical and psychological phenomena. The section's final contribution tackles the problem of materiality in acts of cultural appropriation most painstakingly. Concerned with the evolution of cars during the interwar years, *Gijs Mom* zooms in on "one tiny but crucial aspect," the automotive ignition. His functional understanding of mobility likewise acknowledges the socio-political implications of cultural appropriation. He indicates a general process of taming a technology in order to meet a Western, middleclass decorum by the term *domestication*. Mom's more specific aim, however, is to describe the co-evolution of ignition technologies and engineering discourse. He does so by drawing on a rich set of theoretical resources, most notably the concept of the "dual nature of technology." According to this theory, a given artifact can be analyzed by sketching its properties and its functions as they become realized through its use. The relationship between technical traits and potential functions is not static, but open to intervention by the users; this triggers a further cycle of modification and renewed usage of the artifact. As MOM concedes, some practices will be impossible and some unlikely at best, but the general "fuzziness" of the relation between properties and functions engenders a view of history different from techno-determinist and humanist-instrumentalist accounts. The concept of *affordance*, borrowed from ecological psychology, helps Mom outline users' activities. Affordance designates immediately recognized "information about the environment as a result of purposeful action." While affordances allow for constant re-negotiation by users between properties and functions, and while producers react to consumers' activities, Mom discusses the role of a third element, automotive handbooks, as intermediaries whose discourse influenced the cultural appropriation of automobile ignitions.

All of the assembled texts follow different routes and suggest distinct ways of selecting and connecting key elements toward a theory of cultural appropriation. What they impart, however, is a sense of what Mom calls "highly contingent, variable and continuously changing" phenomena: *machines*. Machines, finally, seem neither indifferent to their contexts nor do they predetermine these; instead, machine and cultural context influence each other. To understand the precise nature of this influence is the task of analyzing cultural appropriation.

References

Carlyle, Thomas (2010). *The Works of Thomas Carlyle. Vol. 27. Critical and Miscellaneous Essays II.* Ed. Henry Duff Traill. Cambridge: Cambridge University Press.

Marx, Leo (1996). Review of Carroll W. Purcell. The Machine in America: A Social History of America. *Isis*, 87, 1, 144–5.

Marx, Leo (2000). *The Machine in the Garden. Technology and the Pastoral Ideal in America.* Oxford: Oxford University Press.

Ford in Interwar Berlin: Perception and Appropriation

Stefan Bauernschmidt

> *Erinnern wir uns daran, dass unser Sehen […] von weither kommt, dass es eine Art «travelling» ist, eine Wahrnehmungstätigkeit, die in der Vergangenheit begonnen hat, um die Gegenwart zu erhellen, das Objekt unserer unmittelbaren Wahrnehmung scharf einzustellen.*
> (Virilio 1987, 34–5)

An American made Ford Model T, completely knocked down and crated for export, shipped from Edgewater, New Jersey, across the Atlantic and national borders to Weimar Germany and assembled in a warehouse at West Harbour in Berlin, is no longer the same good. Something happens to it as it travels from America to Germany—but how? Through a *process of appropriation* Ford becomes invested with cultural meanings distinct from those given it by the American public, in particular by American farmers, the most prominent Model T consumers. In Germany, however, the discussion surrounding Ford revolves around other issues. It is purchased by other social groups and used in other ways. A closer look at the early history of Ford in Germany reveals at least two interwoven phenomena.[1]

First, in Germany during the Weimar Republic, the catchword *American threat* recurs often in reference to American goods, especially Ford automobiles. A twofold distinction is built into this catchword. As Max Prager (1902) writes, there is a difference between competition and threat. The former is a neutral term, whereas the latter is emotionally charged; and it always makes a difference whether something is perceived as innocuous or dangerous. Second, this attitude toward Ford in the Weimar Republic is manifest not only in discursive symbolism (i.e. the use of catchwords), but is also found in the domain of presentational symbolism ('pictorial slogans' or *Schlagbilder*). During the 1920s in Germany (and, to be sure, analogously in other European nations), a particularly prevalent way of perceiving things foreign is organized through the establishment of a link of opposition between German identity and *materialism*—materialism being one element among the spectrum of verbal and visual stereotypes related to the broader phenomenon of *Americanism* (Berg 1963; Schwabe 1978; Peukert 1987; Nolan 1994; Lüdtke et al. 1996; Diner 1996; Wala 2000; Linke and Tanner 2006).

The role of media in determining such perceptions is of utmost importance (Soeffner and Raab 1998). Among the broad range of media, which extends from ephemeral sounds of language to the huge apparatuses of mass media, it is above all the latter that provide visualizations that determine how a given society constructs reality. Furthermore, since perceptions and actions are interrelated (Mitchell 1994; von Saldern 2006; Bohnsack 2008), the appropriation of goods in general and of foreign goods in particular—ranging from acceptance to resistance—depends on how such goods are perceived. In this context, visualizations serve "to provide orientation for our actions and our everyday practice." (Bohnsack 2008, paragraph 8)

In light of the foregoing, I argue that visualizations are not a negligible side issue, but play an important role in the appropriation of foreign goods. In order to demonstrate the importance of mass media visualizations in appropriation processes, this article first examines an advertisement for an anti-theft device known as the 'Auto-Combinator,' the visual rhetoric of which conveys an image of threat. I then provide a chronology of the activities of the Ford Motor Company in Germany until 1927, when the era of the Model T came to an end. Of particular interest here is the way Ford's entry into the German market invoked a certain kind of imagery. Last, I highlight two areas in which *Fordism* is extensively discussed: car manufacturing and construction. The nature of the debate about *Americanism* can help us understand how the German temperament could feel threatened by an infiltration of things foreign. This historical narrative is interspersed with intermediate theoretical reflections about visual rhetoric and the entanglement of culture, consumption and identity.

'Auto-Combinator': an Ekphrasis

The beholder of the scene (see fig. 1) is immediately drawn to the hand. Then, the eyes begin to move across the pictorial surface: the viewer reads the caption and the remaining bits of text and ends up oscillating between the illuminated house in the background and the car in the foreground. Missing from this enumeration, however, is the double circle found over the steering apparatus of the car and the cord bent around the lower arm.

The car represented is an Austrian *Steyr*, easily identified by its typical, expressive radiator. The model here is either a Type II (the so called *Waffen-auto*), produced between 1920 and 1924, or a Type IV, produced between 1921 and 1924. It is, to be sure, an elegant and prestigious six-cylinder motor car typical of its time (Oswald 1990). Corresponding to its status as a high-end car is the particular kind of house depicted in the background. This is no shack, nor is it a flat or a semi-detached house; it is nothing short of a mansion (Veer 2006–2008). Across the oval form, apparently a sprawling lawn suggesting a long driveway, the observer can detect the presence of an entrance separate from the living quarters. The front of the manor, the only visible part, is equally prestigious owing to its borrowings from ancient Greek temples: the high frontage with three-tier fenestration, brightly illuminated, gives an impression of columns, and the flat pitched roof alludes to the pediment triangle of ancient Doric temple constructions. Sobriety is paired with simple and lucid monumentality (Gruben 1980).

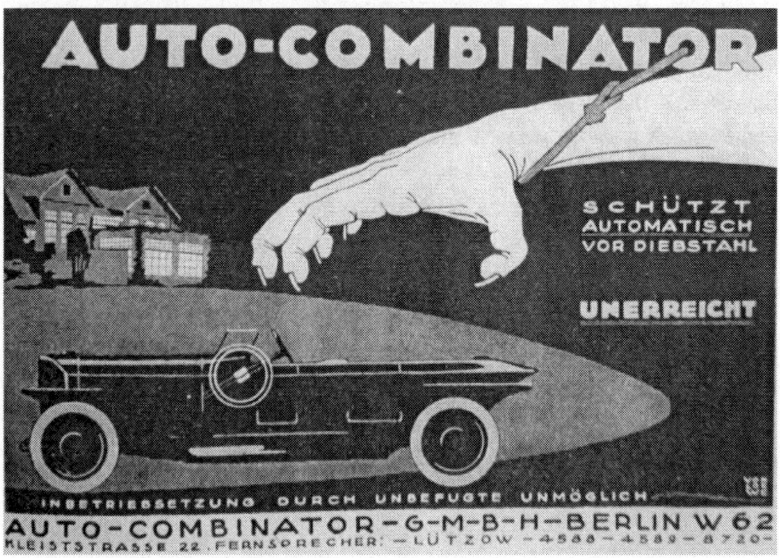

Fig. 1: (Unlawful) Appropriation and Resistance ('Auto-Combinator')
(source: Der Motorfahrer, *XVIII, 5/6, Berlin, February 3, 1921, cover)*

What does it mean that the visualization is composed of elements evoking a specific stratum of society? What does it stand for? Since it is a print-advertisement (by von Loewe), one may assume that these visual elements are taken from the cultural stock of that time not randomly, but by design. "[A]dvertisers do not create the ritualized expressions they employ; they seem to draw upon the same corpus of displays, the same ritual idiom, that is the resource of all of us who participate in social situations, and to the same end: the rendering of glimpsed action (which is so typical for advertising) readable." (Goffman 1979, 84) Furthermore, one may assume that the producer of such an advertisement considers visual forms like these good signifiers of his idea that will speak to the target group, potential upper class consumers. Without exaggeration we can affirm that the two signifiers, car and house, convey a tripartite meaning to the potential viewer: social distinction, technological progress and national wealth. This mixture of cues indicates achievement in terms of a (technologically and materially) progressive civilization, but it is embedded in traditional German *Culture* (with its emphasis on spirituality and the immaterial/ideational).

The depiction of the hand is completely different. It and the lower arm are shaded bright white in stark contrast to the darkened background of the picture, probably indicating night time. Two disproportions are striking. First, the fingers are much longer than the palm of the hand. Most eye-catching, however, is the disproportion among hand, house and automobile. The hand, which is supposedly in the same pictorial plane as the car, is drawn considerably larger than the motor car. For starters, this disproportion could qualify the respective element as central to the picture. But it is also possible to interpret this disproportion as a deformation of the hand and consequently as a visual signifier of ugliness: the ugliness of the insinuated act of theft or pilfering, and the ugliness of the intentions behind such behavior.

It can be justifiably assumed that the configuration of the fingers in conjunction with the extended (but restrained) arm indicates that this hand is in motion and grasping for something, namely for the motor car. By the bent phalanxes, especially of the middle, the pointer finger and the thumb, the hand itself suggests tension. This is not implausible, since the cord bent around the lower arm is holding it back and thereby freezing the motion, making it suitable for a still. The figuration of the fingers insinuates that someone invisible or anonymous (since only hand and arm can be seen) is clawing at something. Just as eye-catching is the unnatural position of the thumb, which should, strictly speaking, point naturally to the picture's vanishing point, but which points instead to the pointer finger. This posture, together with the unpared fingernails, raises a suspicion: this hand is more akin to the claw of a bird of prey than to a human hand. Consequently, the stark visual contrast between the two sets of elements, those of the hand-like object and those of car and house, reflects a contrast between civilization and barbarism, or between culture and nature. It may just as well be both at once: a manifestation of the contrasts between culture and nature and between civilization and barbarism.

The arm and the hand are bound to the caption of the picture by the cord. And the verbal elements of the picture finally reassure the beholder that this image is indeed an advertisement. We can read: "Auto-Combinator—Protects automatically against thievery—Unmatched—Unauthorized use impossible—Auto-Combinator GmbH Berlin, Kleist Street 22, Phone: Lützow—4588–4589–8720". An 'Auto-Combinator' is a combination lock applied to the steering to secure the motor car against unauthorized use (see Memorial des Großherzogtums Luxemburg, Annexe au N° 16 de 1922, Avis.–Brevets d'invention, 33). The 'Auto-Combinator' protects the car against (illegal) appropriation.

First Intermediate Reflection: the 'Visible Arrested Action'

The 'Auto-Combinator' advertisement appeared on the cover of the automotive magazine *Der Motorfahrer* several times in 1921. The publication was the official organ of the popular General German Automobile Club, whose membership at the time was about 40,000. It is obvious from the foregoing description of the advertisement that this visualization, as framed, employs its elements, especially the hand, as "visual formulae charged with highly affective potential." (Assmann 1996, 123)

The composition of the advertisement centers around the hand. The house, in this context, just serves to amplify the status of the car. Within the hand-car-complex, the active, dominant role falls to the hand. The hand, a visual synecdoche, is the primary source of the picture's character as 'threat.' Hands are, as Jack Tresidder (1997) notes, visual elements forceful enough to stand alone in iconography. Hands are essential means for conveying human expressions and intentions. As visual synecdoche, they represent the intentions of those who may be toying with the idea of unlawfully appropriating the property of fellow citizens. Such visual elements, in particular such affectively laden gestures, are called 'pathos formulae.' The term, a neologism coined by the art and cultural historian Aby M. Warburg, "pinpoints the expressive gestures depicted in paintings and other visual media, which he [Warburg] considered to be memory symbols of fears and excitements" (Weigel et al. 1995, 137). Pathos formulae are characterized by their 'stored energy,' or, as we put it today, their 'stored semantics': their built-in binary distinctions and inherent affective dimension (Knape 2008; Assmann 1996). As visual stereotypes, pathos formulae can serve as 'explosives' (*Sprengmittel*) if they are highly energy-laden and have a polarizing impact (Warnke 1980).

Similar visualizations of hands grasping at something can be found in great numbers. A paradigmatic contemporary example is the placard *Hände weg vom Ruhrgebiet!* (Hands off the Ruhr!) from 1923, which depicts a half-clad and disheveled Marianne clawing at the Ruhr. Its creator was the illustrator Theo Matejko, one of the most sought-after graphic designers of his time (Popp 2009).

In short, the visual rhetoric of the 'Auto-Combinator' advertisement stands for fear of unlawful appropriation. Such a notion of impending threat, however, is not confined to the 'hand-car-complex,' as the example of Matejko's 'hand-territory-complex' demonstrates. Presently we shall also see an additional example in the history of Ford in Germany up to 1927. The way Ford entered the German market in the mid-1920s evoked fears that the German car market would be lost—at least symbolically—to foreign companies lead by Ford.

Ford and Germany, 1903–1927

Ever since Mira Wilkins and Frank E. Hill's seminal study *American Business Abroad*, it has been well known that, in the very year the Ford Motor Company was founded, "the stockholders urged their directors to 'take necessary steps to obtain foreign business'" (1964, 1). Before the first annual stockholders' meeting in October 1903, Ford models were already being shipped abroad (Wilkins 2003). Although the internationalization of the company began before the Model T, which came to epitomize mass production and modernity, the exponential increase of output at Ford after 1910 meant rapid expansion of the enterprise, first on the domestic market, then globally. In the 1920s, at the urging of its so-called 'foreign managers' and like many other

American car makers, Ford was beginning to cultivate foreign markets, because the domestic American market of rural first-time buyers was becoming saturated, and the purchasing power of farmers, the foremost buyers and owners of Model Ts, was limiting the growth of automobile production (Wik 2005).

In 1903, Robert M. Lockwood, who "was engaged to manage all Ford Motor Company foreign sales outside of Canada" (Wilkins and Hill 1964, 12), wrote letters to his affiliates in Europe, Asia, Africa, Australia and Latin America asking them whether they would be interested in selling Ford car models. In Germany, Adolph Bernhardt, a businessman who dealt in various goods, received this letter along with one of the 3,000 catalogs that the company had provided to Lockwood, which were "appropriate for introducing to the export trade in foreign countries the [Ford] business" (ibid., 13). Subsequently, only four months after the incorporation of the Ford Motor Company, a German marketing organization, Ford Motor Automobile, was set up in Stolp, a town with much to offer. It was the second largest town in the former Prussian province of Pomerania and home to substantial furniture, machine and wood industries. The Stolpe River gave the town access to the Baltic Sea, and its surrounding district of agricultural and forest resources seemed perfect from both an economic and social standpoint. And yet Ford Motor Automobile never made a profit. Stolp was too far off the beaten track and too remote from centers of modernity.

In the following years, Bernhardt expanded to Berlin, the centre of Germany and, compared to other major European cities like Paris, Rome or Vienna, a metropolis experiencing spectacular, hasty growth. In 1911, Bernhardt rented a showroom at Bismarck Street 97/98 near the station Berlin-Charlottenburg. Bernhard was the first Ford dealer in Germany, and one of perhaps ten dealers in all, doing business with Ford cars before WWI. By 1914 he had sold around 600 Ford Model Ns and Ts in Berlin, mainly T-Models. Compared with other markets, however, these sales were modest. At the onset of the war, the German government closed the market, and after the war the situation did not return to pre-war conditions. Business in the aftermath of WWI remained tough. A clause in the Treaty of Versailles made it more difficult for private citizens to own motorcars (Treaty of Versailles, Part V. Military, Naval and Air Clauses, Article 171), and an import embargo was in effect until October 1925. Consequently, importers of foreign products had to be licensed. In 1921, only three Model Ts were sold (Wilkins and Hill 1964, 55). Bernhardt tried in vain to sell Fords; his Ford Motor Automobile went out of business after 1918, and he finally abandoned his auto business in 1920.[2]

As early as 1919, however, the Board of Directors of the Ford Motor Company resolved "to take all necessary steps to cause said company to be registered as a foreign corporation in the country of Germany" (Acc.85, Bx.1). Charles E. Sorensen travelled around Germany in the winter of 1921/22 to get an idea of the situation there. He sought an ideal site for a plant, focusing on Bremen, Hamburg and Berlin, but uncertain political circumstances forced the plan to be abandoned (Peukert 1987). In *Der Motorfahrer* (XIX, 18, 1922) Sorensen's venture was dealt with in just a short note, and the *Allgemeine Automobil-Zeitung* (XXIII, 12, 1922) reported that the Senate of Hamburg had responded negatively to a Ford query.

By 1923 at the latest, Ford had placed Germany seriously on its agenda again. George Carlson, manager of the assembly plant in Copenhagen, Denmark, sent a letter to Sorensen in April 1923 containing his evaluation of "our German activities" (Acc.38, Bx.48). He based his judgment on the increase in shipped Fordson tractors and on reports about Ford in automotive magazines; in this case, it was an article published in *Der Motorwagen* that caught his attention. Carlson wrote:

> "The March 31 issue of the German motor magazine, called *Motorwagen*, contains a 2 page article for and against our products [...]. This article praises our organization, which from a German automobile manufacture standpoint is a direct warning of the danger its motor industry will soon stand face to face with. Six month [sic] ago it would have been an impossibility to have an article as the attached inserted in a German motor magazine, and this further indicates indirectly that the elimination of the import embargo will no doubt soon become a fact. It is the opinion of some leading German motor car dealers and manufacturers that importation will be permitted this fall." (Acc.38, Bx.48)

Before long, on December 1, 1924, business premises opened at Unter den Linden No. 56. Their initial function was to establish connections to dealers. Eight months earlier, rumors were already circulating that a shipment of Ford automotive parts had arrived in Hamburg's Free Harbor. But this was in fact not true (*AAZ*, XXV, 14, April 5, 1924).

Ford entered Germany through other routes. Paul Cappel was Ford's biggest and most important German dealer in the 1920s. He dealt directly with Ford Anvers (Antwerpen) through his *Cappel & Co. Motorwagen- und Tractoren-Verkaufs-Gesellschaft Aktiengesellschaft* based in the Rhineland city of Aachen (Grosbois 2003). "The assembly plant in Belgian Antwerp was a perfect platform to infiltrate the German market from the West, especially since the region west of the Rhine was occupied by foreign troops, and trade was ineffectively controlled." (Thomas 2003, 154) Another import office (a so-called *Speditionskontor*) was located in the northern city of Lübeck and was the connection to Ford-Denmark and the assembly plant there. By importing cars, trucks and tractors, those Ford plants met the allegedly "heavy demand" for Ford products in Germany. This was, at least, the assessment of William A. Ryan, a Ford sales manager, and of Frank Hadas, a branch, assembly plant and factory inspector, in a cable sent to Edsel B. Ford (Acc.880, Bx.7). Despite their assessment, the initial schedule of 8,500 cars a year was considerably low from the beginning.

On January 5, 1925, the Ford Motor Company Stock Corporation was established in Berlin, and on August 18 of that year, the new corporation was entered into Berlins Commercial Register (Department B Number 36767). Ford began operations effectively on October 1. Carlson, by this time also manager of the German branch, had that same month already suggested renting warehouses cheaply in the West Harbour district of Plötzensee in Berlin. And indeed, they rented the modern warehouses, installed machinery and conveyer lines, and assembly began of Model TT trucks in April of 1926 and of Model T cars in June. 70 S.U.P. (Single Unit Packing) Ford Model T cars were imported to Germany in late 1924, and 750 units (250 passenger cars and 500 trucks) in the last quarter of 1925. But beginning in April 1926, C.K.D. (Completely Knocked Down) Ford Model T cars, Model TT trucks and Fordson tractors were assembled in the following quantities:

- in 1926: 1,577 Model Ts, 1,100 Model TT trucks and 1,250 tractors and
- in 1927: 2,594 Model Ts, 1,627 Model TT trucks and 3,300 tractors.

As a market share of all newly registered passenger cars, these numbers for Model Ts represented 1.4% in 1925, 5.1% in 1926 and 2.7% percent in 1927.

But what image emerges if we examine the two import operations (Aachen and Lübeck) supplying the Ford Motor Company A.G. in Berlin? It looks like Ford is grasping at the German car market (see fig. 2).

Fig. 2: Ford's Access to Germany (author's visualization)

Second Intermediate Reflection: Culture, Consumption, Identity

Thus far, I have argued that the advertisement discussed at the opening is invested with a 'pathos formula' that refers to a resonating universal theme of human experience (the threat of thievery accompanied by a sense of impending evil). However, as the previous section has shown, the formula is not confined to the interactional level but can also be found at the organizational level. The next step will be to look for phenomena which could give rise to a similar notion of impending threat on a societal level. In order to do so, we have to first look at the entanglement of identity, culture and consumption in modern societies. The views on this expressed here are adopted from Grant McCracken (1988, 2005), Tim Edensor (2002) and Richard Jenkins (2008).

In contemporary theory, identity is no longer conceived as an essence but as an ongoing process. Jenkins puts this procedural aspect this way: "This involves knowing who we are, knowing who others are, them knowing who we are, us knowing who they think we are and so on ..." (2008, 5) He defines identity as "the ways in which individuals and collectivities are distinguished in their relations with other individuals and collectivities" (2008, 18). A key element of this dynamic process of identity formation (or *identification*) is the "drawing of boundaries between self and 'other.' For identity is conceivable through identifying differences" (Edensor 2002, 24–5). Identity is established to provide individuals with a "sense of belonging" (Edensor 2002); in the early twentieth century this task prominently falls to national identity.

In order to establish difference from others, and in turn create similarity within peer groups, individuals make use of a variety of resources including history, language or material culture (McCracken 1988; Edensor 2002). In modern-day societies, consumer goods, an instantiation of material culture, are foremost in this function: they help show others who we are or, rather, what we want others to think we are, and last but not least, to show others what we might become. The use of consumer goods constitutes a crucial part of the self and its relation to the world (McCracken 1988). Such things serve on the one hand as identity markers, in that they establish similarities within groups and differences between groups; and on the other hand they serve to stabilize identity on an individual and collective level.

However, under modern conditions many goods are travelling goods: they are produced elsewhere, in a society other than our own, yet are distributed globally for consumption. This holds, for example, for the 'universal car,' an expression for the Model T taken from a Ford brochure, on which apparently 'the sun never set' owing to its having been sold all around the world, albeit with varying degrees of success. Given the lack of spatial and cultural fixity of modern travelling consumer goods, and given the precious relationship among things and peoples and person and object, Edensor notes that these circumstances "provide a discursive and affective focus for reclaiming a sense of situatedness. Any sense of uncertainty requires a terra firma to be sought [...]. Fears like these provide fertile ground for recursive political nationalists to capitalise upon, for the threat of fully decentred identities might seem to lead to epistemological chaos." (Edensor 2002, 28) Against this backdrop of a globalizing material culture (wherein 'material' refers to 'materialism' as a pejorative term for a notion of those societies in which the highest values are material), and in light of the relationship between consumption and identity formation, the following section examines the discussion in Germany during the interwar years about the material foundations of everyday life: *cars* and *houses*.

Ford Cars, Fordist-Built Houses and the *Ford-Mensch*

Even before Ford products were able to enter the German market in greater quantities, another Ford product had appeared in Weimar Germany which had caught Germans' attention: Henry Ford's *My Life and Work*, published in the United States in November 1922. The German edition was released exactly one year later and "caused a sensation" (Zimmermann 1924, 491). Ford's autobiography, particularly in crisis-ridden Germany, became a bestseller. Within the first year it went through thirteen printings, and by the end of the inter bellum 200,000 copies had been sold (Nolan 1994; Eifert 2009). Despite Christine Eifert's claim that Ford's "*Bibel des civilisatorischen Menschen*" disappeared just as fast as it had been euphorically embraced, it had sufficient time to insert its ideas into the minds of engineers and entrepreneurs, politicians, trade unionists, journalists and consumers alike. Above all else, it was on account of *My Life and Work* that Ford was ideologized and that its ideas, previously attached only to Ford cars, trucks and tractors, were detached from these.

In Germany, the term *Fordism*[3] was coined by Friedrich von Gottl-Ottlilienfeld, a distinguished professor at the University of Kiel, in 1924.

> "[His] famous essay on Fordism brought together all the various strands of ideological interpretation, painting a picture of Fordism as a veritable utopia. Material prosperity, harmonious labor relations, joy in work, pride in productivity, a spirit of service, a new style of leadership—all these, he claimed, were realized in Fordism. The result was a new kind of community, a 'white socialism of pure, active conviction.'" (Nolan 1994, 57)

Henry Ford's book, in conjunction with Gottl-Ottlilienfeld's essay, initiated an intense engagement with and debate about Ford's ideas, their transferability from America to Germany, from one domain into another, and about their benefits and risks. The whole debate was ambivalent and followed various strands: prosperity versus poverty, harmonious labor relations versus class struggle, systematic versus partial social change. The last dimension, concerning the scale and scope of social change, was most openly discussed on the material level. The discourse *My Life and Work* precipitated in Weimar Germany was pervaded by two main threads in relation to material culture: cars and houses.

The point of departure is Henry Ford's early interest in technology and machinery, which awakened in his youth. Over the course of the 1880s his interest focused on the development of a horseless carriage. "[W]orking in a shed behind his house in Detroit, [he] was one of many young men across the country experimenting with the new transportation technology." (Casey 2008, 13) These efforts evolved into the Model T, a masterpiece conceived by Henry Ford and his associates. The exclusive concentration on this masterpiece, its mass production and mass consumption, is what elevated Henry Ford and his fellows in the Ford Motor Company into unforeseen dimensions (Nevins and Hill 1957; Hounshell 1984). In the early 1920s, Henry Ford was at the height of his success. The discourse in question here, however, revolved around Ford cars and their American system of manufacture, and on the prospect of that system positively influencing German industry. It is, in the first place, a car-centred discussion.

However, debates about the Fordist mode of manufacturing were also carried on in the construction sector (Andernacht 1995; Fehl 1995b; Bernhardt and Vonau 2009). The application of Ford's ideas in a fundamentally different domain of material culture represents the transfer of a template which until then had been successful only in the automobile sector. Ford himself claimed, however, that this template, characterized by the attainment of simplicity as a product characteristic, "applies to everything—a shoe, a dress, a house, a piece of machinery, a railroad, a steamship, an airplane" (1924, 14). In other words, an idea, in this case a specific mode of manufacturing automobiles, is being generalized.

Ford as an idea, *Fordism*, embodied by a typical American car and by houses built in an American style—material foundations of a way of life (Polster and Voy 1993)—elicited once more a perception linked to a worst-case-scenario; *Fordism* was seen as a threat to the German temperament, or rather, to the German soul. In view of such changing material conditions, under which German children would be socialized and acculturated, communists and capitalists, progressives and conservatives, utopians and ideologues alike were examining the possibility of a new kind of human being. Peter Mennicken, professor for *Lebensphilosophie* at the RWTH Aachen, prefigured a 'Ford-Man' (*Ford-Mensch*) in his book *Anti-Ford*. "In the discourse of which Mennicken was a part, both civilization and progress were negative terms, connoting materialism, pragmatism, fragmentation, superficiality, and conformity. Mennicken regarded Ford, that quintessential representative of America, as the perfect '*Zivilisationsmensch.*'" (Nolan 1994, 114) Right-wing commentator Theodor Lüddecke, by training an economist and head of a media institute, in his book entitled *Das amerikanische Wirtschaftstempo als Bedrohung Europas* (1925), called this new human being a 'luxury helot' (*Luxushelot*), whose aims in life amounted to nothing more than radio, cinema, patent kitchen ranges, refrigerators, parties, mansions and motor cars. This potential appropriation of the so-called American way of life, of American cars and American-style houses, put pressure on *Deutschtum* (German *Culture*) on both the *dwelling* side and *transport* side, and thereby threatened to alter the very character of 'Gullible Fritz.'

Conclusion

This article highlights an aspect of Ford's history in Weimar Germany that comes into focus only through study of *cultural appropriation* informed by an interest in *visual issues*.

The examination of the 'Auto-Combinator' advertisement shows the ad's image of a claw-like hand to be an objectified expression of a designed meaning: an act of theft linked to a sense of imminent threat. The image is not limited to the interactional level; it also appears at an organizational and societal level. Ford's history in Germany in the first three decades of the twentieth century, particularly the 'access roads' formed by its two import centers, again yields an image of imminent threat. The same holds for the main strands of the debate on *Fordism*: the discourse draws a vivid image of the negative consequences of *Fordism*. American materialism, it was thought, would overwhelm and penetrate the German *soul*, which would be destroyed by *Americanisms* (Ford cars, Fordist-built houses), and give rise to a new type of human being, the so-called *Ford-Mensch*.

In this context, Ford—the man, the company and the cars—was not only labeled by the mass media under the catchword *American threat*, but was also visualized, or at least imagined, in a specific manner. Although there were many Ford enthusiasts in the Weimar Republic, a sense of imminent threat prevailed in war-torn, crisis-ridden and relatively impoverished Germany. The privileged position of right wing engineers such as Theodor Lüddecke also contributed to its prevalence. We arrive at a recurring visual form substantially imbued with notions of peril and threat. The phenomenon of *anti-Americanism* was widespread in inter bellum Germany and was not limited to the discursive level, which tends to be more rational. The catchword (*Schlagwort*) of anti-Americanism, in our case, is complemented by a claw that becomes its visual counterpart and a pathos formula or visual slogan (*Schlagbild*).

Since pictures are organized rationally to a lesser extent than are texts, their specific contribution is to give an affective impulse to a society's construction of reality. Germany, the apparent 'belated nation,' seems to be ridden by a fear of loss; a new-found economic prosperity, both on an individual and a societal level, is threatened by the illegal appropriation of personal property by nefarious subjects; and alien companies threaten to appropriate the car market.

Finally, by considering cultural dimensions along with social and economic ones, we are able to arrive at an overall picture of Ford's history in Germany in the first three decades of the twentieth century. From this perspective the discrepancy between the Ford Motor Company's expectation of 'heavy demand' for their automobiles and the reality, sales figures far lower than anticipated, becomes fully comprehensible. Only the demand for Fordson tractors and to some extent the demand for Ford trucks brought profits for Henry Ford and his company in Weimar Germany; Ford cars were not successfully appropriated during this time.

Notes

1 The research for this contribution has benefited from funding from the Clark Travel-to-Collections Research Grant Program. The author would like to thank the staff of the Benson Ford Research Center at The Henry Ford in Dearborn, MI, USA, and above all Linda Skolarus and Judith E. Endelman, director of the Center.

2 The Ford Motor Company had opened another branch in Hamburg's Free Harbor in 1912, which was still in operation after the War. But it vanished during the German hyperinflation of 1923. This branch was, from the beginning, of little importance for the German market.

3 The French press had already coined the term *Fordisme* in 1916 in the wake of the Peace Ship Expedition. Matthew Josephson, editor of the avant-garde magazine *Broom*, is responsible for introducing the phrase in the United States, transforming Ford into a principle, a world view (Fehl 1995a, 35f).

References

Andernacht, Dietrich (1995). Fordistische Aspekte im Wohnungsbau des Neuen Frankfurt. In Stiftung Bauhaus Dessau and RWTH Aachen (eds.). *Zukunft aus Amerika. Fordismus in der Zwischenkriegszeit*, 192–207. Berlin: Movimento.

Assmann, Aleida (1996). Texts, Traces, Trash: The Changing Media of Cultural Memory. *Representations*, 56, 123–34.

Berg, Peter (1963). *Deutschland und Amerika, 1918–1929*. Lübeck, Hamburg: Matthiesen.

Bernhardt, Christoph, and Elsa Vonau (2009). Zwischen Fordismus und Sozialreform: Rationalisierungsstrategien im deutschen und französischen Wohnungsbau 1900–1933. *Zeitgeschichte Online*. 17.09.2011 http://www.zeithistorische-forschungen.de/16126041-Bernhardt-Vonau-2-2009.

Bohnsack, Ralf (2008). The Interpretation of Pictures and the Documentary Method. *Forum Qualitative Social Research*. 17.09.2011 http://www.qualitative-research.net/fqs/.

Casey, Bob (2008). *The Model T: A Centennial History*. Baltimore: Johns Hopkins University Press.

Diner, Dan (1996). *America in the eyes of the Germans: an essay on anti-Americanism*. Princeton: Wiener.

Edensor, Tim (2002). *National Identity, Popular Culture and Everyday Life*. New York: Berg.

Eifert, Christiane (2009). Antisemit und Autokönig. Henry Fords Autobiographie und ihre deutsche Rezeption in den 1920er-Jahren. *Zeitgeschichte Online*. 16.09.2011 http://www. zeithistorische-forschungen.de/16126041-Eifert-2-2009.

Fehl, Gerhard (1995a). Welcher Fordismus eigentlich? Eine einleitende Warnung vor dem leichtfertigen Gebrauch des Begriffs. In Stiftung Bauhaus Dessau and RWTH Aachen (eds.). *Zukunft aus Amerika*, 19–37. Berlin: Movimento.

Fehl, Gerhard (1995b). "Eine Wohnung, gebaut wie ein Auto." Ford und die Industrialisierung des Wohnungsbaus im Nationalsozialismus. In Stiftung Bauhaus Dessau und RWTH Aachen (eds.). *Zukunft aus Amerika*, 250–75. Berlin: Movimento.

Ford, Henry (1922). *My Life and Work*. London: Wyman & Sons.

Goffman, Erving (1979). *Gender Advertisements*. New York: Harper and Row.

Gottl-Ottlilienfeld, Friedrich von (1925). *Fordismus? Von Frederick W. Taylor zu Henry Ford*, 2nd ed. Jena: Fischer.

Grosbois, Thierry (2003). Ford in Belgium. In Hubert Bonin et al. (eds.). *Ford: The European History 1903–2003*, 192–232. Paris: Edition P.L.A.G.E.

Gruben, Gottfried (1980). *Die Tempel der Griechen*. Munich: Hirmer.

Hounshell, David A. (1984). *From the American System to Mass Production, 1800–1932: The Development of Manufacturing Technology in the United States*. Baltimore: Johns Hopkins University Press.

Jenkins, Richard (2008). *Social Identity*. New York: Routledge.

Knape, Joachim (2008). Gibt es Pathosformeln? Überlegungen zu einem Konzept von Aby M. Warburg. In Wolfgang Dickhut, Stefan Manns, and Norbert Winkler (eds.). *Muster im Wandel. Zur Dynamik topischer Wissensordnungen in Spätmittelalter und Früher Neuzeit*, 115–37. Göttingen: V & R Unipress.

Linke, Angelika, and Jakob Tanner (eds.). (2006). *Attraktion und Abwehr. Die Amerikanisierung der Alltagskultur in Europa.* Cologne: Böhlau.

Lüddecke, Theodor (1925). *Das amerikanische Wirtschaftstempo als Bedrohung Europas.* Leipzig: List Verlag.

Lüdtke, Alf et al. (eds.). (1996). *Amerikanisierung. Traum oder Alptraum im Deutschland des 20. Jahrhunderts.* Stuttgart: Franz Steiner Verlag.

McCracken, Grant (1988). *Culture and Consumption: New Approaches to the Symbolic Character of Consumer Goods and Activities.* Bloomington: Indian University Press.

McCracken, Grant (2005). *Culture and Consumption II: Markets, Meaning, and Brand Management.* Bloomington: Indiana University Press.

Memorial des Großherzogtums Luxemburg, Annexe au N° 16 de 1922, Avis.-Brevets d'invention.

Mennicken, Peter (1924). *Anti-Ford oder von der Würde der Menschheit.* Aachen: Die Kuppel.

Mitchell, William J. T. (1994). *Picture Theory: Essays on Verbal and Visual Representation.* Chicago: University of Chicago Press.

Nevins, Allan, and Frank E. Hill (1957). *Ford: Expansion and Challenge (1915–1933).* New York: Charles Scribner's Sons.

Nolan, Mary (1994). *Visions of Modernity: American Business and the Modernization of Germany.* New York: Oxford University Press.

Oswald, Werner (1990). *Deutsche Autos: 1920–1945.* Stuttgart: Motorbuch Verlag.

Peukert, Detlev J. K. (1987). *Die Weimarer Republik. Krisenjahre der Moderne.* Frankfurt/Main: Suhrkamp.

Polster, Werner, and Klaus Voy (1993). Eigenheim und Automobil—Materielle Fundamente der Lebensweise. In Werner Polster et al. (eds.). *Gesellschaftliche Transformationsprozesse und materielle Lebensweise. Beiträge zur Wirtschafts- und Gesellschaftsgeschichte der Bundesrepublik Deutschland (1949–1989)*, 293–356. Marburg: Metropolis-Verlag.

Popp, Susanne (2009). «Marianne» und «Germania». Allegorische Frauengestalten im «Bilderkrieg» der Kriegs- und Nachkriegszeit. In Gerhard Paul (ed.). *Das Jahrhundert der Bilder, Band I: 1900 bis 1949*, 292–9. Bonn: bpb.

Prager, Max (1902). *Die amerikanische Gefahr.* Berlin: Simion.

Saldern, Adelheid von (2006). Selbstbild im Spiegel. Amerikanische Identität im Verhältnis zu Europa—die 1920er Jahre. In Angelika Linke and Jakob Tanner (eds.). *Attraktion und Abwehr. Die Amerikanisierung der Alltagskultur in Europa*, 117–36. Cologne: Böhlau.

Schwabe, Klaus (1976). Anti-Americanism within the German Right, 1917–1933. *Amerikastudien*, 21, 1, 89–108.

Soeffner, Hans-Georg, and Jürgen Raab (1998). Sehtechniken. Die Medialisierung des Sehens: Schnitt und Montage als Ästhetisierungsmittel medialer Kommunikation. In Werner Rammert (ed.). *Technik und Sozialtheorie*, 121–48. Frankfurt: Campus.

Thomes, Paul (2003). Searching for Identity. FMC in the German Market (1903–2003). In Hubert Bonin et al. (eds.). *Ford: The European History, 1903–2003*, 150–95. Paris: Edition P.L.A.G.E.

Tresidder, Jack (1997). *Dictionary of Symbols: an Illustrated Guide to Traditional Images, Icons and Emblems*. London: Duncan Baird Publishers.

Veer, Renate de (2006–08). *Steinernes Gedächtnis: Gutsanlagen und Gutshäuser in Mecklenburg-Vorpommern*, 5 vols. Schwerin: Stock & Stein.

Virilio, Paul (1987). *Das öffentliche Bild*. Bern: Benteli Verlag.

Wala, Michael (2000). Amerikanisierung und Überfremdungsängste: Amerikanische Technologie und Kultur in der Weimarer Republik. In Michael Wala and Ursula Lehmkuhl (eds.). *Europas Blick auf Amerika vom 18. bis zum 20.Jahrhundert*, 121–46. Cologne: Böhlau.

Warnke, Martin (1980). Vier Stichworte: Ikonologie—Pathosformel—Polarität und Ausgleich —Schlagbilder und Bilderfahrzeuge. In Werner Hofmann, Georg Syamken, Martin Warnke (eds.). *Die Menschenrechte des Auges. Über Aby Warburg*, 53–83. Frankfurt/Main: Europäische Verlagsanstalt.

Weigel, Sigrid et al. (1995). Warburg's Schlangenritual: Reading Culture and Reading Written Texts. *New German Critique*, 65, 135–53.

Wik, Reynold M. (2005). *Henry Ford and Grass-roots America: a Fascinating Account of the Model-T era*. Michigan: University of Michigan Press.

Wilkins, Mira (2003). Ford among multinational companies. In Hubert Bonin et al. (eds.). *Ford: The European History 1903–2003*, 71–94. Paris: Edition P.L.A.G.E.

Wilkins, Mira, and Frank E. Hill (1964). *American Business Abroad: Ford on Six Continents*. Detroit: Wayne State University Press.

Zimmermann, Waldemar (1924). Fords Evangelium von der technisch-sozialen Dienstleistung. *Schmollers Jahrbuch für Gesetzgebung, Verwaltung und Volkswirtschaft im Deutschen Reiche*, 48, 3, 87–119.

Unpublished Documents at The Benson Ford Research Center, MI, USA

Acc.38, Box 48: "Copenhagen, Denmark—1923"
Acc.85, Box 1: "FMC-Secretary's Record, June 25, 1919"
Acc.880, Box 7: "Germany–Z / FMC-Germany 1924–1929"

Newspapers and Periodicals

Allgemeine Automobil-Zeitung (AAZ)
Der Motorfahrer
Der Motorwagen

The Dual Nature of Technology: Automotive Ignition Systems and the Evolution of the Car

Gijs Mom

The automobile, with its more than a century of history, its spread across very diverse cultures and the central role it has come to have in many societies is an excellent case for studying cultural appropriation—a process which, in this case, could perhaps better be called *domestication*. The approach developed here builds on an insight first formulated by two Dutch philosophers of technology, Peter Kroes and Anthonie Meijers. Their concept of "the dual nature of technology" (2006) allows us to develop an historical (more specifically: *evolutionary*) account of what I call the process of domestication of the automobile (Pantzar 1997; Aune 1996). Domestication differs from appropriation in that it emphasizes the 'taming' of a technology, its 'civilizing' for integration into Western, middleclass societies. The difference seems particularly relevant for the automobile, which started its career in a more anarchic and adventurous setting (Mom *forthcoming* a). Domestication is a special form of appropriation, relevant where the integration of an object into a middleclass household requires extra effort because the object is potentially dangerous and needs special handling.

Because of the complexity of this phenomenon, and because it has hardly been studied in the detail necessary for this approach, I will focus on one tiny but crucial aspect of the car: the *ignition* as a subsystem of the combustion engine. During the interwar years, the ignition, in a very practical and concrete way, allowed different motorizing cultures to appropriate the car. By adjusting the ignition timing (the moment the spark jumps between the spark plug electrodes) through so-called spark advance, and, later, by delegating this manual practice partly to the machine itself through a process of automation, different automotive cultures such as those in America and Europe were able to evolve, until, just before WWII, a convergence occurred towards one single, universal system: the high-tension battery-fed spark ignition.

Understanding and analyzing the co-evolutionary development of the ignition system and its accompanying engineering discourse requires some preliminary remarks about the dual nature of technology. These are followed by a discussion of technical handbooks published in Europe and the United States since 1900 and, in particular, of one American publication, the *Journal of the Society of Automotive Engineers*. Although this case study covers only a small part of what is needed to fully grasp the varied process of domestication, it nonetheless points toward some tentative generalizations about the overall picture, which will be presented at the end of this contribution.

Domestication as Adjustment of Technical Properties

The concept of the 'dual nature of technology' rests on the assumption that an artifact can be seen as consisting of two sets of characteristics (fig. 1): (technical) properties that describe its inner workings and other intrinsic traits (such as weight, color, tensile strength), and (relational) functions realized (and visible only) through its use (for an introduction see Kroes and Meijers 2006; for a critique see Mitcham 2002).

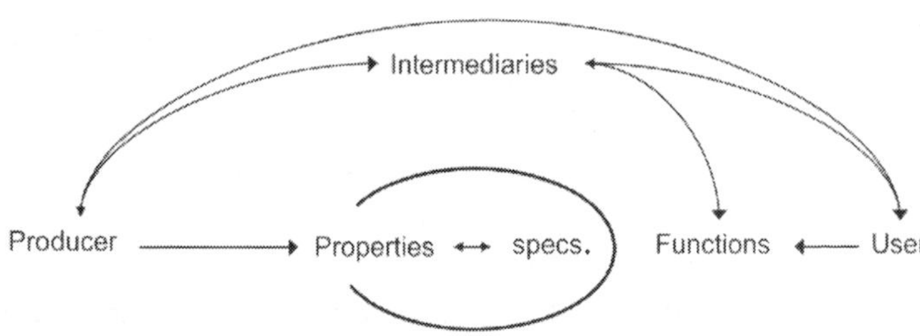

Fig. 1: The dual nature of technology, consisting of (technical) properties and (relational) functions, with (quantitative) specifications in-between; the curved arrows on top symbolize the latent prospective aspects of the practices of the producer and the user; 'intermediaries' (such as handbooks, or consumer organizations) function in between producers and users

Take, for example, the Coca-Cola bottle, as presented by Hans Peter Hahn in this volume: the bottle's properties are, among others things, its weight, its type of glass, the lettering embossed on it, the crown cap used to seal it, and so on; it functions as a drinking vessel, as a flower vase, as a weapon in a bar fight, and so on. From an evolutionary point of view, artifacts exist in variants as diverse and as hierarchically related with regard to properties as they do with regard to functions. Selection and retention of one or a few variants take place when people purchase and use these, or when producers retract variants and replace them with others in anticipation of future changes in use. As soon as a user has acquired an artifact, a second producer, seeing this user handling that artifact, concludes he can do better and develops a slightly different artifact, designedly better suited to the user's intentions. A second user, interested in a slightly different set of functions, acquires another artifact with again slightly different properties, and so on. One can imagine how, in this fashion, variation among artifacts emerges, all of which allow more or less similar activities; in the end one or a few artifacts are selected as those that best enable such activities. The result is a co-evolution of artifact and activities.

This example illustrates two basic insights. First, the relationship between properties and functions is not straightforward, but open for interference by the user. Whether the bottle is to be used as a vase or as a weapon is not inscribed in its technical properties, though some applications will be more difficult than others, and some will be downright impossible (such as using a small number of bottles to support a heavily loaded tabletop). Conversely, certain functions may be enabled by different sets of properties: either special profiles on winter tires or chains may advantage safer driving in snow. This 'fuzziness' between properties and functions drives the process of technological change, a process in which the user is as much involved as the producer (Mom 2007).

The second insight is that artifact populations evolve, split into sub-species, die out, or are (partially) replaced by substitutes, often as a response to changing user practices or sometimes just because the producers deem it worthwhile to modify their products. One way to grasp this process is to create taxonomies (such as is often done in handbooks), which are necessary because the array of variants is, in principle and often in reality, nearly endless. Because no handbook could ever cover a cross section of all variants existing at a given time, let alone cover their changes over time, they may employ one of the following methods: either they present their examples through the construction of a (Jungian) archetype (an actual artifact representative of all artifacts of a certain period), a (Weberian) idealtype (a non-existent, idealized artifact consisting of properties of actual or imagined artifacts), or an 'average type' (Mom 2007). This last type does not exist in fact, but results from a statistical assessment of the frequency of certain properties. For instance, whereas Ford's Model T no doubt functioned in many handbooks (and in many an engineer's or user's mind) as the archetype of the car in the 1910s and 1920s, its ignition system was far from typical in a statistical sense. It had a magneto ignition built into the flywheel of the engine, combined with an equally atypical planetary transmission.

In those days, some journals maintained statistics, for instance in order to determine an average type for models proposed at car shows. When the models are not weighted according to their quantitative occurrence, Ford's idiosyncratic ignition system does not even turn up (fig. 2). The majority of the car models used different types of ignition.

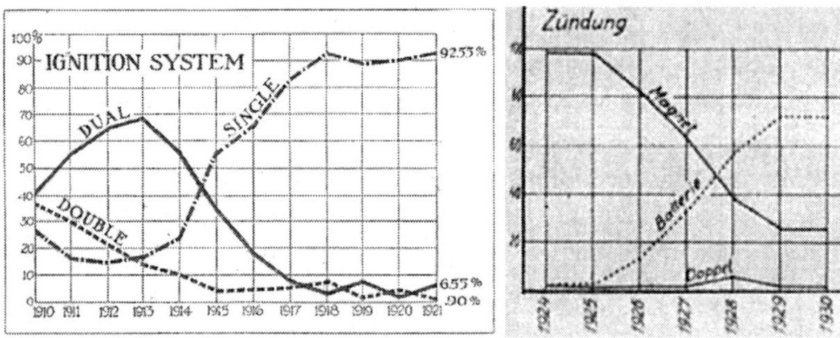

Fig. 2: Construction of average types of ignition systems by calculating the frequency of the subspecies represented at automobile exhibitions (the United States on the left, Germany on the right); note the time lapse of more than a decade between the two countries.A dual ignition is a combination of two ignition types, for instance battery and magneto ignition, while a double ignition has two spark plugs; a single ignition in the American case is a battery ignition. (source: Automotive Industries, *44, 7, 310 [left] and* ADAC-Motorwelt, *27, 33, 15)*

Even if we acknowledge that the relationship between properties and functions is fuzzy, we can still get a better grip on the evolutionary process of variation, selection and retention by applying these concepts. A means of understanding how people are able to use the distinction between properties and functions in their practices of appropriation and domestication was provided by the American psychologist James Gibson. Gibson developed his so-called 'ecological psychology' for the U.S. Army Air Forces during WWII, analyzing pilots' orientation while landing and while dropping bombs. Previously, in 1938, he had done a case study on automobile driving (Reed 1988, 75, 82). According to Gibson, both flying and driving enable a specific kind of space perception. An ardent motorist, Gibson coined the term *affordance*, a quality of an artifact that enables the user to do something; the user perceives affordance through a process of being 'stimulated,' i.e. acquiring information about the environment as a result of purposeful action. Unlike cognitive psychology, ecological psychology assumes an immediate 'grasping,' on the part of the user, of action information from his surroundings (Norman 2002).

Applying Gibson's insights to the dual nature of technology, one can think of as affordance those combinations of technical properties that users perceive as 'invitations' to action. For instance, the form of the Coca-Cola bottle is perceived by users as 'graspability,' inviting them to pick up the bottle. Likewise, the steering wheel of a car offers motorists 'steerability,' especially after they have acquired the necessary skill. Thus skills and affordances are closely related in practice; but importantly, actors perceive affordance even without using the artifact: the information is not incorporated mentally as 'meaning' to a 'neutral' stimulus (as cognitive psychology would have it); it is 'out there' to be perceived by purposeful users, even if they decide not to use the artifact.

The handbooks to be analyzed in the following function as intermediaries (see fig. 1) between producers and users, but do not always account for a Gibson-like 'usability' of the technologies described. Although some handbooks discuss the skills needed to handle the car's systems, in their depiction of the systems themselves they often reflect the designers' biases rather than the viewpoint of the user. One would expect to find user reactions, and evidence of their influence on the evolutionary process of selection and retention, represented more extensively in journals of the car and touring clubs, especially in letters to the editor. However, this source type has not been analyzed for this paper—hence its slant toward the producer perspective. Nonetheless, it is possible using Gibson's insights to infer some information about a technology's potential use from its structure, despite the fuzziness of the relationship between the two.

Equipped with these five tools or concepts (the dual nature of technology, taxonomies, typification, affordance, and intermediaries) one can now approach the 'population' of ignition systems as depicted in the handbooks with the purpose of understanding its evolution in terms of the diversification of, and changes in, the respective automotive cultures of Europe and the United States before WWII.

From Flame to Spark: Overview of Ignition Evolution

The handbooks analyzed here give taxonomies of ignition systems. They often distinguished, at one level, between non-electric systems (gunpowder ignition; catalytic glow ignition; flame ignition) and electric systems (fig. 3). The latter were mostly spark ignition systems, in which the fuel-air mixture in the cylinders was ignited by an electric spark that jumped between electrodes. An intermediary form, a glow ignition heated by electricity instead of a flame (as in the non-electric version), though it did not catch on among the so-called Otto engine types (Sass 1962), was later developed into a starter ignition for diesel engines and is still used as such.

Electric spark ignition systems were said to break down into two major sub-species, magneto ignition and battery ignition; interestingly, these were associated with the respective automotive cultures of Europe and the United States. Magneto and battery ignition systems each split into a low tension sub-group, in which the spark was created by pulling a mobile electrode away from a fixed one (thus 'drawing' a spark), and a high tension sub-group, in which enough high-tension energy was created to get the spark to jump between two fixed electrodes.

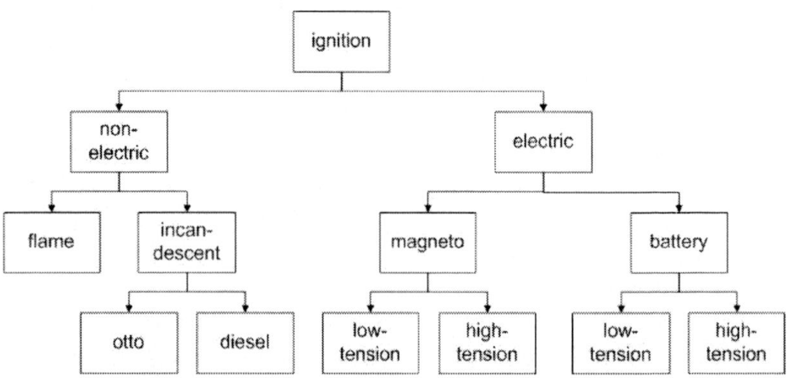

Fig. 3: Hierarchical classification of the population of ignition systems until 1940 as taken from automotive handbooks

The relation between the variants in this diagram (fig. 3) can be understood by situating the selection of preferred species in space and time, i.e. by tracing their appearance at particular moments in particular places (see fig. 4). For the moment, we must assume that the selection process was influenced by consumer responses we have no detailed evidence of. In earlier studies on e.g.

tires, automatic transmissions and the closed car body, I have suggested that automotive engineers translate perceived consumer preferences into changes in their 'state of the art.' (Mom *forthcoming* b)

Based on existing literature, one can propose the following evolutionary hypothesis.[1] The combustion engine's roots in industrial, stationary applications with easy access to gas outlets had made the gas flame ignition a well-known device. It itself evolved from the continuous heating principle of the steam engine, an external combustion engine in which the heat is used to make steam, which does the work within the cylinder after entering through valves. When it came to igniting the fuel-air mixture in an internal combustion engine, this concept of continuous heat provision had to be adjusted, because the flame could not be in constant contact with the mixture in the cylinder. Ingenious valve systems driven by the engine itself through rods and springs were developed to catch the flame and bring it into the cylinder to ignite the mixture.

Evolutionary variation made slides compete with rotating devices, but neither of these could keep up with the consumer's apparent wish to have the engine's rotational speed increase, let alone cope with the requirement that an engine should be able to change speeds continuously in the context of an automobile. In industry, its speed had always been constant. On top of that, both increasing cylinder pressure and the air rushing past the speeding car made it difficult to get the flame near the mixture without it being blown out. This, among other things, prevented the flame ignition system from becoming universal. However, the second non-electric type, glow ignition, was more successful—despite the fact that, initially, it also worked on the basis of a flame that kept a metal tube heated from outside the cylinder.

Glow-tube ignition, several versions of which had been proposed, was ultimately developed for use in automobiles by Gottlieb Daimler from a pre-existing English patent. It became the mainstream ignition during the first decade of automotive technology, between 1883 and 1893. As late as 1896, no single British-produced car was equipped with an electric ignition. Glow ignition heated by electricity was out of the question because of the poor reliability of lead-acid accumulators, and their alternative, primary dry batteries, discharged too quickly and thus had to be replaced too often. Early driving was a delicate practice: it was more a functional adventure, characterized by tinkering, maintenance and repair rather than by racing and touring. Operating an automobile required the constant attention of a knowledgeable user or his—most often these early adopters were men—mechanic or chauffeur.[2]

Once motorists started to define their hobby as something characterized by speed, in evolutionary terms, the flame ignition subspecies died out. The shift to electricity thus seems to have been determined by technically informed arguments (such as about the vulnerability of flame ignition to wind pressure), but whether engineers opted for magneto ignition or not depended at least as much on culture. Whereas the lead-acid battery was developed to a comparable degree of sophistication on both sides of the Atlantic, European car producers highlighted 'reliability' (as a proxy for 'high quality') and opted for magneto ignition, although the original incentive to go for this option might have come from engineering considerations.

When Robert Bosch, as early as 1887, started to develop the magneto alternative, light-version (grid plate) lead batteries were a cause of great concern among experts because they were perceived as unreliable. Like the flame ignition, magneto ignition (which did not need a battery, because it generated its own electricity by rotation in a magnetic field) also had its non-automotive predecessors, in this case systems, used to detonate mines, which generated electricity by a manual cranking mechanism. Remarkably, the Bosch low-tension magneto ignition squeezed all other alternatives out of the European market, including the low- and high-tension battery ignition systems employed by Carl Benz in his first car in 1886 (improved in 1893) or by De Dion Bouton in 1895 (whose design was equipped with an interruptor to generate the spark). When the Simms-Bosch magneto ignition (1898) came on the market, the battery version seemed doomed to extinction.

The low-tension version of the magneto ignition system (so called only after a high-tension version emerged in 1902), known as the 'make and break' system in English-speaking cultures (as opposed to the 'jump spark' high-tension variants), was considered very beneficial to car engine designs because of the "fat" spark it produced (Whitman 1907, 89, 92). Bosch and its competitors, such as Eisemann, Lucas and others, devised various mechanisms to enable the moment at which the spark was produced to vary relative to the piston position in the cylinder. This ignition timing soon became the core focus of research and of descriptions of the various systems in the handbooks, because it was through this mechanism, called 'spark advance' in the terminology of automotive engineers, that the user could influence the behavior of the engine. In Gibsonian terms, this means that, however different their technical properties, the proposed ignition systems all had to *afford* the user the ability to change the ignition timing depending on the situation (starting; climbing a hill; high-speed cruising). Starting the car, for instance, had to begin with cranking at a late spark setting, achieved by turning a 'manette' near the steering wheel; but as soon as the engine caught, the motorist had to hurry back to the manette to advance the spark and thereby get the engine to run regularly. Increasing the engine (and thus the driving) speed initially did not even involve an accelerator pedal but could be done partially by advancing the spark, which ensured that, even at higher engine revolutions, the fuel-air mixture still had enough time to burn and generate pressure upon the pistons, which, through the clutch and transmission, turned the wheels. When "slowing down for a hard pull," i.e. climbing a hill, the skilled motorist had to advance the ignition timing to compensate for the fact that a—as one would now call it—'richer' mixture of fuel relative to the amount of air sucked in took longer to burn (Libby 1920, 289).

It was consumers' desire to drive faster (or at least, this desire as perceived by the producers) while maintaining control of the car which subsequently drove innovation. It set in motion an interesting competition between alternatives and a transfer of functions between them. As mentioned previously, low-tension magnetos worked according to the 'make and break' principle, in which a mobile electrode drew a spark as it separated from a fixed electrode. Increasing car speeds meant higher compression pressures in the cylinders, which led to sealing problems involving the mobile shafts protruding into the cylinders. High-tension battery ignition did not have this problem because it worked with two fixed spark plug electrodes, so proponents of the magneto solved the sealing problem by introducing a high-tension version of this ignition type, despite the fact that the sparks produced were not as 'fat.' Thus the functional requirement 'reliability,' which could be achieved with non-leaking sparkplugs, was adopted by mainstream technology from an alternative that had threatened to take the lead in the market.

In 1912, Bosch sold its millionth magneto and three years later had sold its second millionth. Before WWI, cars with magneto ignitions were also being sold in the US, but even though 87% of the models at the 1920 Paris car show and 80% of the models at the 1926 London show were equipped with a high-tension magneto ignition, the majority of American cars used a battery ignition. The reason for this was that American engineers had meanwhile integrated the ignition into an electrically operated starting-lighting-system, so the battery was needed anyhow for the lighting system. Because no one could deny that the magneto was more reliable, double and dual ignition systems (fig. 2) were in use on luxury cars, but from the end of the 1920s onward, even European car makers started to introduce the less expensive battery ignition, although this resulted in the ignition becoming the most common defect in daily automobile use (Mom *forthcoming* a).

There were also technical reasons why producers shifted toward the battery, such as better spark quality at low engine speeds compared to magneto alternatives, and the handbooks deal with these extensively; but in the end production costs and the relative simplicity of the design of battery ignition eventually led to the extinction of the magneto in cars. In motorcycles and other light road vehicles, as well as in airplanes with piston engines, however, magneto ignition systems were in use until long after WWII. In light of the substantial penetration of American cars on the Dutch market, it is no wonder that around 40 % of the cars on display at the 1924 and 1927 Amsterdam car exhibitions had battery ignitions. In the UK, which had its own auto industry, the share of magneto ignitions had decreased to one-tenth by the outbreak of the war, even though in 1929 half of the cars on exhibit at the London automobile show were still equipped with this device. An overview of the differences between American and European cars from 1921 in the American trade journal *Automotive Industries*, delivered in the US by the American representative of Rolls-Royce, stated that some European makers started to adopt the American system "probably as a matter of justified economy," but that on "small cars without self-starter, the magneto is almost universal and seems correct, since in this way the car can always get home, battery or no battery" (Olley 1921, 551).[3] As late as 1926, according to the handbook writer P. M. Heldt, a knowledgeable observer, "practically all of the cars [in Europe] carry ignition magnetos, those with simple battery ignition being the exception." (1926, 254)

The remainder of the pre-WWII ignition history is about control: the spread of the car to less knowledgeable users had increased the impetus to automate, that is, to delegate the skill of spark timing to the hardware.[4] Given ample evidence from letters to the editor in club journals, this process can be characterized as a struggle between knowledgeable users and engineers about who had the say in determining the behavior of the car (Franz 2005). This struggle started well before the post-WWII 'electronic revolution,' which shows that automation was originally a fully mechanical, pneumatic and hydraulic affair, and not a matter of electronics. Automatic spark advance was first accomplished by introducing centrifugal weights that advanced the spark as a function of the rotation speed of the engine. By the end of the 1930s it had been fine-tuned with the addition of a vacuum control, which corrected the rather straightforward rotation-speed control algorithm to one of so-called engine load, measured by the amount of vacuum in an engine's inlet system. We know today that high speed/high load driving, for instance on a freeway, requires more spark advance than high speed/low load driving, as when accelerating on a city street; however, the spread of the car to users not well versed in automotive technology necessitated a restriction of Gibsonian *affordances* related to spark advance and ignition timing, hence the solution of automated spark advance.

Analysis: Embedding Ignition in its Car Culture

In his analysis of airplane development, engineer-turned-historian of technology Walter Vincenti has argued that the deeper one descends into the 'bowels' of technology, the more difficult it will be to connect technical changes to societal processes (2000; in general see 1990). But in the case of car engine ignition we have no problem embedding the evolution of ignition technology within a broader car culture, or distinguishing between a European and an American car culture to explain the divergence and, later, the convergence of the magneto and battery ignition sub-species within the family of ignition systems. The problem is rather to avoid stereotyping—we must not create a dichotomy between a comfort-oriented American motorist and a sporting European haunted by high taxes and consequently blighted with high-revving engines—in a hitherto vastly under-researched area in the history of technology and of mobility.

Striking is the relatively modest attention paid to this 'problem of problems' (as Karl Benz called the ignition) in engineering circles. *The Journal of the Society of Automotive Engineers,* over more than two decades, contains less than half a dozen articles dedicated to this subsystem. On the other hand, the handbooks devoted an unusually large amount of space (in number of pages per total book size) to it.[5]

The level of attention paid to ignition was at its height in the years the two systems were competing head-on against each other, just before the 'American' variant started to make inroads into 'European' technology in the mid-1920s. Around one-fifth of the total volume of some handbooks was then being dedicated to the ignition. The comparatively modest level of attention to ignition systems in the journals may be explained by two factors. First, from the very beginning, the problem was owned, so to speak, by a supplier industry that quickly grew into a powerful force prepared to tackle a problem of considerable complexity with its specialized precision and electrical engineers. Like the tire, which was also produced by a separate branch of specialized manufacturers, car manufacturers left ignition alone. The problem was big (as reflected in the handbooks), but not so much for the car industry (as reflected in *The Journal of the Society of Automotive Engineers*).

Second, during the 1920s the American car industry became more self-confident with respect to the European example, and came to see its own solution, the battery ignition, as the universal solution. They were right, but not in the technical sense: Bosch only very reluctantly gave up its superior technology in face of an 'invasion' of cheap, American technology that it could not resist. In Gibsonian terms, the two systems afforded largely the same practice: skillful spark advance. Though the battery system was less reliable, this was easily compensated in the United States by a more extensive service system (Franz 2005; Mom *forthcoming* b). Figure 4, a dynamic diagram of the early automotive ignition, illustrates this sequence of events: the arrows between the alternatives represent a transfer of 'functions' and suggest that by borrowing from encroaching technologies, some other technologies managed to survive and eventually achieved dominance through purchasing and the broader appropriation and domestication processes.

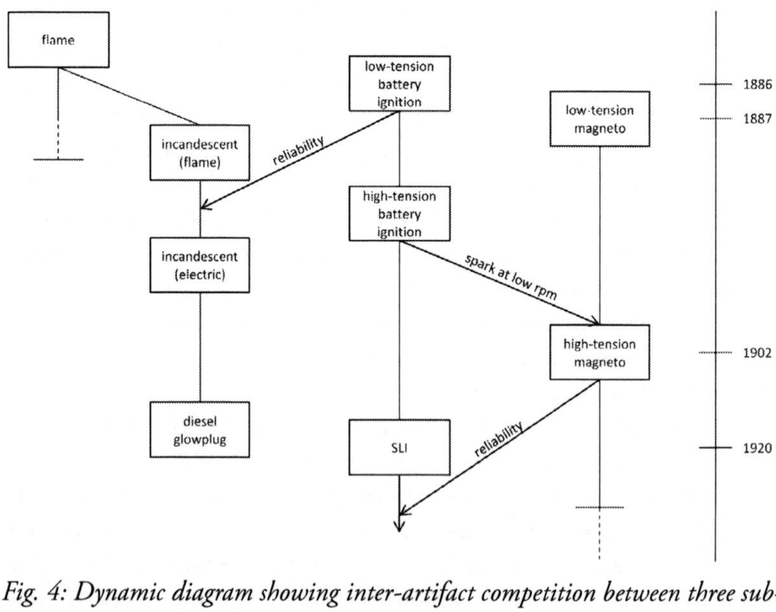

Fig. 4: Dynamic diagram showing inter-artifact competition between three sub-species of ignition systems and the transfer of functions

It is remarkable that this process is accompanied, in the handbooks, by a gradual rewriting of the system's history. If we take the Dutch handbook *De automobiel en haar behandeling* (*The Automobile and Its Handling*) [sic: *automobiel* is masculine so it should be: *zijn* (his) instead of *haar* (her)] by former Spyker employee J. W. Brand as an example, we can trace this modification of the system's history as a repeated 'rolling-back' of the new 'winner' into the past, because multiple editions of this handbook appeared over nearly half a century until at least 1950.[6] In the first available edition, thought to date from 1911, Brand presented the battery as an auxiliary component only used for starting (74).[7] In the post-WWI twelfth edition (1921) the battery ignition still receives its due in Brand's handbook, although he comments that it was "not anymore applied as separate ignition, unless on very old engines" (104). Only one year later, in the 'improved' thirteenth edition of 1922, Brand presents the battery ignition as a system that "witnesses a comeback during the last years. Modern cars are all equipped with a complete electrical installation" (103–4).[8] One year earlier, Brand's former colleague and boss, G. F. Steinbuch, in the first edition of his famous handbook, further cements this story by acknowledging that in "the beginning of automobilism the glow tube ignition was applied often. It became rather famous, mostly because of the many defects associated with it and the load of misery it caused for the motorists." (1922, 259)

In 1932, Brand formulated the definitive, consolidated story by presenting the magneto ignition as an aberration on the battery ignition's road to triumph: "Although the magneto ignition had supplanted battery ignition almost completely, the battery has reconquered its place again. [...] Because [...] a good and solid electricity source is [...] present, the magneto ignition is very often entirely left out." (1932, 151) In the post-WWII 25th edition, battery and magneto ignitions are both presented as alternatives, without any comments on the frequency of their use, and knowledgeable readers would have known that the battery was a car system, while the magneto was to be found here and there on other vehicles, such as mopeds (1950, 151).

Remarkably, Brand's history is compatible with a 'story' constructed on the other side of the Atlantic as early as 1917. As a result, the American story became the universal story, and the magneto's European past was more or less forgotten. In 1917, when sales manager H. Rice, of ignition manufacturer Atwater Kent, wrote about "Problems in Ignition Development," he presented battery ignition as the "first ignition used for automobile engines," altogether forgetting or ignoring all flame and glow ignition variants. He emphasized that "today out of a total of 109 manufacturers of cars, 87 use battery ignition exclusively," while 22 used either low- or high-tension magnetos (154-5). One of the latter 22, by the way, was the Model T, which at that time comprised about half of the world's total car production (Mom *forthcoming* b).

Three years later most American engineers agreed that there was no difference in quality and performance between the competing systems, despite American proponent of the magneto A. D. Libby's suggestion that this competition was comparable to the majestic struggle between direct and alternating current systems in the realm of electricity production. During the discussion of Libby's presentation, some even opined that not even the costs could help decide the competition in favor of one or the other (Libby 1920, 277, 287–289).[9] In other words, the battery became predominant by way of coincidence, not technical superiority: the breakthrough of battery ignition in the US was conditioned by the introduction of battery-powered lighting. In that sense, it *was* cheaper, because the battery was there anyway. After 1920, both systems managed to eliminate whatever differences had existed between them in quality and performance, and ignition became a matter of national identity rather than of technology. It disappeared as such from the pages of the major American engineering journal and became a part of the users' discourse on comfort (fig. 5).

Conclusion

In 1986, on the occasion of the centenary of the German automobile, just as automotive electronics were breaking through, the development chief at Volkswagen complained that outsourcing the development of electronic systems jeopardized the very character of the Volkswagen. In doing so he voiced a concern that would have been unthinkable fifty years earlier (Mom 1996, 41). During the interwar years, as we have seen, users and producers alike shaped national automotive cultures, materially and ideologically, using stereotypes to fine-tune their cultural automotive practices. Ironically, the automation of ignition functions half a century earlier (together with a comparable development in the formation of the fuel-air mixture in the carburetor, see fig. 5) triggered this process of increasing automation. The process had reached its nadir a century later, when spark advance became fully programmable as part of an 'electronic motor management system,' inaccessible even to the tinkering motorist, let alone the lay user. Technological reliability (better: the promise

Fig. 5: Ignition (spark advance) and carburetor (fuel-air mixture adjustment) were the first functions to be automated, and a process of shifting skills to the hardware began (source: The Journal of the Society of Automotive Engineers, *39, 6, 37)*

of reliability, because 'electronification' caused new problems of reliability related to the complexity of these new systems) had been achieved by deskilling the motorist and delegating the skills of knowledgeable users to the hardware. It was no coincidence that this process started at the moment, shortly before WWI, when a new, less technically educated user appeared on the market. The potential for further domestication of the car increased again when, during the heyday of mass motorization after a full century, the character of the car was now fully electronically defined by the producer. Culture (including the way one climbed a hill or started the engine) was now built into the car's technology, attitude had become electronics and had 'hardened' to bits and pieces.

The process described in the foregoing pages was characterized by a high degree of contingency: it is hard to justify either one of the two technological paths, the American or the European, on the basis of technical superiority. It was rather a specific event, the emergence of a very effective entrepreneur (Robert Bosch) who managed to carve out a special path called 'magneto ignition' that, if engineering excellence had been the sole criterion for technological evolution, might have become the hegemonic technology. Instead, the competing American technology managed to live up to the consumers' expectations of reliability by compensating for its technical inferiority with a well-developed garage infrastructure. In the end, Bosch's alternative had to be given up in favor of a solution that suited the entire electrical system. This was an American revival of the battery ignition that, meanwhile, had taken over the advantages of the magneto ignition to the extent that experts could find no major differences in quality or performance. As such, costs and simplicity made the final difference; they were aided by the position of the American automobile, which had meanwhile become hegemonic. The convergence of the original evolutionary variety had advanced to the point where the system was ready to be subsumed within a general trend of ongoing automation; spark advance turned from a token of skilled masculinity into a covert property of the hardware. Appropriation, from this perspective, is a highly contingent, variable and continuously changing phenomenon, a result of the dialectic between production and use, engineering and lay culture. Domestication is perhaps a better term in this context, because automation was aimed at 'taming' the technology into a 'comfortable' car for a lay public of new users, whose masculinity was better not too seriously challenged by adventurous exercises in self-governed acceleration using manual spark advance.

Notes

1 This reconstruction is based upon Mom (1986). See also Schildberger (1952) and Lehr (1961). For contemporary specialized handbooks see Klaiber and Lippart (1928), Sainturat (1910) and Smith (1931).
2 For an analysis of this tripartite adventure (racing, touring, tinkering) see Mom (2001).
3 The presentation was delivered to the Society of Automotive Engineers. For an overview (based on a survey by the American Department of Commerce) of major ignition systems used in most motorizing countries in the world, see anon. (1926). According to this survey, 22 of the 47 countries (including China, Bulgaria and Paraguay) still had exclusively magneto ignition, 14 had exclusively battery ignition; the rest had both.
4 For efforts by the American car industry to push knowledgeable users out of the realm of automotive technology, see Franz (2005). On the development of automotive (and aviation) skills in the interwar years also see Möser (2009).
5 For an analysis of these handbooks, see Mom (*forthcoming* b). I thank the *Nederlands Centrum voor Autohistorische Documentatie* (NCAD, Dutch Centre for Automotive-Historical Documentation), Helmond, The Netherlands, for making a large portion of the set of handbooks available to me.
6 Brand had already published the fourth edition of his handbook in 1911; the last traceable edition (the 25th) dates from 1950 and contains *zijn* instead of *haar* in the title.
7 If an engine was still warm, the handbook recommends restarting it on the ignition alone (without using the hand-crank) (Brand 1911, 133).
8 The fifteenth edition contains text identical to the 1922 edition (Brand 1926, 97).
9 Libby argued that the magneto ignition had a hotter spark, but most of his colleagues who took part in the discussion, printed in the journal, did not agree with him in this.

References

anon. (1926). What Buyers Want on Their Cars in Foreign Countries. *Automotive Industries*, 54, 18, 766–8.

Aune, Margrethe (1996). The Computer in Everyday Life: Patterns of Domestication of a New Technology. In Merete Lie and Knut H. Sørensen (eds.). *Making Technology Our Own? Domesticating Technology into Everyday Life*, 91–120. Oslo: Scandinavian University Press.

Brand, J. W. (1911). *De automobiel en haar behandeling,* 4th ed. Rotterdam: Nijgh & Van Ditmar.

Brand, J. W. (1921). *De automobiel en haar behandeling,* 12th ed. Rotterdam: Nijgh & Van Ditmar.

Brand, J. W. (1922). *De automobiel en haar behandeling,* 13th ed. Rotterdam: Nijgh & Van Ditmar.

Brand, J. W. (1926). *De automobiel en haar behandeling,* 15th ed. Rotterdam: Nijgh & Van Ditmar.

Brand, J. W. (1932). *De automobiel en haar behandeling*, 19th ed. Rotterdam: Nijgh & Van Ditmar.

Brand, J. W. (1950). *De automobiel en zijn behandeling*, 25th ed. Rotterdam: Nijgh & Van Ditmar.

Franz, Kathleen (2005). *Tinkering: Consumers Reinvent the Early Automobile*. Philadelphia: University of Pennsylvania Press.

Heldt, P. M. (1926). What is a European Light Car? *Automotive Industries*, 55, 7, 252–4.

Klaiber, E. and W. Lippart (1928). *Die elektrische Ausrüstung des Kraftfahrzeuges, Teil I: Zündung*. Berlin: de Gruyter.

Kroes, Peter, and Anthonie Meijers (2006). Introduction: The dual nature of technical artefacts. *Studies in History and Philosophy of Science*, 37, 1–4.

Lehr, W. (1961). Die Enstehung der elektrischen Kraftfahrzeugausrüstung. *Automobiltechnische Zeitschrift*, 6, 9, 260–5 and 11, 380–4.

Libby, A. D. (1920). Advantages of Magneto Ignition. *The Journal of the Society of Automotive Engineers*, 7, 3, 277–90.

Mitcham, Carl (2002). Do Artifacts Have Dual Natures? Two Points of Commentary on the Delft Project. *Techné*, 6, 2, 9–12.

Mom, Gijs (1986). De elektrische installatie in historisch perspectief. In Henk de Boer et al. (eds.). *De elektrische installatie*, 17–51. Deventer: Kluwer Technische Boeken.

Mom, Gijs (1996). De auto-elektronica in historisch perspectief. In A. G. Visser and Gijs. P. A. Mom (eds.). *Elektronica in de auto*, 17–46. Deventer: Kluwer Bedrijfsinformatie.

Mom, Gijs (2001). Civilized adventure as a remedy for nervous times: early automobilism and Fin-de-Siècle culture. *History of Technology*, 23, 157–90.

Mom, Gijs (2007). Translating Properties into Functions (and Vice Versa): Design, User Culture and the Creation of an American and a European Car (1930–1970). *Journal of Design History*, 20, 2, 171–81.

Mom, Gijs (*forthcoming* a). *Atlantic Automobilism: Emergence and Persistence of the Car in Europe and the USA, 1895–1940.*

Mom, Gijs (*forthcoming* b). *Constructing the State of the Art: Innovation and the Evolution of Automotive Technology (1898–1940).*

Möser, Kurt (2009). *Fahren und Fliegen in Frieden und Krieg: Kulturen individueller Mobilitätsmaschinen 1880–1930*. Heidelberg et al.: Verlag Regionalkultur.

Norman, Joel (2002). Two visual systems and two theories of perception: an attempt to reconcile the constructivist and ecological approaches. *Behavioral and Brain Sciences*, 25, 73–144.

Olley, M. (1921). Why American, British and Continental Car Designs Differ. *Automotive Industries*, 44, 10, 547–53.

Pantzar, Mika (1997). Domestication of Everyday Life Technology: Dynamic Views on the Social Histories of Artifacts. *Design Issues*, 13, 3, 52–65.

Reed, Edward S. (1988). *James J. Gibson and the Psychology of Perception*. New Haven: Yale University Press.
Rice, H. E. (1917). Problems in Ignition Development. *The Journal of the Society of Automotive Engineers*, 1, 2, 154–8.
Sainturat, Maurice. (1910). *Allumage électrique des moteurs*. Paris: Dunod et Pinat.
Sass, Friedrich (1962). *Geschichte des deutschen Verbrennungsmotorenbaues von 1860 bis 1918*. Berlin: Springer-Verlag.
Schildberger, Friedrich (1952). *Bosch und die Zündung*. Stuttgart: Bosch Schriftenreihe.
Smith, S. Parker (1931). *The electrical equipment of automobiles*. London: Chapman & Hall.
Steinbuch, G. F. (1922). *De automobiel: Handboek voor automobielbestuurders, monteurs en reparateurs. Deel I: De motor*. Deventer: Æ. E. Kluwer.
Vincenti, Walter G. (1990). *What Engineers Know and How They Know It: Analytical Studies of Aeronautical History*. Baltimore: Johns Hopkins University Press.
Vincenti, Walter G. (2000). Real-world variation-selection in the evolution of technological form: historical examples. In John Ziman (ed.). *Technological Innovation as an Evolutionary Process*, 174–89. Cambridge: Cambridge University Press.
Whitman, Roger B. (1907). *Motor-Car Principles: The Gasoline Automobile*. New York: D. Appleton and Company.

Ghost in the Machine: Mechanization in a Philippine Frontier, 1898–1941

Patricia Irene Dacudao

[S]ocieties transform objects and ideas …
[but] societies as such are transformed as they integrate new things.
Hans Peter Hahn (in this volume, 30)

The creation of an abaca stripping machine born out of the needs of a frontier plantation economy in the southern Philippine region of Davao became an experience of cultural appropriation that fused together different traits and values in a population of mostly settlers that included Americans, Filipinos and Japanese nationals. It also resulted in the transformation of the Davao frontier itself from a remote and isolated wilderness into an urbanized region during the period of American rule in the Philippines during the first half of the twentieth century.

In Davao, the American traditions of individualism and mechanization (Turner 1920, 37), which had originated in Greco-Roman secular humanism (Gabriel 1963, 3) and the Industrial Revolution (Adas 2006, 78–9), came to co-exist with the communal cooperation practiced in Asian societies such as the Philippines and Japan (Nakane 1970, 2–22; Sugimoto 1997, 245–59; Pertierra 2002, 85; Rodell 2002, 197–8). Accordingly, heterogeneous values were appropriated, discarded and/or transformed in a quest for the ultimate abaca stripping machine, a quest determined by the particular conditions of labor scarcity in the frontier zone vis-à-vis the labor-intensive and time-consuming process of stripping abaca. The American notion of machines as the embodiment of progress was imbibed and transformed by the Davao settlers, and the end product of this process was the *hagotan*, a machine utilized as communal equipment and shared by Filipino and Japanese workers on the Westernized agro-industrial abaca plantations of Davao. Thus, the *hagotan* is illustrative both of Western-initiated industrialization achieved through the appropriation of Asian values and of an Asian environment appropriating the Western notion of industrial mechanization.

America's Last Western Frontier

The United States acquired the Philippines as a colony from Spain in 1898 through the Treaty of Paris that ended the Spanish-American War. The Philippine archipelago is comprised of three main island groups: Luzon in the north, the Visayan Islands in the center, and Mindanao to the south. Davao, the geographical setting of the processes described in this paper, is located in southeast Mindanao along the Davao Gulf. One of the southernmost areas in the Philippines, far away from the capital of Manila in Luzon, Davao was thickly forested and sparsely populated when the first group of Americans, mostly U.S. army soldiers, arrived in December 1899.

At that time, Davao was a string of small coastal settlements populated by a few thousand members of (Hispanized) local tribes, and less than a thousand Spanish missionaries and landowners. Spanish rule in Davao was tenuous, having only begun fifty years earlier in 1848, when Jose Oyanguren brought an expedition of soldiers and settlers (Tiu 2005, 22). The majority of the native inhabitants[1] was scattered over a vast territory of over 20,200 square kilometers, and by 1903 just a small percentage of the indigenous tribes had been Hispanized by the Recollect and Jesuit missionaries (Commission of the Census 1941, 4). The local tribes were hunter-gatherers and barter traders who practiced slash and burn farming. This enabled them to remain mobile most of the time, but they also inhabited temporary communities called *rancherias* (Tiu 2005, 24; Hayase 2007, 163). It was near or within these *rancherias* that the Spaniards established a few permanent settlements (*reduccion*) resembling small villages, with house lots, streets, a church and a government center that exercised authority through the whip or by spiritual conversion (Tiu 2005, 24–5). Within these *reducciones*, the villagers began new lives as farmers, tending their fields adjacent to the village, paying tributes to the Spanish government, hearing mass, and abandoning their old hunter-gatherer lifestyle and human sacrifice rituals (as practiced by some tribes); in theory, because they were now under the protection of God and Spain, they would no longer be attacked by intra-tribal warriors (*bagani*) and Muslim raiding parties from Western Mindanao (Arcilla 1998, 407, 432–3, 454; Tiu 2005, 47). However, desertions, uprisings and flight to the mountainous interior were widespread among the inhabitants, especially when their fields failed to produce (Arcilla 1998, 411–2, 422). The small villages were located along the Davao Gulf coast, without interconnecting roads, while the vast interior, filled with primary growth forest, was relatively unexplored and uninhabited (ibid., 273, 536).

It was thus a wilderness into which the American soldiers came when they reached Davao's shores, and they promptly set about building their lodging and roads, for "there were none" (anon. 1926a, 11). After their tour of duty had expired and with the encouragement of the military governors of Mindanao such as Generals Leonard Wood and John J. Pershing, a number of these soldiers settled in Davao, applied for public lands, and started establishing coconut and hemp plantations along the coast (anon. 1926d, 9). These soldiers-turned-settlers saw themselves as pioneers of the "last American frontier," as they liked to call Davao. After all, with little capital but "plenty of grit," they saw themselves as following in the footsteps of their fathers and grandfathers who had tamed the American West a generation or two earlier (ibid.).

These Davao pioneers came from an America that instilled in its school children the "saga of the rise of their nation as an epic struggle by sturdy yeoman farmers to civilize a continent thinly peopled by savages" (Adas 2006, 73). By the 1890s, Frederick Jackson Turner's essays on the enduring influence of the moving frontier on U.S. history provided what was "then believed to be an empirical and objective validation by a professional historian for this settler perspective" (ibid.). Among the "striking characteristics" of Americans that Turner (1920, 37) enumerated were "that masterful grasp of material things [...] powerful to effect great ends," and "that dominant individualism," the twin traits of industry and rugged individualism frontiersmen were known for. From the popularity that Turner received as a result of his essay, it can be deduced that many Americans thought this way. Theodore Roosevelt himself acknowledged that Turner had enunciated a "thought that has been floating around rather loosely" (Ridge 1991, 10).

It has been noted that Turner's background as a child of the frontier was influential in his formulating this thesis. He grew up in Midwestern Wisconsin with a father involved in railroads and other pioneer enterprises and experienced for himself the progress of his home state through the years (ibid., 5). Just as Turner was influenced by his childhood environment, many American pioneers of Davao were products of this same America, with their "coming of age in towns transformed by new systems of transport and communication" where new technologies had altered work patterns and lifestyles (Adas 2006, 149). Among them was Captain J. L. Burchfield, who grew up in Kentucky and was among the first Americans to settle in Davao. He aptly named his first plantation 'The Kentucky Plantation.' This son of the Bluegrass Region was called a "Pioneer Border Man," and his sturdy character was likened to that of Davy Crockett, an American Midwestern hero (anon. 1926a, 11). Another was James Martin Welborn, born in McDonough County, Illinois, who had plantations on both coasts of the Gulf (Tiu 2005, 150–1).[2] The Pacific coastal state of California was home to several Davao pioneers, notably O. V. Wood and Edward E. Christensen, Thomasite[3] schoolteachers turned plantation owners (anon. 1926d, 8). Even the Klondike gold mining region had a Davao connection in the person of Peter Harding, a partner at Piso Plantation known for his ability to handle indigenous laborers (Mindanao Herald 1909, 73).

In their Davao special edition, the *American Chamber of Commerce Journal* (January 1926) wrote about the Americans in Davao with apparent allusions to the American west, as the following titles suggest: "Veterans Turn Davao Jungle into Rich Plantations: Teach Industry to Tribes" (Boyle 1926, 9), "Epic in Pioneering—Americans in Davao" (anon. 1926b, 12) or "Independence on Davao Homestead—What may be done with Sixteen Hectares" (anon. 1926c, 28). These articles often evoke images of the American frontier itself—in Davao.

Machines to Tame the Wilderness

Part and parcel of frontier expansion were the role of machines and the importance of industry in taming the wilderness. It was that special point in time, as the fruits of the industrial revolution merged with the acquisition of a colony, that American 'exceptionalism' was engendered. In the American frontier of the 1830s and 1840s, John Deere's 'singing plow,' usually pulled by horses, not men, tilled and cut the North American prairies into one of the most productive agricultural regions in the world (Adas 2006, 78). By 1890, when the American frontier was deemed officially closed by the U.S. Census, the use of internal combustion engines had just begun (ibid., 79). In 1898, the United States acquired the Philippines, and, as a matter of course, Davao in the Philippine frontier, touted as America's last frontier, began using these engines to power its machines. Perhaps sharing in the belief that "nature was to be mastered, resources exploited to the fullest, and technologies invented" (ibid., 74), these plantation men ventured into the wilderness of Davao. Machines were used and, if none was available, created.

One such machine, which had to be invented, innovated upon and mass-produced, was the hemp-stripping machine. Hemp was one of the most popular crops on the Davao plantations. One of the first accounts written about Davao highlights the nature of its soil, sandy loam, which was ideal for growing abaca, also known as Manila hemp. Its fiber was used for cordage on many ships (anon. 1926a, 11). The Philippines, due to its tropical climate and topography, had a natural advantage in growing the crop, which was greatly demanded on the international market, especially by the naval industries of Great Britain, Germany, the United States and Japan. However, the traditional hemp growing regions in Luzon and the Visayas could not meet the demand, partly because they practiced the then usual method of cultivation in small plots, and partly because the extraction of the plant's fiber, often by hand, yielded only a small volume (Saleeby 1911, 307; Hayase 1985a, 508). Davao was seen as an alternative production district, and was *tabula rasa* at that.

In Davao, where land was plentiful, hemp was usually grown on plantations of a hundred to a thousand hectares. The few thousand inhabitants of Davao at the turn of the last century, mostly indigenous tribes accustomed to the mobility of slash and burn agriculture, barter trading, and hunting and gathering more so than to sedentary farming, had to be co-opted and convinced to work on the plantations. In early 1906, a tribal ward system was created through the installment of an American planter as headman in place of the traditional tribal leader, the *datu* (Hayase 1985b, 141–2). This was an attempt to raise indigenous labor for the plantations, but it resulted in the destruction of the tribal people's traditional way of life and was met with widespread resistance in the form of a fanatical dance movement whose tone was anti-American and which culminated in the assassination of the American Governor, Edward Bolton (ibid., 143; Tiu 2005, 30). Using superior force, the Americans were able to suppress the insurgence in August 1906 after two months of fighting that cost the lives of many innocent people (Tiu 2005, 30).

Contending with resistance often made the creation of an indigenous working class a difficult undertaking, and labor was the "worst problem" confronting the planters (anon. 1909b, 633). One solution to the labor shortage was importing workers, among whom were Japanese nationals, from the Visayas and Luzon (ibid.; Cody 1958, 23; Hayase 1984, 133). The Filipinos from Visayas and Luzon were hired on the assumption that they were better adjusted to plantation life, since they had come from areas in the Philippines where sedentary agriculture had been practiced for centuries; but a number of these workers were also found to be inefficient and prone to sleeping on the job (Cody 1959, 173). The importation of labor and the subsequent success of the plantation economy in Davao resulted in an influx of Filipino and Japanese settlers, who soon outnumbered the local tribes in Davao during the first half of the twentieth century (Commission of the Census 1941, 4). However, despite daily wages in Davao which were often the highest in the Philippines, the labor supply never sufficed, because the number of plantations and business establishments continued to increase throughout the following decades (Dacudao 2010, 118).

In abaca production, the two important labor-intensive processes were cultivation and fiber extraction. The American pioneers would employ machines for these two processes. Captain Burchfield's Kentucky Plantation was one of the first to adjust the spacing of hemp plantings to enable plows and disc harrows to pass between rows of newly planted seedlings, which prevented weed growth. Farm machinery would traverse newly-planted hemp fields for four months, or until the hemp leaves were large enough to shade the ground and prevent weeds from growing (Mindanao Herald 1909, 73). The traditional Filipino way of planting was to let the abaca stalks grow wild, usually without replanting; the practice was prevalent in the older abaca-growing regions of Luzon and the Visayas, but in Davao, the plantations adopted the systematic planting arrangement, thereby accommodating the use of machinery (anon. 1926d, 9; anon. 1931, 7).

Fiber extraction, the second part of the process, was more labor-intensive. The traditional method was to strip manually with a knife. This resulted in a lot of wasted fiber, time, and effort. Separating the fibrous strips from each sheath left only a quarter of the fiber; another quarter of that was lost in pulling and scrapping the remaining strips under the crude knife (Saleeby 1914, 10). This hand-stripping method employed a stripping knife held up by a bamboo frame stretched to a certain tension (Robb 1931, 25). This simple Filipino contraption, used in the abaca plantations of Davao in its early years, yielded only 20 kilograms of cleaned fiber a day.

To a certain extent, the scarcity of labor on the frontier plantations and the highly labor-intensive process of abaca stripping made it a necessity for Davao plantation owners to use stripping machines as soon as they became available. Whereas the American colonial government encouraged mechanization for ideological reasons, for the Davao plantations the machines were a necessity born out of the realities of the jungle frontier. In 1909, the government-affiliated *Philippine Agricultural Review* published a study showing that the tensile strength of machine-stripped fiber was greater than that of a hand-stripped fiber (Bacon 1909, 452). Despite this mechanical benefit, the older abaca-producing regions continued the manual process of extraction, in sharp contrast to the abaca industry of Davao, which proceeded to use machines. In 1931, the National Fiber Board actively campaigned for the mechanization of abaca production in Luzon and the Visayas. They cited the rapid development of Davao's abaca industry and the success the sisal industries of Yucatan, East Africa, and the Dutch East Indies had attained through their use of machinery (Saleeby 1931, 4).

At first, Davao plantations experimented with imported automatic sisal strippers such as the Corona and Prieto machines, but their use was never widespread. The bulky Corona was able to strip 3,000 kilograms of hemp a day, but it could not produce as high grade[4] a fiber as the manual method. Moreover, a big, heavy sisal machine had an unattractive acquisition cost of 60,000 Pesos (ibid., 18; Alvarez 1934, 6). The perfect abaca stripping machine continued to be the 'holy grail' for those engaged in abaca production in Davao.

It was this labor-scarce frontier environment, with its imperfect machines, in which the Western spirit of invention and experimentation took hold and became widespread. It should be noted that various machines were showcased at trade expositions and to the press throughout the first three decades of the twentieth century. Their inventors were people and companies from all over the world. In 1909, H. H. Behrendt, a New York-based American, introduced an improved version of an invention of his, a compact machine with a gasoline motor (anon. 1909a, 522). The British created the Clarke Hemp Machine, built in Hong Kong, which underwent several changes in order to strip longer fibers; the company Burn & Co., Ltd. based in Calcutta, India, patented their hemp stripping machine for the Philippine market in 1909 as well (Mindanao Herald 1909, 82; anon. 1909, 709).

However, most of the machines that came to be used on Davao plantations were invented and built in the Philippines, either by Americans, Filipinos or Japanese, the same nationalities directly engaged in abaca production. The McLane Hemp machine, which stripped 400 kilograms of fiber per day, was built in Cebu and Zamboanga, while the Universal Hemp Company of the Philippine-based American inventors Patrick Henry Frank and William Henry Gohn manufactured their machine in Manila. The Americans initiated this love affair with machines, but Filipino inventors were not far behind in creating machines of their own, in seeking patents for them (as did one Mr. Salas), and in exhibiting them at trade fairs and expositions (as did one Mr. Molo and one Mr. Perez) (Salas' Patent No. 1334262; anon. 1909a, 522).

Many machines were invented only to be discarded after short trials because they could not meet the four major criteria for effective abaca stripping. The first requirement was portability. Hemp strippers had to be light enough to be moved around the abaca fields in order to save on the laborious process of consolidating heavy abaca stalks. Second, the volume of hemp produced by the machines had to outstrip what could be done by hand. Third, the machine-stripped quality had to be equal to or greater than that of hand-stripped fiber. The fourth criterion was the machine's affordability (anon. 1921, 28).

The first and fourth criteria, namely portability and affordability, were not often met. The early machines were heavy, ranging in weight from the 180 kilogram Elser Machine to the 820 kilogram Corona. And as with any machine requiring a good deal of metal, those exhibited at the fairs were expensive. A McLane Hemp Machine cost 1,500 Pesos; a Corona machine cost 60,000 Pesos (Mindanao Herald 1909, 82; Alvarez 1936, 6). Most of the machines did meet the second criteria: they could strip a greater volume. With output ranging between 230 kilograms per day for the Buffalo Pons No. 3 to 3,000 kilograms daily for the Corona, the machines were able to beat the 20 kilogram output of the manual method (ibid.). But other factors such as price and portability reduced the benefit of using these new machines on the plantations.

Experimentation was rife, and several years of trial and error were usually required before a particular invention could be marketed. Manuel Perez spent four years designing his machine, while Patrick Henry Frank's took 14 years to develop (Patent No. 1334262; anon. 1921, 28). In almost no case did the inventor of a machine claim that he had designed his machine from scratch. 'Improvement' was an often-used term, because common to all these hemp machines was the basic fundamental of the traditional Filipino contraption, the stripping knife.[5] Innovations usually involved the mechanization of the stripping knife with the addition of a spindle and fly wheel to draw the hemp across the blade (U.S. Patent Office 1924, No. 1519579; Supreme Court Decision G.R. No. L-38010 December 21, 1933; Boyle 1926, 10).

The Spirit of Innovation in a Multi-National Frontier

Eventually, the machine that came to be used extensively and successfully on the Davao plantations was the *hagotan*, because it fulfilled all the requirements for a practical stripping machine. It was movable and could be disassembled, it stripped a satisfactory 150 kilograms per day, it produced medium-to-high grade hemp, and at a cost of at most 450 Pesos (Alvarez 1934, 6), it was affordable. By 1928, more than 75 percent of the output of Davao abaca was being stripped with the *hagotan*. The numerous Japanese plantations and laborers in Davao were using 723 *hagotans* in the field by 1934 (Hayase 1984, 190). Perhaps because the Japanese were the first to use the *hagotan* extensively, the machine came to be associated with them; but the Japanese did not invent the *hagotan*. Rather, it was an innovation on various preexisting hemp stripping machines, which themselves were based on the original Filipino stripping knife. The name *hagotan* implied that it was not of Japanese, but of Filipino origin. It is based on the verb *hagot*, meaning 'to strip, scrape off.'[6] A *hagotan*, then, was a device for stripping.

The idea for the *hagotan* was said to have come from an old Spanish priest from the settlement of Santa Cruz, which lies south of the main town, who had suggested it to the American B. A. Crumb, the owner of a nearby plantation (Hayase 1984, 202). In 1920, a Japanese man employed by the Ohta Development Company built a similar machine. He added a fly-wheel, making use of a *carabao*[7] cart wheel for the purpose, and employed the principle of the hand apparatus used in most fiber producing districts in Luzon and the Visayas. Crumb's machine had a three-horsepower gasoline engine, but the Japanese inventor erected his machine near a river and used a waterwheel to power twelve machines connected to the energy source (Boyle 1926, 10).

In the meantime, Crumb had passed his machine on to William Henry Gohn and Patrick Henry Frank, who added improvements such as a conical spindle. They patented their modified design and created the Universal Hemp Machine Company to manufacture it. At the same time as Gohn and Frank were patenting and building their machine for mass production, a group of Japanese machinists, led by G. Kosuyama, were working on something similar. They sold about four thousand of their *hagotan* to the Davao plantations (Supreme Court Decision G.R. No. L-38010 December 21, 1933; Hayase 1984, 202). In 1933, Frank and Gohn filed suit against Kosuyama for patent infringement; they were perhaps encouraged by a 1928 Supreme Court decision providing for an injunction against a Filipino inventor of a hemp machine, for sale at a trade fair, that had a conical spindle similar to the one used in their machine (Supreme Court Decision G.R. No. L-27793 March 15, 1928). However, in the Kosuyama case, the Supreme Court upheld a lower court's decision letting Kosuyama keep his profits from the sale of the machines. Frank and Gohn's machine was held to be "not novel and original" and similar to ones already in use on the plantations of Davao at the time of its invention (Supreme Court Decision G.R. No. L-38010 December 21, 1933).

Fig. 1: Stripping Hemp by Power
(source: American Chamber of Commerce Journal, Dec. 1936, n. pag.)

This narrative of the creation of the *hagotan* reveals the immersion of the multinational settlers of Davao in a very American industrial spirit. Of the many people involved, not all were Americans who had grown up in an industrializing America, with the saga of the frontier imprinted onto their psyche. The Filipino settlers imbibed this American frontier mentality as well, embraced the plantation system and thereby joined in the scramble to invent a hemp stripping machine at a time when fellow Filipinos in Luzon and the Visayas were reluctant and unable to mechanize their small-plot abaca farms (Saleeby 1911, 307; Saleeby 1931, 19; Robinson and Johnson 1953, 14). The Japanese, most of whom were displaced agrarian workers from the non-industrial prefectures of Okinawa and Fukushima, were also quick to adjust to Davao's mechanized abaca industry, and were among those who appreciated and implemented the rational cultivation and mechanized extraction of the abaca plant (Hayase 1984, 161; Yu-Jose 1997, 121; Abinales 2000, 81).

Perhaps the most lasting legacy of the American pioneers was their spirit of enterprise, fine-tuned as they tamed the American west with their machinery, which served as a template for taming the jungles of Davao. But the mechanization of the Davao frontier, and in this case the evolution of a homegrown machine, produced another outcome far removed from the rugged individualism evoked by the American frontier.

The Communal Effect

In the abaca fields, the *hagotan* encouraged a cooperative spirit among those extracting hemp. Workers on the plantations were mostly a mixture of Filipino and Japanese laborers (Alvarez 1934, 7), and the machine required them to cooperate. Coordination and timing among workers was important: one worker would operate the machine while others assisted in gathering the hemp, running it through the machine and gathering the stripped product (Kaneshiro 2002, 77–8). Moreover, due to its portability, the *hagotan* allowed for cooperative sharing by farmers, because one machine, even a borrowed or rented one, could be used and transferred from one group of farmers in one part of a field to a group in another part of the field. A pool of farmers, facilitated by cooperatives or associations, could rent the machines (Alvarez 1934, 7). Through the use of machinery, abaca plantations in Davao came to resemble the typical rice fields of the Philippines, which are organized on a principle Filipinos call *bayanihan*, or communality, wherein neighbors help each other harvest the rice on each other's plots. Traditional rice-farming Filipino societies, like those found in the lowlands of Luzon and the Visayas, practice *bayanihan* when most members of the community help in the seasonal work rhythms of the agricultural process, especially in "preparing the soil, transplanting, irrigation management and harvesting" the grains (Villegas 1998, 173; Rodell 2002, 198). Over the years *bayanihan* has become so ingrained that a 1988 survey of Filipinos showed it to be one of their foremost values (Pertierra 2002, 85).

This community spirit was also a hallmark trait of the Japanese. The Japanese formed the very effective Davao Japanese Association, which began providing loans and community assistance to its members in 1916 (Saniel 1966, 120). Associations such as this trace their roots to Tokugawa Japan, when five-family neighborhood groups were created; their influence can be seen today in the collective (*han*) units of school, companies and government networks (Sugimoto 1997, 246–9). By 1925, the Japanese had initiated a co-ordinated auction system open to every grower and buyer of abaca, regardless of nationality. By 1936, the Americans themselves were crediting Davao's agro-industrial success to its cooperative nature (anon. 1936, 7). Though the American pioneers showed a streak of individualism, life on the Philippine frontier also brought the need for cooperation. By 1905, Americans had already formed the Davao Planters Association, and in 1932, inspired by the Japanese cooperatives, they formed a coconut marketing cooperative (ibid.; Gleeck 1993, 88–9; Abinales 2000, 75).

These settler groups in Davao cooperated among themselves and were conscious of how they related to one another. The local Rotary Club, formed in 1938, had Filipino, American, Japanese, Spanish and Chinese founding members (Cody 1959, 177). Filipinos and Japanese often mingled in the streets, at work, in the bazaars, and on the golf courses (ibid., 182–3). Davao was spared the race riots that had occurred in other parts of the Philippines and in America before WWII. Davao residents, especially the Japanese and Filipinos, and to some extent the Americans,[8] especially aware of their differences, were mindful of the need to maintain cordial relationships and not offend the sensibilities of the others—a very Asian trait of non-confrontation (ibid., 182–4).

Perhaps illustrative of this multi-national cooperation is one photograph from an International Night at the Davao Carnival on 20 May 1941, where five pairs of children of different nationalities (Filipino, Spanish, American, Chinese and Japanese) posed for the camera in Filipino traditional garb after having performed a Filipino dance—a symbolic gesture wherein the younger generation was to be taught the values of society (fig. 2). The photo is also telling, in the absence of any representation of Davao's indigenous inhabitants, of the children being attired in traditional Hispanized Filipino dress instead of in tribal dress. By the twentieth century, the indigenous tribes had become minorities; many integrated and inter-married into the Japanese and majority Filipino settler societies (Commission of the Census 1941, 4; Tiu 2005, 48; Hayase 2007, 178).

Davao May 1941 Carnival

Fig. 2: Davao May 1941 Carnival
(source: Bulletin of American Historical Collection, *July–September 1981, 80)*

Conclusion

The creation of Davao has its origin in the American concept of extending a frontier through the application of machinery and industry, and to a certain extent, this was realized. Davao was transformed from an undeveloped outpost at the turn of the century into the top taxpayer in Mindanao in the early 1930s, and it was inaugurated as a chartered city in March 1937 (Corcino 1997, 85; Abinales 2000, 87). However, Davao did not turn completely into "a sort of glorified Iowa" (Adas 2006, 166) due to the fact that the Filipino and Japanese settlers who had arrived shortly after the Americans, though they did absorb the American penchant for mechanization, also contributed their own traits and practices. This sufficed to counter Turner's "dominant individualism" (Turner 1920, 37). It is also interesting to note that, although the *hagotan* was modified and used by people of different nationalities, including by Americans and Japanese, it was known by its Filipino name. In this particular Davao case study, Western attitudes and methods were adopted and adapted by the settlers of a Philippine frontier in order to create a machine that mirrored the particularities of their environment. This experiment of national groups living in proximity to one another proved that trans-national relations can also be trans-cultural. The mechanization of the Davao frontier, thus, did not completely Americanize Davao, but created a specific, new culture.

The creation of the *hagotan* was a process that placed the settlers (Filipino, Americans or Japanese), who had been separated from their places of origin, in what Michel de Certeau has called the "in between" (1984, 30). The settlers created a space for themselves by finding "ways of using" the realities of an isolated frontier and meeting the challenge of operating a labor-intensive hemp stripping process in a labor-scarce environment. They achieved this by "making do" with the industrial spirit they had appropriated from the Americans; they took the less effective mechanisms of the earlier machines and ultimately created for themselves the *hagotan* (see further Hahn in this volume). It was their status "in-between" milieus of industrialization and agriculture, modernization and tradition, American and Filipino, Western and Asian, that enabled these Davao settlers to fashion the *hagotan*.

What was appropriated in this process was not only a spirit of industry or a fascination for things mechanical, but a technological concept of how the machines work. This conceptual appropriation was the basis for the new and improved machines created afterwards, with their modified features such as a conical spindle or a *carabao* cartwheel arising as needed. The *hagotan* as an object became a sort of a focal point in the abaca fields. It transformed them and gave them what Kaneshiro (2002, 77) calls a "factory-like appearance," a result of the division of labor that required several men to coordinate their actions in putting a hemp sheath into a machine and taking out the stripped fibers. From the number of men involved in stripping, to the practice of groups of workers taking turns using a machine that was often rented from cooperative associations, the *hagotan* changed the way workers fulfilled their tasks on the plantation. The cooperative spirit became a trait celebrated by observers as being one of the reasons why the Davao abaca industry became such a success (anon. 1936, 7).

The foregoing considerations lead us to the transformation of the Davao frontier on both the physical and the psychological level (Hahn in this volume). The Davao landscape changed from a primeval forest into rows and rows of abaca and coconut plantations. In the realm of mentalities, the frontier spirit itself was transformed from the rugged individualism of the American west to the *bayanihan* spirit of mutual cooperation in a Philippine agro-industrial setting, of which communality was just as integral a part as the mechanized industrial endeavor. The process of mechanization of this frontier thus created new spaces of meaning that give the Davao experience its unique character.

Notes

1 Indigenous tribes include the Atas, Bagobos, Blaans, Dibabawons, Giangans, Kalagans, Kulaman Manobos, Mandayas, Mangguwangans, Mansakas, Matigsalogs, Obos, Samals, Sangils and Tagacaolos, among others (Hayase 1985b, 139–50; Tiu 2005, 47–88).

2 James Martin Welborn would eventually return to America to settle and die in Kansas in 1956, but his children remained in Davao (Tiu 2005, 148, 359).

3 *Thomasite* was a name given to the American schoolteachers who arrived in the first decade of the twentieth century, after the ship U.S.S. Thomas, which had brought many of them to the Philippines. See O. M. Habana's article in this volume for more details.

4 Hemp stripped by sisal machines was dull in color and lacked luster, with some pulp still sticking to the strands (Saleeby 1931, 18).

5 In the race to create the perfect machine, their creators often litigated alleged similarities among the machines being built and sold to the plantations.

6 An idea pointed out by Shinzo Hayase in a conversation in 2007, Tangub City.

7 *Carabao*, an oxen, is the traditional agricultural work-animal in the Philippines.

8 The Americans usually stayed in their plantations, rather than reside in the town proper. But they were also wont to contract Japanese laborers to maintain their plantations.

References

Abinales, Patricio N. (2000). *Making Mindanao: Cotabato and Davao in the Formation of the Philippine Nation State*. Quezon City: Ateneo de Manila University Press.

Adas, Michael (2006). *Dominance by Design: Technological Imperatives and America's Civilizing Mission*. Cambridge: Belknap Press of Harvard University Press.

Alvarez, David (1934). Why the Davao hemp industry is successful. *Philippine Journal of Commerce and Industry*. 10, 11, 5–7.

anon. (1909a). Hemp Stripping Machines. *Philippine Agricultural Review*, November, 2, 11, 522.

anon. (1909b). Davao Hemp Planters. *Philippine Agricultural Review*, November, 2, 11, 632–3.

anon. (1909c). A New Hemp Stripping Machine. *Philippine Agricultural Review*, December, 2, 12, 709.

anon. (1921). Inventions: The Frank Hemp Stripping Machine. *American Chamber of Commerce Journal*, June, 1, 6, 28–9.

anon. (1926a). Son of Blue Grass Region Famous in Davao: J. L. Burchfield—Pioneer Border Man. *American Chamber of Commerce Journal*, January, 6, 1, 11, 14.

anon. (1926b). Epic in Pioneering—Americans in Davao. *American Chamber of Commerce Journal*, January, 6, 1, 12–3.

anon. (1926c). Independence on Davao Homestead—What may be done with Sixteen Hectares. *American Chamber of Commerce Journal,* January, 6, 1, 28–9.

anon. (1926d). Hemp Coconuts and Dividends at Padada: Davao's Christensen of California Manages Two Growing Plantations. *American Chamber of Commerce Journal,* December, 6, 12, 8–9.

anon. (1931). The Manila Hemp Industry's Growth. *American Chamber of Commerce Journal,* August, 11, 8, 7, 20.

anon. (1936a). Davao. *American Chamber of Commerce Journal,* August, 16, 8, 5–7, 10–1, 29–30.

anon. (1936b). Stripping Hemp by Power: Talomo, Davao. *American Chamber of Commerce Journal,* December, 16, 12, n. pag.

Arcilla, Jose S. J. (ed.). (1998). *Jesuit Missionary Letters from Mindanao, vol. 3: The Davao Mission.* Quezon City: University of the Philippines Center for Integrative and Development Studies.

Bacon, Raymond (1909). The Tensile Strength of Machine and Hand Stripped Abaca Fiber. *Philippine Agriculture Review,* 452–4.

Boyle, H. H. (1926). Veterans Turn Davao Jungle into Rich Plantations: Teach Industry to Tribes. *American Chamber of Commerce Journal,* 6, 1, 9–10.

Certeau, Michel de (1984). *The Practice of Everyday Life.* Berkeley: University of California Press.

Commission of the Census, Commonwealth of the Philippines (1941). *Census of the Philippines: 1939, vol. I, II: Davao.* Manila: Bureau of Printing.

Corcino, Ernesto (1997). *Facets of Davao's History.* Davao City: Philippine Centennial Movement Davao City Chapter.

Cody, C. E. (1958). The Consolidation of the Japanese in Davao. *Comment,* 7, 3, 23–36.

Cody, C. E. (1959). The Japanese Way of Life in Pre-War Davao. *Philippine Studies.* 7, 2, 172–86.

Dacudao, Patricia Irene (2010). Pioneer Migrants in the Land of Promise. *Philippine Population Review,* 9, 10, 109–24.

Gabriel, Ralph H. (1963). *Traditional Values in American Life.* New York: Harcourt, Brace and World, Inc. in cooperation with the United States National Commission for UNESCO.

Gleeck, Lewis E. (1993). Davao in American Times. *Bulletin of the American Historical Collection,* January–March, 86–103.

Hayase, Shinzo (1984). Tribes, Settlers and Administrators on a Frontier. Economic Development and Social Change in Davao, 1899–1941. PhD dissertation. Murdoch University.

Hayase, Shinzo (1985a). American Colonial Policy and the Japanese Abaca Industry in Davao, 1898–1941. *Philippine Studies,* 33, 4, 505–17.

Hayase, Shinzo (1985b). Tribes on the Davao Frontier, 1899–1941. *Philippine Studies,* 33, 2, 139–50.

Hayase, Shinzo (2007). *Mindanao Ethnohistory Beyond Nations: Magindanao, Sangir and Bagobo Societies in East Maritime Southeast Asia*. Quezon City: Ateneo de Manila University Press.

Kaneshiro, Edith (2002). 'The Other Japanese': Okinawan Immigrants to the Philippines, 1903–1941. In Ronald Y. Nakasone (ed.). *Okinawan Diaspora*, 71–89. Honolulu: University of Hawaii Press.

Mindanao Herald (1909). *Historical and Industrial Number Commemorating a Decennium of American Occupation of the Land of the Farthest East and Nearest West*. Zamboanga, Philippine Islands: Mindanao Herald Pub. Co. [=special issue of the weekly *Mindanao Herald*, 6, 11 (3 Feb. 1909)]

Nakane, Chie (1970). *Japanese Society*. Berkeley, Los Angeles: University of California Press.

Pertierra, Raul (2002). *The Work of Culture*. Manila: De La Salle University Press.

Ridge, Martin (1991). The Life of an Idea: The Significance of Frederick Jackson Turner's Frontier Thesis. *Montana: the Magazine of Western History*, 41, 1, 2–13.

Robb, Walter (1931). Odell Abaca Plantation. *American Chamber of Commerce Journal*, 11, 11, 12–3, 25–6.

Robinson, Brittain B., and Falba L. Johnson (1953). *Abaca: A Cordage Fiber*. Beltsville, MD: US Department of Agriculture.

Rodell, Paul A. (2002). *Culture and Customs of the Philippines*. Westport, CT: Greenwood Press.

Saleeby, M. M. (1911). Abaca (Manila Hemp)—Agricultural Extension Work Lecture No.3. *Philippine Agricultural Review*, 4, 6, 298–307.

Saleeby, M. M. (1914). *Abaca (Manila Hemp) in the Philippines*. Manila: The Government of the Philippine Islands, Department of Agriculture.

Saleeby, M. M. (1931). New Aspects of the Abaca Industry. *American Chamber of Commerce Journal*, 11, 4, 18–9.

Saniel, Josefa M. (1966). The Japanese Minority in the Philippines Before Pearl Harbor: Social Organization in Davao. *Asian Studies*, 4, 1, 103–26.

Sugimoto, Yoshio (1997). *An Introduction to Japanese Society*. Cambridge: Cambridge University Press.

Tiu, Macario D. (2005). *Davao: Reconstructing History from Text and Memory*. Davao City: Ateneo de Davao Research and Publication Office and Mindanao Coalition of Development NGOs.

Turner, Frederick Jackson (1920). *The Frontier in American History*. New York: Henry Holt and Co.

Villegas, Bernardo M. (1998). *The Filipino Phenomenon*. Metro Manila: University of Asia and the Pacific Foundation, Inc.

Yu-Jose, Lydia N. (1997). Japanese OCWs to the Philippines, 1903–1917. *Philippine Studies*, 45, 1, 108–23.

Institutional Archives

Philippine Supreme Court Decisions.
___(1928). G.R. No. L-27793. March 15. 03.01.2011 www.chanrobles.com.
___(1933). G.R. No. L-38010. December 21. 03.01.2011 www.chanrobles.com.

United States Patent Office.
___(1920). Patent No. 1334262. March 16. 03.02.2011 www.uspto.gov.
___(1924). Patent No. 1519579. December 16. 03.02.2011 www.uspto.gov.

Theory Revisited

Trans-Cultural Appropriation

Christian Huck and Stefan Bauernschmidt

Introduction

It might seem bold, even somewhat audacious, to make another contribution to the polyphonic, often discipline-bound debates concerning the concept of 'appropriation.' As early as 1967, Frithjof Rodi had begun his article "*Zur Metaphorik der Aneignung*" ("On the Metaphoricity of Appropriation") with a similar complaint. He was asking how to use such a concept properly; and rightly so, because it is, in its generality, both trivial and empty. Nonetheless, at least since the 1980s, the concept has come into common use in the discourse of many disciplines: anthropology, communication science, cultural studies, history (including art history), law, linguistics, media studies, pedagogy, philosophy, political science, psychology, sociology—to name but a few. In most cases, the concept is first of all a 'collective singular' (Koselleck 2006, 67–8); it is detached from concrete actions, detached from (living) actors and (material) things, and from any specific historical circumstances. It looks as if anything can be appropriated by anyone at any time; and even appropriation itself, as a form of action, does not limit itself to a specific kind of practice.

Even a quick glance at the contents of the volume in which this essay appears will reveal some of the wide ranging application of the term 'appropriation.' American dime novels and American cars cross the Atlantic and are read or driven in Weimar Germany; fish and chips is transferred from Great Britain to Germany—albeit with little success; Chinese food is eaten in American homes; the Japanese-inspired *hagotan*, a fibre stripping machine, was used by Americans in the Philippines in the early twentieth century. All these phenomena are analyzed as processes of appropriation. As we can see, many different things can be appropriated: cars, literary genres, food styles, technologies and so on. Additionally, different social groups enter the stage; they may desire or resist such things. Dominant groups might appropriate the culture of subordinated and/or marginalized groups (on a cross-cultural level, for example, in the context of colonialism; see Ziff and Rao 1997; Ashley and Plesch 2002; critical: Büyükokutan 2011).[1] On an individual, interactional level, we can study such highly diverse manifestations of appropriation as borrowing, collecting, purchasing, stealing, eating, reading, adopting and so on.

The career of the term 'appropriation' advanced in the 1980s (Franz and Tramsen 2000), a decade that witnessed the so-called *cultural turn* in the humanities and social sciences. In this context, 'appropriation' was (and still is) frequently under-theorized, and only rarely defined (Rogers 2006). To guarantee that the term should be used consistently at least *within* a given discipline, subdivisions have arisen and proliferated expansively in recent years. We are confronted with 'social appropriation' (Beck 1989; Algra 2003; López and Cámara 2007), 'communicative appropriation' (Hepp 2005; Braun and Wetzel 2009; Sutter 2010), 'legal appropriation' (Coombe 1998; Merry 1998; Mellisaris 2007), 'medial appropriation' (Charlton 1993; Jäger 2008), 'white appropriation' (Hill 1992), 'feminist appropriation' (Dixson 1988), and of course, with 'cultural appropriation.' Each modifying adjective reflects the choice, or rather the implicit application of, a certain theory or theoretical tradition and its corresponding methods and research techniques. Researchers working within such frameworks are also confronted with different kinds of raw data.

For us, the concept of 'cultural appropriation,' which is at the centre of our theoretical approach, can be interpreted in at least two ways. We can speak of 'cultures' appropriating some sort of entity. Here, 'culture' can be used synonymously with society, a (large) group of people. However, we can also talk of certain modes of appropriation, cultural or otherwise. There is a huge difference, as Hans Peter Hahn emphasizes in this volume, between appropriating a quadriga by physically removing the object, and appropriating it by making one yourself, adapting its design to the demands and values of your own culture. There is a similar difference between appropriating Chinese food by eating it, i.e. literally incorporating it, and appropriating it by adapting its recipes to the tastes and values of your own culture. Central to our approach will be a combination of both aspects.

In order to re-conceptualize the term in a way we hope will be both innovative and helpful, we must limit the reach and scope of our concept in two ways. The first of these limits is historical: since the empirical studies that our theoretical reflections are based on are all concerned with the past two centuries, we shape our concept with the demands of a global modernity in mind. This means that our structural frame of reference is characterized by a liberal, competitive economic order with industrial overproduction for a faceless mass of consumers; by a social order based on liberty and democracy, on open access to goods and on social rule of law; and by the presence of global transport networks. To be sure, many actors involved in processes of appropriation do not perform under such circumstances. Nonetheless, the conditions of Western modernity provide at least the background for the instances of 'cultural appropriation' we analyze here. The second limit to our perspective is related to the first one, but involves the scope of the objects of appropriation: we concentrate on (consumer) 'goods,' because these are the most common things to be appropriated under the circumstances of global modernity.

With these limitations in mind, three aspects of cultural appropriation become central for us and are therefore emphasized in what follows. First, specific attention is given to the role of *actors*, and especially of *mediators*, in the appropriation process. We believe that the concept of cultural appropriation allows us to break down highly abstract and somewhat vague claims about the effects of globalization—including *McDonaldization*, homogenization, and the clash of cultures—to the level of individual acts. Second, the role of *things* in cultural appropriation processes will be highlighted. Things play a quasi-active role because they allow only certain ways of handling them.[2] Third, since cultural appropriation is, above all, a process of signification, we highlight the role of *contexts* in these processes; in our view social, spatial, and temporal contexts are central to the production of meaning.

To clarify our conception of cultural appropriation in this article, we first offer a tentative definition of the term 'cultural appropriation' as it is used in the literature. Next, we concern ourselves with the individual components of the concept's name: we scrutinize the term 'appropriation' and offer a strategic interpretation of 'culture' as it underlies the qualifying term 'cultural.' Finally, we unite these strands in our conception of 'trans-cultural appropriation,' which we obtain partly from our discussion of the theoretical background, and partly from the empirical studies in this volume.

Cultural Appropriation

One definition of the term 'cultural appropriation' that is widespread in the literature stems from a resolution of the Writers' Union of Canada. It provides a fitting preliminary basis for further exploration. 'Cultural appropriation' is defined there as the "taking—from a culture that is not one's own—of intellectual property, cultural expressions or artifacts, history and ways of knowledge and profiting at the expense of the people of that culture" (see for example Ziff and Rao 1997, 1). While such a definition casts the appropriator in a position of dominance, the roles can easily be reversed. Dick Hebdige's position, which is rooted in cultural studies, constitutes a second central strand in the discourse on appropriation. Hebdige grants some power to those in a seemingly subordinate position: "The basis of style is the appropriation and reorganisation by the subject of elements in the objective world which would otherwise determine and constrict him." (1993, 93–4) While the first definition highlights 'cultures' in the sense of a group of people, the second definition highlights 'the cultural' as a sphere of signification. Both definitions, however, imply a prior evaluation and appear to involve moral judgment: whereas it is apparently wrong to take from the powerless, 'stealing from the rich' seems legitimate. This limits the range of application of the concept of cultural appropriation. In order to extend its applicability to a greater variety of situations, we would like to free the concept up from such prejudices. We would attempt instead to unravel the dimensions and distinctions that give structure to the term's meaning in order to make 'cultural appropriation' a versatile tool for examining a specific range of phenomena.

Broadly speaking, we take 'cultural appropriation' to be a form of (social) action; its common feature is the use of something valued by members of one culture by members of another culture, as well as all forms of dealing with such things (Rogers 2006, 136; Young 2005; Hahn 2004; Ashely and Plesch 2002; Ziff and Rao 1997, 1).

About Appropriation

Etymologically, the word 'appropriation' is derived from the Latin verb *appropriāre*, which means 'to make one's own' or 'to take to oneself.' The verb, which is transitive, is composed of the prefix *ad-*, meaning 'to,' and a root 'proprius' meaning 'own' or 'personal' (Hoad 1986, 20; see also de Certeau 1988; Ashley and Plesch 2002; Nelson 2003; Büyükokutan 2011).

Originally, the things appropriated were common goods—land, for example—that were made private property through the act of appropriation; today, this is still the legal meaning of the German term *Aneignung*. However, as Adam Smith argued, the times of common goods have passed: "But this original state of things, in which the labourer enjoyed the whole produce of his own labour, could not last beyond the first introduction of the appropriation of land and the accumulation of stock." (1776, I.8.2) In a world where everything always seems to be owned by someone already, appropriation often takes on a negative connotation—that of theft—or it becomes imbued with some swashbuckling mentality that resists capitalist notions of property. Appropriation accordingly means that things, viewed as belonging to someone else, are now treated by others as their own, or at least, as if they were their own.

Appropriation, as we understand it, may not only be the act of taking, of making something—legally or not—part of one's property; it may also be the act of giving, of preparing or shaping something in order to 'sell' it to others, in other words: of making it an appropriate and proper object of desire. For us, appropriation also includes acts of individuals or companies preparing objects in order to make them seem like potential property, either within their own culture or within another.

This brings us to a closer look at the various dimensions of appropriation,[3] i.e. the *objects*, *actors*, *means*, *circumstances* and *aims* of appropriation. We will try to answer the following questions: what can be appropriated? Who can appropriate? How are things being appropriated? When and where can appropriation take place? What for is appropriation performed?

Objects of appropriation: what can be appropriated? When reviewing the literature on 'appropriation' one is struck that the act of appropriation can relate to almost every 'thing,' be it tangible or intangible, consumer good or otherwise, or of domestic or foreign origin. It can relate to Chinese cuisine (Weishaupt in this volume), German sausages (Schulte Beerbühl in this volume), means of transportation such as Ford cars (Bauernschmidt in this volume), and to dime novels, schoolbooks or travelogues (Huck, Habana and Felcht, all in this volume). But it can also relate to social and political institutions like the German university system (*Universitätswesen*) and parliamentary standing orders (*parlamentarische Geschäftsordnung*) (Paulmann 1998), to musical forms such as jazz, blues, soul, rap, and others emanating from the 'Black musical experience' (Ziff and Rao 1997), to Shamanistic rituals or to artworks and architecture (Hahn in this volume). These are but a few examples.

Though there may seem to be little logic in this great variety of objects, the things mentioned here all share at least three core properties. First, in the cultural universe of a specific collective, they are deemed worthy of playing a role (of any kind whatsoever); they are *valued* and *meaningful*. However, "nothing has value by itself [...]. Since value is conferred by human judgments, each thing's value depends on its place in a series of complementary other objects." (Douglas and Isherwood 1996, xxii) The value of a good, therefore, depends on its place within a specific cultural pattern, i.e. within both a set of practices and a horizon of norms and values. Second, the things in question share the quality of *sociality* (Appadurai 1986; Kopytoff 2001), meaning that their value goes beyond individual attachment, and that they can be exchanged. In modern societies, things valued by more than one person tend to bear a price tag indicating their exchange value. It is on such *goods* as these that we concentrate here. Third, the appropriated object is deemed, at least at the beginning of the process, to be *alien*, whether because it is foreign, or because it is new, or both.

The objects of appropriation, we can conclude, must be socially valued and desired by others. That not every object is socially valued should be obvious. Mirroring Joseph Schumpeter's famous economic distinction between *invention* und *innovation* concerning inventors and producers (Flik 2001, with reference to cars), consumers can either *accept/adopt* or *refuse/repel* new goods (Bode 1902). The results of consumers refusing to accept the value of an imported good can be seen in the papers by Sparenberg and Bauernschmidt (in this volume). Consumer choice based on those consumers' cultural parameters is what decides the success of a good; the process of appropriation can be interrupted or even completely abandoned. Ultimately, only the social acceptance of a thing can complete the process of appropriation. Both aspects, that of evaluation and that of sociality, refer to a further dimension of appropriation, one that can be distinguished from the object only heuristically: the *actor*, to whom we will return in a moment.

It is important to emphasize here that we assume a material basis for every 'thing' appropriated. Even concepts and institutions do not simply spread, as if moved by an invisible hand (progress? civilization?); they are brought to other places—materialized in some form or another, be it even only in the memory or habitus of an individual—through very mundane and material means of transport. It is important, therefore, to be on the lookout for actors who move things and bring them into new context, and for what motivates them. Moreover, the materiality of the object of appropriation limits the valuation of the thing, because it conditions its potential functions and uses. These can be called its 'affordances' (Mom in this volume). Things, consequently,

> "participate in social practices just as human beings do. To be sure, these things are 'interpreted' by the human beings in certain ways, but at the same time they are applied, used, and must be handled within their own materiality. As things, they are not arbitrarily interchangeable. [...] 'Things' thus have the status of 'hybrids': On the one hand, they are definitively not a physical world as such, within practices they are socially and culturally interpreted and handled. On the other hand, these quasi-objects are definitively more than the content of cultural 'representations': they are used and have effects in their materiality." (Reckwitz 2002, 208–9)

Actors of appropriation: who can appropriate? As with the objects of appropriation, the potential manifestations of individual or collective actors are manifold. At least three fields have been distinguished. In social terms, we can differentiate between *powerful* and *powerless* groups (Ziff and Rao 1997; Young 2005; Hahn 2008); in economic terms, the field is divided between *producers* and *consumers* (Mom in this volume); and in cultural terms we can differentiate between *natives* and *foreigners*. Indeed, only two core distinctions seem to give structure to this dimension of the actor. On the one hand, the distinction between 'strong' and 'weak' (Füssel 2006; Young 2005; Ziff and Rao 1997) emphasizes power relations in a relationship between at least two cultural entities.[4] On the other hand, the distinction between 'we' and 'them,' though it can address power relations too, addresses different (oppositional) groupings. The identities of these groupings emerge from a dialectic of (perceived) differences towards out-groups and (perceived) similarities within in-groups (Jenkins 2008; Bateson 1935).

However, we think it necessary to complicate this neat picture involving just two parties, since there are always *mediators* at work in appropriation (Huck in this volume). Of course, mediators often belong to one or the other side: advertising agencies do outsourced business for producers, and consumer watchdogs do their work of (resisting) appropriation (Carrier 1995, 106) on the side of consumers. Nonetheless, they must also be distinguished from either side and established as an autonomous position in the structural model of appropriation (Mom in this volume). The role of the mediator is especially relevant in recent historical times, i.e. in modernity, which is characterized by structural conditions that lead to a strict (geographical and social) separation between two interacting parties, and by social groups that are too large to act collectively. Often, mediators will use media in order to distribute information to large collectives across great distances.

Modes of appropriation: how are things being appropriated? Depending on the position we attribute to the appropriators, we can construct different modes appropriation ranging from illegal stealing to rightful occupancy and from appreciation to incorporation. We have already examined how the exploitation model of appropriation is supplemented by a resistance model. In the former, a dominant group appropriates both the material and the immaterial culture of a structurally subordinate group, while in the latter the powerless take what they need to make do with. The paradigm for this resistance model stems from Michel de Certeau's *Practice of Everyday Life* (1988): "His essay argued that the products imposed by a dominant [economic] order can undergo numerous transformations by the ways in which ordinary people make use of them." (Dikötter 2006, 8)

In a modern consumer society, however, the economic transaction of purchasing becomes the paradigmatic moment of appropriation: "An object is appropriated at the point at which it is sold, at the point at which it leaves the world of the commodity [...] and is taken possession of by an individual or household and owned." And Roger Silverstone, Eric Hirsch, and David Morley add: "It is through their appropriation that artefacts [...] achieve significance." (1997, 21) However, the act of buying (*Marktentnahme*; Vershofen 1959) represents only a narrow aspect of the overall process of appropriation. Whereas Silverstone, Hirsch and Morley restrict 'appropriation' to an initial phase, we follow Hahn (in this volume) in understanding cultural appropriation to mean the entire process the former authors describe: (material) modification, objectification, incorporation, and transformation. We will return to these steps when we talk about the time and place of appropriation.

As the previous quotation indicates, signification and the attribution of meaning are crucial to the appropriation process, since only through such acts can the actors perceive the objects as significant. To make an object one's own means giving it meaning and/or value. However, values and meanings are culture-specific. Through people's handling of certain objects in specific ways, and through their acts of possessing, protecting, presenting, withdrawing or representing them, the objects become placed upon the "mattering maps" (Grossberg 1992, 287) of cultures. Thus, appropriation becomes a continuous process of integrating things and concepts into a "culturally constituted world," a "world of everyday experience in which the phenomenal world presents itself to the senses of the individual, fully shaped and constituted by the beliefs and assumptions of his or her culture" (McCracken 1991, 72–3). Appropriation therefore describes the activity behind objects being first perceived as strange, foreign or new and gradually becoming more familiar—it describes how things become integrated into a particular cultural fabric. Appropriation, however, does not mean that all former connotations of the object in question are necessarily erased; rather, the framed foreign or new appeal can become part of its attraction.

Appropriation is by no means a unidirectional activity. Often, the few individuals who introduce a thing (which, especially in modern times, is more often than not a globally distributed consumer good) into a new culture are unable or unwilling to determine its meaning or value. Migrants (Schulte Beerbühl in this volume), multinational corporations (Mom in this volume) or state agencies (Sparenberg in this volume) may all try their best to determine the meaning of a thing within a culture. However, consumers and other users appropriate a new thing according to their particular needs and desires or according to their fears or anxieties of a certain thing. In most cases, the appropriate(d) meaning of a (new) thing within a culture is determined through a reciprocal process of negotiation between those that introduce a thing and those that receive it—and quite often yet another group mediates this process. Sometimes, however, things refuse to accept the meaning the various actors try to attach to them, and develop a life of their own.

Circumstances of appropriation: when and where does appropriation take place? Dominik Schrage (2009) argues convincingly for the acute relevance of accounting for spatial and temporal conditions of the general concept of 'appropriation.' Appropriation does not happen all at once, nor can it easily be determined where it begins or ends. Similarly, since the work of appropriation takes time and involves various actors and activities, the place of appropriation (*contact zones*, see below) is not easy to ascertain.

As mentioned previously, Silverstone, Hirsch and Morley distinguish among a number of phases in the process of appropriation; Hahn (in this volume) interprets these as: (material) *modification*, *objectification*, *incorporation*, and *transformation*. Although Hahn emphasizes that these steps are not all necessary and do not have to proceed in this order, the distinct phases constitute a model that can be a valuable tool for breaking down the amorphous process of appropriation. As a further preliminary step, or phase, of appropriation, we would like to add *mobility*.

For a new or foreign thing to present itself for appropriation, it and the prospective appropriator—at least one of the actors involved in the process of appropriation—must come together. To enable such meetings, either the actor or the object of appropriation must be *mobilized* so as to enter the reach of the other. The same or other actors must then decide to keep the foreign thing: they buy, claim, steal or copy it and thereby *modify* its status, if not its material form. The same or other actors might *objectify* the thing in question by giving it a place within their culture's 'universe of things'; the object is named and discursively grouped with other objects and thereby put on a culture's mattering map. The same or other actors might then *incorporate* the object by granting it a place within their culture's habitual practices. This incorporation might lead to a *transformation* of the thing or of the receiving culture. For example, a pair of jeans on an American cowboy is not the same object as on a German foreign minister, neither symbolically nor literally. Or, American culture has been transformed since it incorporated the railway, although in different ways than has the British culture (Schivelbusch 1987). Each moment in the process of appropriation carries its own specific potential and should be analyzed according to its duration and situatedness.[5]

Each phase in the process of appropriation takes place in a specific geographical, material and social setting. The 'contact zones,' where thing and appropriator meet, can be mediated, as in when we get to know things initially through depictions and descriptions of them; or they can be the result of a direct encounter facilitated by, say, business travellers, migrants, explorers or others (Schulte Beerbühl in this volume). The conditions prevailing in these contact zones are important determiners of how the thing will fare in the appropriation process. Similarly, the specific material circumstances of the *place* of appropriation influence the modifying, objectifying, incorporating and transforming appropriation processes; the Philippine jungle, for example, has influenced the design of a machine originally devised for the plains of Idaho, as well as its use (Dacudao in this volume).

Aims of appropriation: why is appropriation performed? Just as diverse as the appropriated objects, actors, acts and instances are the motivations and purposes of appropriation. Nonetheless, we can specify a number of factors that seem central to its aims and motives. These are *exoticism*, *social advancement*, *identity formation*, *problem solving*, *economic profit*, *ideological concerns* and *fear of the unfamiliar*. We explain them in greater detail here.

Rachel Rowlby claims "that modern consumption is a matter not of basic items bought for definite needs, but of visual fascination and remarkable sights of things not found at home" (1985, 1). Elizabeth Kowaleski-Wallace adds: "there is no thrill in shopping for what one can obtain at home"—"the mentality of the consumer necessarily partakes of a craving for the novel or the different, the unusual or the *exotic*" (1997, 9; emphasis added). Whatever the reasons for this 'charm of the unfamiliar,' be it anthropological craving or a mimetic desire created by economic actors, the desire for new and foreign things is surely a powerful driver of appropriation.

Related to this desire for unfamiliar goods is the role goods play in the process of collective and individual *identity formation* (McCracken 1991). Ashley and Plesch note specifically "that appropriation is aimed at creating and/or consolidating identity" (2002, 6; Hahn 2004; Hahn 2005). A key element of this dynamic process of identity formation, or *identification*, is the "drawing of boundaries between self and 'other.' For identity is conceivable through identifying differences" (Edensor 2002, 24–5). In order to establish such differences (and create similarities within peer groups), individuals make use of a variety of resources including history, language and material culture (McCracken 1991; Edensor 2002). Consumer goods—an instance of material culture—are often in this function in modern-day societies: they help show others who we are, or more precisely, who we want others to think we are (Bauernschmidt in this volume).

Similarly, appropriating things can be a matter of enhancing one's *social status*: exotic textiles and rare materials used for clothes and ornamentation, in ancient times, were difficult to obtain and could therefore be considered indexical of the specific (structural, organizational, or economic) powers necessary to acquire them. However, not only can appropriated goods represent social status (or at least the desire for social advancement), but they can also actually better one's social standing in a more pragmatic way: by appropriating the bicycle, for example, certain segments of African societies improve their economic prospects by opening up new job opportunities for themselves (Hahn in this volume).

The appropriation of technology in particular is often motivated by the search for solutions to *problems* shared among different cultures (Mom in this volume)—even in cases where the 'problem' might only have been discovered on the basis of knowledge of another culture, i.e. by comparison. The appropriation of the railway in the USA, for example, solved the problem of traversing huge distances far better than had any previous solution (coach, ship); however, during the process of appropriation, European compartment design was adapted to American travellers' desires (Schivelbusch

1987). 'Technologies' are not limited to machinery, however: the recognition that Chinese methods of preparing food were superior to American ones (in that they were healthier and more energy efficient) motivated the appropriation of Chinese meals into American households (Weishaupt in this volume).

A further motivation for appropriating a good is, of course, to gain *economic profit*. Specific products are imported and adapted to the tastes and lifestyles of the receiving culture in order to sell them, often at the expense of other goods already on the market there (Sparenberg and Schulte Beerbühl, in this volume). The adaptation of tastes (and lifestyles) to local palates by multinational companies like Kellogg's or McDonalds is obviously driven by the will to sell more goods. The marketing of Native-American dream catchers or Indian massage techniques is often motivated by similar pecuniary desires. One should emphasize, however, that such economic considerations are not the exclusive domain of global companies looking for new markets; they are also a primary concern of migrants or deprived travellers trying to earn a living.

The example of the Indian massage technique shows that economic considerations are often accompanied by, or even secondary to, *ideological concerns*. The appropriation of Native-American or Asian goods, rituals or techniques into Western cultures (or vice versa) is often motivated by a desire to change the morals, manners and values of a society. Owing to this potential to transform societies, the appropriation of media has often been met with especially fierce criticism from those who would like to maintain a status quo (Huck in this volume). Similarly, new technologies are often desired or feared not solely for economic reasons, but also for their potential to change traditional ways of living (Bauernschmidt in this volume).

Finally, appropriation, the process of making something unfamiliar one's own, can be motivated not by a desire for something new but by a *fear of the unfamiliar*, the uncategorized, unincorporated, or unnamed: "what really disturbs cultural order is […] when things fail to fit any category—such as a substance like mercury, which is a metal but also a liquid, or a social group […] ambiguously in some unstable, dangerous, hybrid zone of indeterminacy in-between" (Hall 2003, 236). As soon as new things appear on the radar of a given culture, and for as long as they do not fit the structures and categories of this culture, appropriation becomes a necessity for those who cannot tolerate such a state.

About Culture

No less problematic than the term 'appropriation,' unfortunately, is its modifier: 'cultural.' "Culture," Raymond Williams famously lamented, "is one of the two or three most complicated words in the English language." (1985, 87) Not the best choice of terms, it appears, to qualify 'appropriation.' Nonetheless, two central dimensions of the modifier seem most relevant to us and can help us delineate the concept.

Our first reading turns the adjective 'cultural' into a descriptor of an actual actor in the process: *appropriation by a culture*, as opposed to an 'individual appropriation,' which might signify appropriation by an individual. 'Culture,' here, is a group of human beings ranging in dimension from families to nations. In this sense, 'culture' is a synonym for 'society,' a structured cluster of human beings and a collective whose members are integrated by patterns of acquired knowledge and conduct (as opposed to genetic dispositions). According to this definition, we may say that a Ford automobile (an object of appropriation) is appropriated by some group such as the Miller family, the Bavarians, the French, the Mercedes company, men, women, workers, farmers and so on (actors of appropriation). Which specific groupings are relevant and how they are composed (*who*), their situation (*where* and *when*) and their behaviour (*how* they act), become central questions for research on cultural appropriation.

The definition of culture as a social group seems to follow the tradition of understanding culture in a totalistic, homogeneous way (Reckwitz 2008), but such a tradition also seems out of place with respect to the heterogeneous, open societies of (Western) modernity. Moreover, such an understanding would seem to lack analytical utility, because it signifies, in Williams' terms, "a whole way of life" (1985, 13): everything, it appears, is culture. The culture of a culture seems to determine every aspect of living.[6]

However, talk of 'a culture' can be seen as a mere heuristic simplification of a more complicated process. Cultures, from the moment they emerge through an act of *schismogenesis* (Bateson 1935), are always already defined by their other, or by that which they exclude; they are an entity and at the same time a relational way of observing others. Cultures come into being through a process of recognizing difference by acknowledging sameness, which is why they can only exist in plurality, or in terms of comparison. Consequently the identity of any culture ('we') is never 'pure,' but is always 'contaminated' by that from which it distinguishes itself ('them'). As soon as such distinctions between 'we' and 'them' are drawn, hierarchies such as between the 'powerful' and the 'powerless' can be established (Baecker 2003, 12–6). Once certain customs are recognized as particular to one's own peer group, they can then be perpetuated through (ritualized) mnemonic practices; they can be identified, represented and passed on. A culture, in this sense, could be a nation or a regional or ethnic group, but it could also be a social segment or subset of society, a class or a gendered group.

This comparing, leading to the distinction between 'us' and 'them,' takes as its point of departure precisely those patterns that are neither naturally given nor individually willed: *they act* like that, but *we act* like this. Only contingencies are comparable, not necessities or arbitrary features. Comparison applies to actions based on norms, meanings, values and so on. Thus, what creates 'cultures' is 'the cultural'—a specific structuring dimension in the cohabitation of humans.

A second reading of 'cultural appropriation,' therefore, understands 'cultural' as a modification of a more general process, *a cultural way of appropriation*, instead of, for example, an economic, organic or religious way of appropriation. 'Cultural appropriation' is thus an appropriation based on cultural parameters, i.e. on values and meanings. 'Culture' here denotes "an historically transmitted pattern of meanings embodied in symbols, a system of inherited conceptions expressed in symbolic forms by means of which people communicate, perpetuate, and develop their knowledge about and attitudes toward life" (Geertz 1973, 89). Keeping its schismogenetic origin in mind, we can thus understand a particular culture as reflecting the shared "horizons of norms and values in which [interactional, albeit often mediated, forms of action] are embedded" (Böhme et al. 2007, 104).

To speak of 'cultural' appropriation means to find explanations for appropriation processes that are based on meaning-making, and to do so neither by referring to natural necessities (genes), nor to an individual, autonomous free will (consciousness), but to contingent processes of signification. However, it is important to bear in mind that such processes of signification do not take place wholly independently of materialities and mentalities, but are still not reducible to these. 'Culture' in this sense is no longer identical with a society as a whole, but is a specific dimension motivating and orienting (social) actions within societies.

For example, Chinese food as an artifact is culturally appropriated—or not—because of meanings and values that actors in a specific setting attribute to it, or because it transports meanings and values that have been inscribed by other actors in other settings. An appropriation solely for *organic* purposes, i.e. to prevent starvation, must be distinguished from this. Appropriation, in the cultural sense, means to domesticate material entities into the cultural universe inhabited by *homo symbolicus*, wherein the reasons for appropriation or refusal also reside.

The 'cultural' denominates the symbolic dimension of the appropriation process. Meanings and values that motivate and direct the actions of members of a society are decisive in the appropriation of foreign, unfamiliar things, more specifically in the appropriation of *travelling*—i.e. of globally distributed—*goods*. Such an understanding observes a 'meaning and knowledge based definition of culture.'[7] When concentrating on meanings and values, however, one must keep in mind the media-material basis of culture (the ways meanings are stored, distributed and formed by media) as well as the pragmatic circumstances of the signifying actors (the way social, mental and natural dispositions determine the actors' meaning-making abilities). Also, it is important to emphasize that things, not just humans, can appear as actors of some kind (Latour 2005; Felcht in this volume); things have 'affordances' (Mom in this volume) that suggest certain activities, enable them or make others impossible. As a consequence, the things influence signification. Ultimately, meaning-making is a process negotiated by various actors and determined—but not predetermined—by their mental and material contexts.

Conclusions: Trans-Cultural Appropriation

In the course of our discussion of the concept of 'cultural appropriation,' we have tried to point out several crucial positions that complement existing theoretical frameworks dealing with the appropriation of globally distributed consumer goods. The theory of 'trans-cultural appropriation' developed here provides a suitable frame of reference for interpreting specific dimensions of collective interaction with unfamiliar things. In conclusion, we highlight five main features of our conceptualization: first, 'trans-cultural appropriation' must be conceptualized both as an open concept and as a relational concept; second, the decisive moment in the relationship among different (collective) actors is to be found in the process of making a thing fit into a particular culture; third, the notion of culture is used both in a descriptive and an analytical sense; fourth, in the process of trans-cultural appropriation we have to take mediators into account; and fifth, the appropriated thing plays a quasi-active role.

First: To cope with both the multi-dimensionality and multi-directionality of 'trans-cultural appropriation,' we think it is useful to re-conceptualize the term as an *open* and *relational* concept. The concept is *relational* in character, because it puts things and actors in a mutual relationship. The relata of the concept are various, culturally embedded actors: in economic terms, for example, we have producers, consumers, and mediators such as advertising experts or consumer watchdogs, all playing key roles in the overall process of appropriation. The relationship is formed by the process of 'trans-cultural appropriation,' in which the discrete acts of the different actors are interlocked, but which at the same time creates the very positions the actors take up. Only in the process of recognizing some 'thing' as *culturally* alien—only by recognizing it as unfamiliar among the meanings and values shared within one's peer group—are both peer groups created, the 'we' and the differential 'them' to whom the appropriate use of the 'thing' is attributed. Trans-cultural appropriation, then, necessarily involves the attribution of a good to a specific cultural other. The concept is *open* in character, because it can only say something about the actors and things involved by providing examples of these. As soon as we start thinking about a concrete thing, for example the sculpted marble freezes from the Parthenon, we have to reckon with certain actors; in this example the responsibility for taking these artifacts from a culture that was not his own falls to Lord Elgin, a former British ambassador to the Ottoman Empire (Nelson 1995; Ziff and Rao 1997). Thus the concept is not a theory that provides foregone conclusions, but a research tool to analyze contingent phenomena.

Second: We hold that the particular moment of making a consumer good fit into a particular culture is a decisive element in the overall process of 'trans-cultural appropriation.' Such appropriation can be performed both by actors participating in the target culture and by actors participating in the culture of origin of a consumer good (Bauernschmidt 2011). Hahn, among others (de Certeau 1988; Ashley and Plesch 2002; Dikötter 2006), "emphasize[s] the creative aspect of subjects' dealings with consumer goods in different cultures" (Hahn 2004, 213). He views appropriation as defining the "types of modification an object undergoes before it is at some point viewed as a personal good which is an unquestioned and integral part of local society and identity" (ibid., 219). These modifications are carried out by actors of the target group only; consequently, Hahn views this as a process of localizing global goods. As we look specifically at the cultural transfer (Rogers 2006) of goods between at least two cultures, we see that those goods are not necessarily produced by multinational corporations acting globally and indifferently—even insensitively—to local or regional cultural differences. Instead, we find actors (on the scene of action) who want to make their good appropriate to a specific culture. Often, the appropriative acts of members of the respective cultures—the original culture and the target culture—feed into one another reciprocally.

The concept of 'trans-cultural appropriation' focuses on globally distributed consumer goods, specifically on their transfer from one cultural entity into another. These cultural entities are characterized by similarities within groups and differences among groups; but only over the course of such processes are the similarities and differences established. For this reason we must be alert to *boundaries*; boundaries in physical terms (oceans, mountains, rivers), juridical terms (national borders) and above all in cultural terms (appropriateness). The above-mentioned 'contact zones' are the site of "boundary work" (Gieryn 1983).[8] Here, a new social type emerges on an intermediate level: the so called "boundary spanner" (Metcalfe et al. 2008). We will come back to this type shortly.

'Boundary work,' and as such, the 'work of appropriation,' deals with selection. Its results can be such that:

a. The (materially unmodified) thing becomes integrated into a completely new pattern and thereby a different good. The book, for example, became a form of entertainment rather than enlightenment as new sections of society adopted it. (*cultural selection*)
b. The (culturally unreconstructed) thing can encounter similar patterns in the new culture as existed in the original culture ('shared values'); mobility, for example, seems to be a value in most cultures, and consequently, most of the time cars and bicycles, however materially fitted or modified, are used for similar purposes across cultures. (*material selection*)
c. Finally, a thing can be dropped and become a valueless some-'thing.' (*de-selection*)

Third: In our concept of 'trans-cultural appropriation' the idea of 'culture' occupies, at minimum, a two-fold position. On the one hand, the term designates a 'culture' in the sense of a collective. It is therefore similar in meaning to the term 'society.' Used this way, the term 'culture' should be understood as descriptive, supplemental to the analytical term 'appropriation.' On the other hand, our use of 'the cultural' is intended to explain specific actions in parallel to the way 'the social,' 'the economic' or 'the political' are employed to explain actions; here, 'the cultural' is an analytical term. In both cases, the aim is to distinguish the specified, specific activity (*appropriating*) from other activities (*stealing, borrowing* and so on). *Cultural* appropriation looks for specifically *cultural* moments that determine the performance of actors, whereas appropriation by *a culture* situates the actor and his/her/its actions within a cultural setting. To be sure, the two uses of the term are not mutually exclusive; on the contrary, they supplement each other. It is important, however, to keep these aspects separate; only then we can relate each to the other.[9]

Fourth: We think it important to take into account *mediators* in the process of 'trans-cultural appropriation.' Especially when it comes to larger groups—modern nation states, for example—appropriation is no simultaneous collective act. Instead, specific sub-groups either *take* the thing in question—as the French military did on behalf of the French nation in the case of the Quadriga (Hahn in this volume)—or *receive* it—as the rocker subculture did when it was the first group to adopt jeans. Similarly, designers shape goods to suit specific consumer groups, and advertisers try to place goods within the value system of a certain target group (McCracken 1991, 77–83). The position of mediators in modern societies is often assumed by the media, who perceive new objects and provide them with meanings and values; and by corporations, who want new markets for their products. These mediators can act as 'boundary spanners' or 'gate keepers' (Huck in this volume) as they try either to police or to open the borders between cultures.

Fifth: Things play a quasi-active role in the process of appropriation. That is, they are not merely passive recipients of processes of meaning attribution. Consumer goods are not blank slates; their materiality allows, suggests or makes impossible certain, limited practices. By determining, through their very form, the way users can handle them, things condition their own pragmatic use and, consequently, their own meaning. Only certain functions can be attributed to any given thing, and because each thing's meaning is based on its usage, only certain meanings will be available.

We would like to offer a final paraphrase of trans-cultural appropriation: it is a process of signification that weaves selected (global, travelling) consumer goods into the cultural fabric of a (given) local community. The specific focus of this concept is the delicate process of making something appropriate, of turning an alien 'thing,' or at least a thing construed as alien, into something that come across as proper, fitting, suitable and acceptable for use and valued possession within a culture.

With this conceptualization of trans-cultural appropriation we hope to have provided a terminological grid that is both theoretically well-reflected and empirically supported; it should serve as a research tool for cultural and social studies focussing on the construction of meaning, value and desire inherent in the global circulation of goods.

Notes

1 Of course, such processes take place on an intra-cultural level as well (Marx 1964; Rogers 2006; Lutz 1990); we concentrate on trans-cultural processes here.

2 We disagree with the purely (postmodern) semiotic point of view that "the object is nothing" and that "it matters little what object is involved" (Baudrillard 1981, 63, 64) in the meaning-giving process of a culture.

3 See Ziff and Rao (1997), Young (2005) and Büyükokutan (2011) for such distinctions: *objects* of appropriation (Ziff and Rao 1997, 2; Young 2005, 136); *modes* of appropriation (Ziff and Rao 1997, 4); *actors* of appropriation (Büyükokutan 2011, 622); *milieus* of appropriation (Büyükokutan 2011, 622).

4 We can speak of an *exchange* between two equals in a symmetrical relationship; in an asymmetrical relationship we can speak of *taking* (dominant) or *resisting* (subordinate); see Rogers (2006, 491).

5 However, when it comes to designing specific research projects, we suggest excluding the effects of appropriation on the structure of a given society. Although appropriation surely plays an important role in the development of cultures, it would become difficult to determine the conclusion of such processes.

6 This understanding of 'culture' is like that proposed by the writers who first established the modern term: Herder (1967), Tylor (1958) and the early Williams (1958), to name a few.

7 Such an understanding of 'culture' was put forward by Williams (1981) in the context of cultural studies, by Geertz (1973) in the context of ethnology and Alexander (1990) in the context of sociology—just to name a few.

8 In fact, the concept of 'boundary work' might just be another term for James G. Carrier's "work of appropriation" (1995), taking into account 'boundary'-phenomena.

9 Such a distinction is also central to Bourdieu (1997, 17).

References

Alexander, Jeffrey C. (1990). Analytic Debates: Understanding the Relative Autonomy of Culture. In Jeffrey C. Alexander and Steven Seidman (eds.). *Culture and Society. Contemporary Debates*, 1–27. Cambridge: Cambridge University Press.

Algra, Keimpe (2003). The Mechanism of Social Appropriation and its Role in Hellenistic Ethics. *Oxford Studies in Ancient Philosophy*, 25, 265–96.

Appadurai, Arjun (ed.). (1986). *The Social Life of Things: Commodities in Cultural Perspective*. Cambridge: Cambridge University Press.

Ashley, Kathleen, and Véronique Plesch (2002). The Cultural Processes of 'Appropriation.' *Journal of Medieval and Early Modern Studies*, 32, 1–15.

Baecker, Dirk (2003). *Wozu Kultur?* 3rd ed. Berlin: Kulturverlag Kadmos.

Bateson, Gregory (1935). Culture Contact and Schismogenesis. In *Steps to an Ecology of Mind*, 61–72. New York: Ballantine [1972].

Baudrillard, Jean (1981). *For a Critique of the Political Economy of the Sign*. St. Louis, MO: Telos [1972].

Bauernschmidt, Stefan (2011). *Fahrzeuge auf Zelluloid. Fernsehwerbung für Automobile in der Bundesrepublik des Wirtschaftswunders. Ein kultursoziologischer Versuch.* Bielefeld: transcript.

Beck, Klaus (1989). Telefongeschichte als Sozialgeschichte: Die soziale und kulturelle Aneignung des Telefons im Alltag. In Forschungsgruppe Telefonkommunikation (ed.). *Telefon und Gesellschaft. Beiträge zu einer Soziologie der Telefonkommunikation. Reihe Telefon und Gesellschaft*, vol. 1, 45–75. Berlin: Spiess.

Bode, Wilhelm (1902). *Die Macht der Konsumenten*. Weimar: Wagner.

Böhme, Hartmut et al. (2007). *Orientierung Kulturwissenschaft: Was sie kann, was sie will*, 3rd ed. Reinbek: Rowohlt.

Bourdieu, Pierre (1997). *Die feinen Unterschiede. Kritik der gesellschaftlichen Urteilskraft*. Frankfurt/Main: Suhrkamp [1979].

Braun, Karl-Heinz, and Konstanze Wetzel (2009). Sozialreportage—Zur kommunikativen Aneignung von historischen Sozialräumen. In Karl-Heinz Braun and Konstanze Wetzel (eds.). *Methodenbuch Sozialraum*, 213–34. Wiesbaden: VS Verlag.

Büyükokutan, Barış (2011). Toward a Theory of Cultural Appropriation: Buddhism, the Vietnam War, and the Field of U.S. Poetry. *American Sociological Review*, 76, 4, 620–39.

Carrier, James G. (1995). *Gifts and Commodities: Exchange and Western Capitalism since 1700*. London: Routledge.

Certeau, Michel de (1988). *Die Kunst des Handelns*. Berlin: Merve [1980].

Charlton, Michael (1993). Methoden der Erforschung von Medienaneignungsprozessen. In Werner Holly and Ulrich Püschel (eds.). *Medienrezeption als Aneignung. Methoden und Perspektiven qualitativer Medienforschung*, 11–26. Opladen: Westdeutscher Verlag.

Coombe, Rosemary J. (1998). *The Cultural Life of Intellectual Properties: Authorship, Appropriation, and the Law*. Durham: Duke University Press.

Dikötter, Frank (2006). *Exotic Commodities. Modern Objects and Everyday Life in China.* New York: Columbia University Press.
Dixson, Miriam (1988). The Ideal Type, the Sociologist and the Contemporary Historian: A Case Study in a Feminist Appropriation of Psychoanalysis. *British Journal of Sociology*, 39, 4, 545–53.
Douglas, Mary, and Baron Isherwood (1996). Introduction. *In The World of Goods: Towards an Anthropology of Consumption*, 2nd ed., xx–xxvii. London et al.: Routledge.
Edensor, Tim (2002). *National Identity, Popular Culture and Everyday Life.* Oxford, New York: Berg.
Flik, Reiner (2001). *Von Ford lernen? Automobilbau und Motorisierung in Deutschland bis 1933.* Köln et al.: Böhlau.
Franz, Michael, and Eckhard Tramsen (2000): Aneignung/Subjektivität und Aneignung. In Karlheinz Barck et al. (eds.). *Ästhetische Grundbegriffe. Historisches Wörterbuch in sieben Bänden*, vol. 1, 153–93. Stuttgart, Weimar: Metzler.
Füssel, Marian (2006). Die Kunst der Schwachen. Zum Begriff der 'Aneignung' in der Geschichtswissenschaft. *Sozial.Geschichte. Zeitschrift für historische Analyse des 20. und 21. Jahrhunderts*, 21, 3, 7–28.
Geertz, Clifford (1973). *The Interpretation of Cultures: Selected Essays.* New York: Basic Books.
Gieryn, Thomas F. (1983). Boundary-Work and the Demarcation of Science from Non-Science: Strains and Interests in Professional Ideologies of Scientists. *American Sociological Review*, 48, 781–95.
Grossberg, Lawrence (1992). *We Gotta Get Out of This Place. Popular Conservatism and Postmodern Culture.* London: Routledge.
Hahn, Hans Peter (2004). Global Goods and the Process of Appropriation. In Peter Probst and Gerd Spittler (eds.). *Between Resistance and Expansion. Dimensions of Local Vitality in Africa*, 213–31. Münster: Lit.
Hahn, Hans Peter (2005). *Materielle Kultur: Eine Einführung.* Berlin: Reimer.
Hahn, Hans Peter (2008). Consumption, Identities and Agency in Africa—Introduction. In Hans Peter Hahn (ed.). *Consumption in Africa. Anthropological Approaches*, 9–43. Münster: Lit.
Hall, Stuart (2003). The Spectacle of the 'Other.' In Stuart Hall (ed.). *Representation: Cultural Representations and Signifying Practices*, 223–90. London et al.: Sage.
Hebdige, Dick (1993). The Meaning of Mod. In Stuart Hall and Tony Jefferson (eds.). *Resistance Through Rituals: Youth Subcultures in post-War Britain*, 87–98. London: Routledge [1976].
Hepp, Andreas (2005). Kommunikative Aneignung. In Lothar Mikos (ed.). *Qualitative Medienforschung. Ein Handbuch*, 67–79. Konstanz: UVK.
Herder, Johann Gottfried (1967). *Auch eine Philosophie der Geschichte zur Bildung der Menschheit.* Frankfurt/Main: Suhrkamp [1774].
Hill, Richard (1992). One Part per Million: White Appropriation and Native Voices. *Fuse*, 15, 12–22.

Hoad, Terry F. (ed.). (1986). *The Concise Oxford Dictionary of English Etymology*. Oxford: Clarendon Press.
Jäger, Jens (2008): 'Heimat' in Afrika. Oder: die mediale Aneignung der Kolonien um 1900. *Zeitenblicke*, 7, 2, 14.06.2012 http://www.zeitenblicke.de/2008/2/jaeger/.
Jenkins, Richard (2008). *Social Identity*, 3rd ed. New York: Routledge.
Kopytoff, Igor (1986). The Cultural Biography of Things. In Arjun Appadurai (ed.). *The Social Life of Things. Commodities in Cultural Perspective*, 64–91. Cambridge: Cambridge University Press.
Koselleck, Reinhart (2006). *Begriffsgeschichten. Studien zur Semantik und Pragmatik der politischen und sozialen Sprache*. Frankfurt/Main: Suhrkamp.
Kowaleski-Wallace, Elisabeth (1997). *Consuming Subjects: Women, Shopping, and Business in the Eighteenth Century*. New York: Columbia University Press.
Latour, Bruno (2005). *Reassembling the Social: an Introduction to Actor-Network-Theory*. Oxford: Oxford University Press.
López Cerezo, José A., and Montaña Cámara (2007). Scientific Culture and Social Appropriation of the Science. *Social Epistemology*, 21, 1, 69–81.
Lüdtke, Alf (1997). Alltagsgeschichte: Aneignung und Akteure. Oder—es hat noch kaum begonnen. *WerkstattGeschichte*, 17, 83–92.
Lutz, Hartmut (1990). Cultural Appropriation as a Process of Displacing Peoples and History. *Canadian Journal of Native Studies*, 10, 167–82.
Marx, Karl (1964). *Die Frühschriften. Von 1837 bis zum Manifest der kommunistischen Partei*. Stuttgart: Kröner [1837–57].
McCracken, Grant (1991). *Culture and Consumption: New Approaches to the Symbolic Character of Consumer Goods and Activities*. Bloomington: Indiana University Press.
Melissaris, Emmanuel (2007). The Concept of Appropriation and the Offence of Theft. *Modern Law Review*, 70, 4, 581–97.
Merry, Sally Engle (1998). Law, Culture, and Cultural Appropriation. *Yale Journal of Law & the Humanities*, 10, 575–604.
Metcalfe, Jenni et al. (2008). Situating Science in the Social Context by Cross-Sectoral Collaboration. In Donghong Cheng et al. (eds.). *Communicating Science in Social Contexts. New Models, New Practices*, 181–99. Wien: Springer.
Nelson, Robert S. (2003). Appropriation. In Robert S. Nelson and Richard Shiff (eds.). *Critical Terms for Art History*, 160–73. Chicago et al.: Chicago University Press.
Paulmann, Johannes (1998). Interkultureller Transfer zwischen Deutschland und Großbritannien: Einführung in ein Forschungskonzept. In Rudolf Muhs et al. (eds.). *Aneignung und Abwehr. Interkultureller Transfer zwischen Deutschland und Großbritannien im 19. Jahrhundert*, 21–43. Bodenheim: Philo.
Plourde, Eric (2000). The Dubbing of the Simpsons. Cultural Appropriation, Discursive Manipulation and Divergences. *Texas Linguistic Forum*, 44, 1, 114–31.
Rao, Pratima V. (1997). Cultural Appropriation: A Selected Bibliography. In Bruce Ziff and Pratima V. Rao (eds.). *Borrowed Power. Essays on Cultural Appropriation*, 321–5. New Brunswick, NJ: Rutgers University Press.

Reckwitz, Andreas (2008): *Die Transformation der Kulturtheorien. Zur Entwicklung eines Theorieprogramms*. Weilerswist: Velbrück Wissenschaft.

Reckwitz, Andreas (2002): The Status of the 'Material' in Theories of Culture: From 'Social Structure' to 'Artefacts.' *Journal for the Theory of Social Behaviour*, 32, 2, 195–217.

Rodi, Frithjof (1967). Zur Metaphorik der Aneignung. *Bildung und Erziehung*, 20, 6, 425–38.

Rogers, Richard A. (2006). From Cultural Exchange to Transculturation: A Review and Reconceptualization of Cultural Appropriation. *Communication Theory*, 16, 4, 474–503.

Rowlby, Rachel (1985). *Just Looking: Consumer Culture in Dresier, Gissing, and Zola*. New York: Methuen.

Schivelbusch, Wolfgang (1987). *The Railway Journey: the Industrialization of Time and Space in the 19th Century*. Berkeley: University of California Press [1977].

Schrage, Dominik (2009). *Die Verfügbarkeit der Dinge. Eine historische Soziologie des Konsums*. Frankfurt, New York: Campus.

Silverstone, Roger, Eric Hirsch and David Morley (1992). Information and communication technologies and the moral economy of the household. In Roger Silverstone and Eric Hirsch (eds.). *Consuming Technologies: Media and Information in Domestic Spaces*, 15–29. New York: Routledge.

Smith, Adam (1776). *An Inquiry into the Nature and Causes of the Wealth of Nations*. London.

Sutter, Tilmann (2010). Zur Bedeutung kommunikativer Aneignungsprozesse in der Mediensozialisation. In Dagmar Hoffmann and Lothar Mikos (eds.). *Mediensozialisationstheorien*, 131–45. Wiesbaden: VS Verlag.

Tylor, Edward B. (1958). *Primitive Culture: the Origins of Culture*, vol. 1. New York: Harper & Row.

Vershofen, Wilhelm (1959). *Die Marktentnahme als Kernstück der Wirtschaftsforschung*. Berlin: Heymann.

Williams, Raymond (1958). *Culture and Society, 1780–1950*. London: Chattoo & Windus.

Williams, Raymond (1985). *Keywords. A Vocabulary of Culture and Society*, rev. ed. New York: Oxford University Press.

Williams, Raymond (1981). *Culture*. Glasgow: Fontana.

Young, James O. (2005). Profound Offense and Cultural Appropriation. *The Journal of Aesthetics and Art Criticism*, 63, 2, 135–46.

Ziff, Bruce, and Pratima V. Rao (eds.). (1997). *Borrowed Power. Essays on Cultural Appropriation*. New Brunswick, NJ: Rutgers University Press.

Ziff, Bruce, and Pratima V. Rao (1997). Introduction to cultural appropriation: A framework for analysis. In Bruce Ziff and Pratima V. Rao (eds.). *Borrowed Power. Essays on Cultural Appropriation*, 1–27. New Brunswick, NJ: Rutgers University Press.

Authors

Stefan Bauernschmidt is an associated member at the University of Bayreuth, Germany (Chair of Sociology of Culture and Religion). His fields of research include visual culture, car culture, theory of culture, sociology of culture, sociology of knowledge, and methods of social research (especially qualitative methods). His most recent publications are "Leonardos Abendmahl: Zwischen Kunst und Kommerz. Soziologisches für '*Dazwischen*'," *kunsttexte.de*, 1/12 (2012); "Bumpy Road: The History of Ford in Germany," *Automotive History Review*, 54 (2011); *Fahrzeuge auf Zelluloid. Fernsehwerbung für Automobile in der Bundesrepublik des Wirtschaftswunders. Ein kultursoziologischer Versuch* (2011).

Frederike Felcht teaches Cultural Theory and History at the Humboldt-University of Berlin and Scandinavian Studies at the University of Greifswald. She has written a dissertation on Hans Christian Andersen's texts from a global perspective and published on Scandinavian literature and thing theory, German literature and globalization, hunger and literature, and postcolonial intellectuals. Her most recent publication is "Die Politik globalisierten Lebens in Ulrich Peltzers *Teil der Lösung*," in Anna Kochanowska-Nieborak et al. (eds.), *Literatur und Literaturwissenschaft im Zeichen der Globalisierung* (2012).

Doris Feldmann is Professor of English Literature and Culture at the University of Erlangen-Nuremberg. Her research and teaching cover English literature and culture from the Renaissance to the present, with special emphasis on the complex relations between literature and other discourses (economic, philosophical, political, etc.) and media (film, digital media). She has written a monograph on *Politik und Fiktion* (1995), translated Henry Mayhew's *London Labour and the London Poor* (1996), and she has co-edited *Anglistik im Internet* (1997) and *Theorising Cultural Difference and Transdifference* (2006). Her current projects include a translation of Gayatri Ch. Spivak's *A Critique of Postcolonial Reason* and an introduction to Victorian culture.

Patricia Irene Dacudao is Instructor at the Department of History at the Ateneo de Manila University in the Philippines. She teaches Philippine History and Western History classes while doing research on Philippine frontier history during the American colonial era. Her most recent publication is "Pioneer Migrants in the Land of Promise" in the *Philippine Population Review* (2010).

Olivia Anne M. Habana, PhD, is Assistant Professor at the Department of History, School of Social Sciences, at the Ateneo de Manila University in the Philippines. She has co-authored a series of textbooks in English and Filipino on Philippine, Asian and World History for the high school level (*Lupang Hinirang*, 2000, 2003), *Asia: History, Civilization and Culture* (2007), and *World History for Filipinos* (2011). Her publications include *Gold Mining in Benguet: 1900–1941* (2001) and *Rebuilding Democracy: The Ateneo de Manila University in the 1980s* (2010). Her current research interests are the history of colonial childhood and education in the Philippines. She is also active in cultural heritage preservation studies and is part of the research consortium called the Ateneo Cultural Laboratory, which gives students hands-on experience as historical and cultural researchers, while also contributing to the tourism marketing and cultural preservation needs of selected communities.

Hans Peter Hahn is Professor for Social Anthropology at the University of Frankfurt and vice-speaker of the research training group "Value and Equivalence." His research topics include Western Africa (Burkina Faso, Ghana, Togo), material culture, consumption, migration and mobility, and globalization. His most recent publications include the edited collections *People at the Well. Kinds, Usages and Meanings of Water in a Global Perspective* (2012) (with Karlheinz Cless and Jens Soentgen), *Urban Life-Worlds in Motion. African Perspectives* (2012) (with Kristin Kastner) and *Consumption in Africa. Anthropological Approaches* (2008).

Christian Huck is Professor for English and American Cultural and Media Studies at the University of Kiel, Germany. He has published on popular culture and literature, cultural and media theory, music videos, Irish poetry and nationalism, dime novels, football, film and fashion. His most recent monograph is *Fashioning Society, or, The Mode of Modernity: Observing Fashion in Eighteenth-Century Britain* (2010).

Dr. ing. *Gijs Mom* is Associate Professor at Eindhoven University of Technology, and programme director for Mobility History. He is the founder of the European Center for Mobility Documentation (ECMD, since 1997). In 2003, he co-founded the International Association for the History of Transport, Traffic and Mobility (T^2M). In 2004, Johns Hopkins University Press published his book on *The Electric Vehicle: Technology and Expectations in the Automobile Age*. For this book, he received the 2004 ASME Engineer-Historian Award as well as the Best Book Award from the Society of Automotive Historians. He is editor of the new journal *Transfers: Interdisciplinary Journal of Mobility Studies*, which he founded in 2011. His recent publications include "'Historians Bleed Too Much': Recent Trends in the State of the Art in Mobility History," in Peter Norton et al. (eds.), *Mobility in History: Reviews and Reflections (T^2M Yearbook 2012)* (2011). He is currently finishing a monograph on the history of Atlantic Automobilism.

Carsten Schinko is a post-doctoral fellow at the University of Kiel, Germany. He has published on a variety of topics, including systems theory, black cultural studies, media theory, and popular culture. Most recently, he published *Addressing Modernity: Social Systems Theory and U.S. Cultures* (2011, co-edited with Hannes Bergthaller). He is currently finishing a monograph on the intermedial ties between literature and popular music in the USA.

Susanne Scholz is Professor of English Literature and Culture at the University of Frankfurt/Main. She has held teaching posts at the universities of Frankfurt, Siegen and Paderborn. Her main research interests and publications are in the field of early modern, eighteenth- and nineteenth-century English literature, gender studies, medical humanities and visual culture studies. Her major book publications are: *Body Narratives: Writing the Nation and Fashioning the Subject in Early Modern England* (2000) and *Objekte und Erzählungen. Subjektivität und kultureller Dinggebrauch im England des frühen 18. Jahrhunderts* (2004). She is currently working on a research project on English literature and the scientific gaze 1880–1930.

Margrit Schulte Beerbuehl, PhD, is Professor (apl.) at the Department of Historical Studies II (Modern History) at the Heinrich Heine University of

Düsseldorf. She has published widely in the fields of British social and economic history, Anglo-German relations, British naturalization policy and the history of consumption. Her latest publications include *Deutsche Kaufleute in London: Welthandel und Einbürgerung 1660–1818* (2007); with Stefan Manz and John Davis (eds.), *Transnational Networks: German Migrants in the British Empire, 1670-1914* (2012).

Ole Sparenberg is a research assistant for Economic and Environmental History at the University of Saarbrücken, Germany. He has written a doctoral thesis on fishery and whaling under the National Socialist autarky policy. Currently he is working on the history of deep-sea mining from the 1960s to 1980s.

Sonja Weishaupt is a PhD-student at the Department of Cultural Anthropology at the University of Kiel. She studied *Europäische Ethnologie*, American Studies and Central Asian Studies at the Humboldt University Berlin and has published on the problem of exhibiting Nazi art in museums.

Index